Mysterious Regions

Great Mysteries

Aldus Books London

Mysterious Regions

by Beppie Harrison

Series Coordinator: John Mason
Art Director: Grahame Dudley
Designer: Juanita Grout
Editor: Nina Shandloff
Research: Sarah Waters

SBN 490 004369

© 1979 Aldus Books Limited London

First published in the United Kingdom
in 1979 by Aldus Books Limited
17 Conway Street, London W1P 6BS

Printed and bound in Hong Kong by
Lee Fung-Asco Printers Ltd.

Introduction

The earth is full of dark and mysterious
regions, remote or desolate territories far
from the cozy, snug domestic patchwork
of town and country which forms the
backdrop for the lives of most of us. But
for the adventurous, those faraway places
—the icy poles, the vast burning deserts,
the perilous mountain peaks, and the dense
impenetrable jungles—have always exerted
an overwhelming attraction. What
mysteries do these places still hold? What
of those who dared to venture into these
strange regions? What hardships did they
experience? How many returned to tell the
tale, and how many were believed when
they did come back? Who were the
explorers and adventurers who searched
for a Northwest Passage through the icy
waters north of Canada; who were
obsessed with setting foot on the North
Pole before anyone else; who stubbornly
believed in an undiscovered continent or a
city of gold; or underwent incredible
hardship and courted incurable fevers to
map the source of the Nile? It is the stories
of these people, who pitted themselves
against sometimes impossible odds to
fulfill their quests, which make up this
book. Their intriguing reports, along with
their very personalities, provide answers
to some of the enigmas. But will we ever
know all the answers—or will our strange
and challenging world retain some of its
secrets forever?

Contents

Chapter 1 The Riddle of the Northwest Passage

For centuries Europe coveted the spices and treasures of the mysterious East, which reached the West through the hands of Arab merchants. To bypass these middlemen was an obvious objective. A route west and north, past newly discovered North America, seemed a logical possibility, especially to armchair navigators, and for nearly 500 years sailors and explorers struggled through the Arctic's frozen wastes to find it. Was there ever a Northwest Passage? What happened to those who went to search for it? What was learned about life in the frozen north, and what sacrifices were necessary to obtain that knowledge?

The wind had dropped. In the chill Arctic air of the morning of July 26, 1845 two ships, the H.M.S. *Erebus* and the H.M.S. *Terror*, stirred restlessly, waiting for a strong breeze to fill their sails and take them west across the icy waters of Baffin Bay off the coast of Greenland to the mouth of Lancaster Sound. Aboard the ships were 129 officers and men led by Sir John Franklin, a well-known and respected British explorer who had several grueling years of Arctic experience behind him. He and his men were impatiently awaiting the opportunity to solve one of geography's most enigmatic puzzles.

For nearly 400 years seamen had been searching for the elusive strait that they believed connected the Atlantic and Pacific Oceans across the northern reaches of the immense American continent, convinced that logic demanded the existence of a Northwest Passage. Bold explorers, most of them British, had endured the appalling hardships of the Arctic—cold that froze the flesh, barren wastes of ice that covered land and sea alike, and terrifying storms which tossed sturdy ships recklessly between jagged ice floes and forbidding cliffs—to search for the Passage. Although none had succeeded, most of those who returned were sure that they would have found it, if only the ice had not forced them back.

In 1840 Britain's admiralty secretary, Sir John Barrow, believed success was at last in sight. A route had been explored on the Pacific side of the North American continental coastline

Opposite: frozen wastes of the Canadian Arctic. Conditions in the area in which generations of seamen searched for a Northwest Passage were almost intolerable for humans, but impelled by a combination of scientific curiosity and commercial motives numerous bold explorers made the attempt.

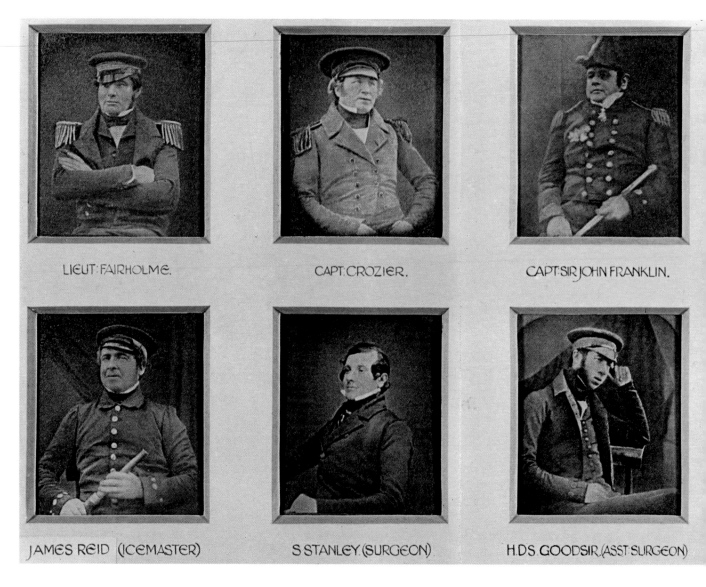

LIEUT. FAIRHOLME.

CAPT. CROZIER.

CAPT. SIR JOHN FRANKLIN.

JAMES REID (ICEMASTER)

S. STANLEY (SURGEON)

H.D.S. GOODSIR (ASST. SURGEON)

from Bering Strait as far east as the mouth of Back River and from the Atlantic side as far up the broad channel past Lancaster Sound as Melville Island. Only a few hundred miles remained to be crossed, argued Sir John. Surely it was time for a final expedition, the one that would complete the task. So plans were meticulously made, ships were supplied with provisions for three years, and in May 1845 they sailed down the Thames to the sea.

By July 26, the *Erebus* and the *Terror* had crossed the Atlantic and taken aboard their stores from the supply ship which had accompanied them to Greenland. All they needed now was the wind. As they waited the whaler *Prince of Wales* drifted nearby, and 10 of Franklin's officers took a boat over to it to invite her captain to dine with their commander that evening. The whaler's log recorded that all Franklin's men were well and that they were confident and in good spirits. But that afternoon, before Captain Dannett could take up Sir John's invitation, the long-awaited strong breeze came up. White sails swelling with the wind, the *Erebus* and the *Terror* sailed off west past the icebergs and into the world's naval history.

The Enigmatic Arctic Region

COM^DR FITZJAMES.

LIEUT·GRAHAM GORE.

C. OSMER. (PURSER)

H.F. COLLINS (ICEMASTER)

Left: some of the officers of the *Erebus*, which sailed from England on May 19, 1845 and was never heard from again. Its commander, Sir John Franklin, is pictured in the middle of the upper row, wearing a medal that would later be used as a means of identification.

Of all the world's mysterious regions, the North American Arctic was among the most reluctant to yield its secrets to the persistence of explorers. Men battled the savage climate and hostile landscape for five centuries to discover its secrets. Some found the puzzle so fascinating that they could not leave it alone: after limping, half-dead, back to civilization they were straining to be off again as soon as their health was restored, back to the cold, hunger, and the mysterious lure of the unknown. It is from the carefully collected maps and notations of these men that we now know what the Canadian Arctic archipelago looks like — roughly, a triangle shattered into a mass of fragmented islands. Its base lies just north of the Arctic Circle, and the point curves over toward Greenland.

Between the islands runs a broad waterway from Baffin Bay to the Beaufort Sea, part of the Arctic Ocean. Although a single channel, it is called (from east to west) Lancaster Sound, Barrow Strait, Viscount Melville Sound, and McClure Strait. On the map it appears that, were it only ice-free, the channel would be one of the world's great waterways, a direct route from Europe

Right: map of northern Canada and Greenland, showing the area through which Sir John Franklin's ships and those of later explorers tried to find a passage from the northern Atlantic across to Asia. Their efforts added greatly to geographical knowledge of the Arctic.

to the Far East. Unfortunately, the heavy permanent pack ice of the Arctic Ocean, forced through the funnel of McClure Strait, forms an insuperable obstacle. About 300 miles south of this great channel is a much narrower, shallower waterway which runs from the Beaufort Sea in the west along the northern coast of the American continent until it is blocked by Boothia Peninsula, jutting northward like a fat thumb. This waterway, like that to the north, has many names: from east to west it is called Simpson Strait, Queen Maud Gulf, Dease Strait, Coronation Gulf, Dolphin and Union Strait, and Amundsen Gulf. Between these two east/west channels, threading between the islands which separate them, are four channels running north/south. We now know that not all are navigable even in a good year: shallows or thick pack ice forced eastward and southward by the currents of the Arctic Ocean make them impassable.

Franklin's maps were considerably less comprehensive. By the time he sailed, Lancaster Sound had been discovered and explored to the extent that headlands had been named and charted as far west as Melville Island. Sir William E. Parry had overwintered at Winter Harbor on Melville Island in 1819–20 and while there had explored the northern coast, so the outlines of that island were fairly clearly drawn. Several land expeditions had mapped the southern shore of the narrower channel, skirting the continental coastline, but the northern edge was unexplored. Both Parry in 1824 and the Scottish explorer Sir John Ross in 1829 had sailed down Prince Regent Inlet and mapped the eastern coasts of Somerset Island and Boothia Peninsula, which were

The Elusive Shortcut

Left: Sir William Edward Parry (1790–1855), whose first journey (to Baffin Bay and Lancaster Sound) was made when he was only 29 years old. He was very ambitious and had already won a fellowship to the Royal Society for his knowledge of hydrography (the study and charting of bodies of water), nautical astronomy, and magnetic research. He was also well known in the navy for his seamanship, navigation, and sensitive leadership qualities.

thought to be connected. Ross' nephew, Sir James Clark Ross, was the second-in-command on his voyage, and he had made land journeys westward across Boothia during the winters when their ship was frozen in, crossing what is now named James Ross Strait to what he called King William Land. In the frozen landscape where land and sea alike were sheathed in ice, Ross decided that King William Land was part of Boothia and therefore part of the mainland rather than an island. It was an error with far-reaching consequences.

A few of the dead ends which had trapped many of Franklin's predecessors were at least clearly recognized as such. Hudson Bay was for centuries seen by geographers as the obvious possibility, but dozens of men, starved, scurvy-ridden, and frozen, had died there vainly seeking a westward opening. Parry spent two years in Hudson Bay on his second voyage which began in 1821, discovering, as he explained later, where *not* to find the Passage. He did eventually locate a narrow, icebound strait far in the north of Foxe Basin, but it was not then clear where it led. Since it was not navigable in any case, the strait was not considered a promising lead, and from then on the ships went elsewhere.

Even with maps which indicated approximately what lay ahead (a luxury denied to most of Franklin's predecessors, who headed north into uncharted territory), navigation in Arctic waters is a hazardous business. There is the everpresent ice—a solid, unbreakable sheet in winter, a shifting, floating maze in summer. Clouds lie low over the land and water; there is fog during the

Above: Sir James Clark Ross (1800–1862). He was very experienced in arctic conditions (his first journey was with his uncle Sir John Ross when he was only 18 years old) and crossed James Ross Strait. There he assumed that King William Island was attached to the Boothia peninsula.

The Frozen Desert

Right: drawing by Sir John Ross of a strange iceberg he encountered in Baffin Bay in 1818.

summer, while winter brings weeks of storms during a perpetual night. A magnetic compass is often useless for navigation because of the proximity of the magnetic North Pole. The water is so bitterly cold that the life expectancy of a man unfortunate enough to fall into it is about two minutes. The land is hardly more hospitable: it is barren, with little vegetation. The Arctic is one of the world's deserts, albeit a frozen one.

The temperature of the Arctic waters Franklin set out to explore is so low that even the sea water freezes. The ice first forms in areas of low salinity (saltiness), generally near coasts and particularly near the mouths of rivers. It was this phenomenon which for centuries led geographers to believe that ice formed only near the land, and that if you sailed far enough into the ocean you would find clear water, a belief that led many to look for an ice-free passage over the North Pole. Sea ice actually begins as a thin crust which grows into continuous sheets of young ice. At the end of an Arctic winter the young ice is usually about 5 feet thick, but during the summer much of it melts, creating pools of fresh water which seep under the remaining ice and freeze again underneath. As the ice becomes older and (through this melting process) less salty, it also grows harder until, as polar ice, it is as hard as steel. Ice floes—single sheets of polar ice—can be as small as a dining table or cover an area many

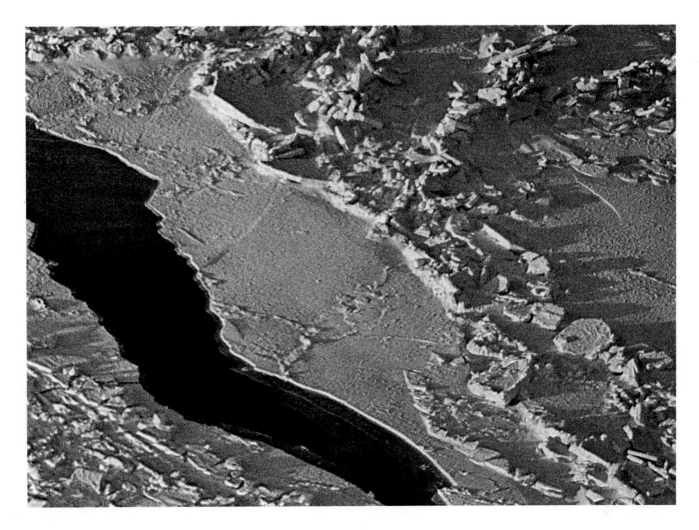

miles square. When ice floes are driven by the wind and tides to collide with each other, they form pressure ridges as high as 50 feet. Between the floes are *leads* or channels of open water, and the traditional method of ice navigation is to sail as quickly as possible through these ever-changing channels. There is always the danger of a ship being crushed between floes or pinched fatally between ice and shoreline rocks, or of the lead closing behind the ship so that retreat becomes impossible and the ship is imprisoned in the ice.

In the winter ice blocks all channels. By April or May with longer, warmer days the accumulated snow and ice begin to melt until, generally by August, the resulting patches of clear water permit some movement along the channels and straits. In October winter begins again, and the ice becomes solid once more. The "season" for exploration is thus August and September, with luck, and it was to reach the Arctic in time for that short season that Franklin was aiming. Of course, in a bad year the season may not come at all. More than one explorer has seen his ship remain frozen in winter ice while the two precious months slipped past, knowing that he and his crew would have to endure another long winter before they could hope to break free into open water.

Had it not been for the silks and spices of the East, the adven-

Above: aerial view of a lead—a strip of open water in the Arctic pack ice. The watery lanes provide channels for ships to pass through, but they are only temporary openings and can quickly close up again, thus trapping a ship within the ice.

turing seamen of Europe would undoubtedly have felt little interest in penetrating hostile Arctic waters. But there were treasures in Cathay, and medieval Europe was eager for a route that would bypass the Arab middlemen who controlled overland routes to Asia. In the 15th century, while the Portuguese rounded the Cape of Good Hope at the southern tip of Africa and prepared to strike out for India from there, the Italian Christopher Columbus sailed west and in 1492 reached what he was convinced were the Indies. The Venetian John Cabot, sailing for the English, was the first to head northwest across the Atlantic in 1497. He, too, thought he had reached Asia.

As it became obvious that the newly found lands were not part of Asia, but a previously unsuspected land mass that would have to be bypassed in order to reach the Indies, there was no shortage of men eager to find the way. The Portuguese navigator Ferdinand Magellan succeeded, in the service of Spain in 1519–21, by going south around South America's Cape Horn. Others went

Below: map drawn by order of the Danish explorer Vitus Bering in 1729, illustrating his first expedition of 1727–29. The map shows the people of Siberia as Bering saw them and also records a line of soundings he and Alexei Chirikov made, reaching above 67° north. It was there Bering decided that "our task had been carried out and that the land did not extend farther north."

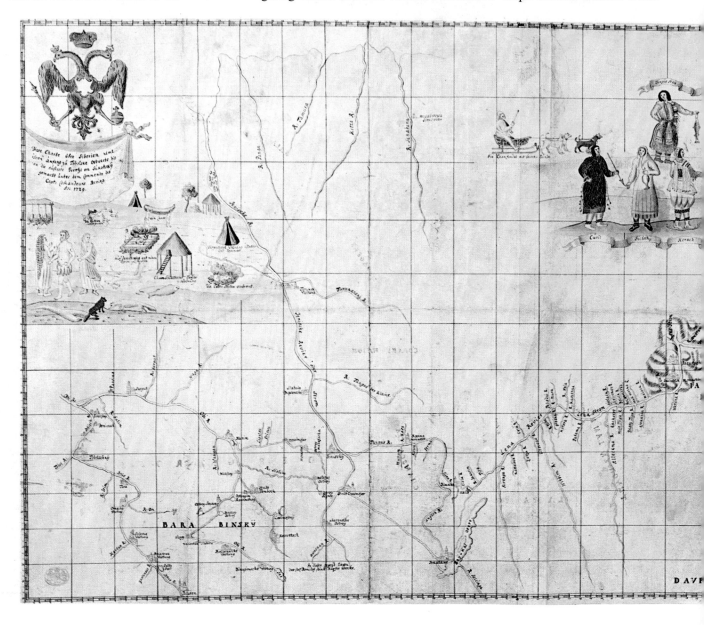

north. Gradually, as their search led into higher and higher latitudes, it became obvious that the Passage did not exist in the more southerly, ice-free waters and therefore was unlikely to be commercially useful. The hopes of a shortcut to the wealth of the East flickered and dimmed. But the pure challenge glittered brighter than ever. Did the Passage exist at all? When so little was known anything seemed possible. Could it be found? If dogged determination could overcome the ice, the Passage would be found. For the British by the 19th century the search had acquired the role that space exploration would have for the United States a century later. The Napoleonic Wars had ended in 1815 and the British Navy, unquestioned ruler of the seas, had ships and experienced sailors with little to do. The question of the Northwest Passage, now a purely geographical problem, was still unsolved. The ice (like outer space and Mount Everest to later adventurers) was *there*, and for some men that was reason enough. In addition, there were Russian challengers. Vitus

Unsolved Problem

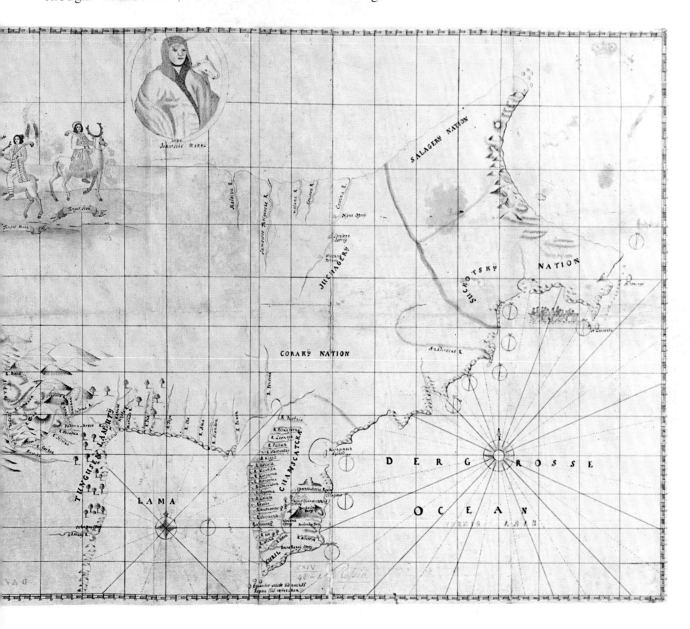

Franklin's Expedition

Bering, a Dane sailing for the Russians, had in 1728 set off around Kamchatka Peninsula and sailed northward through what became known as Bering Strait. In 1784 Russian traders had established the first white settlement in Alaska—and hence the only governing power. A clearly desirable side effect of British ships in the Arctic would be to counteract Russia's imperialistic claims.

Out of this confusion of motives, and urged on by reports that the waters off Greenland were freer of ice in 1817 than they had been for decades, the British Parliament in 1818 offered a series of prizes for Arctic exploration. Expeditions set off immediately: Parry sailed west down Lancaster Sound to Melville Island, and there were expeditions to Baffin Bay, Hudson Bay, and the Prince Regent Inlet area northwest of Baffin Island. Meanwhile land expeditions, two commanded by the then Lieutenant John Franklin, traced out the north coast of the American continent, and by 1840 the stage was set. The existence of the two east/west channels was established, and what remained was to connect these two channels by a strait running north/south. Then the elusive Passage would be complete. It was a tempting prospect, and if not perhaps as straightforward as armchair geographers in England made it sound, it did seem possible. The solution to the centuries-old mystery might be close at hand.

An expedition was thus organized in a climate of optimism. The officers and crew were hand picked, and many were Arctic veterans. John Franklin, by now 59 years old and honored by a knighthood, volunteered to lead the expedition, and after some doubts were expressed about his age he was eventually accepted. His instructions were to fill in the empty places on the map. He

Below: the then Lieutenant Franklin's party encamped during his 1819–21 overland expedition from the Hudson Bay to the mouth of the Coppermine River. It was these expeditions, made after the British Parliament offered a series of prizes for Arctic exploration, which helped to trace out the details of the north coast of the American continent.

was to proceed through Lancaster Sound and Barrow Strait and then go southwest as directly as ice and yet-undiscovered land permitted. If that were not possible, he could turn north up Wellington Channel (the first channel to the north after entering Lancaster Sound) and see if an opening to the west existed from there. The two ships selected, the *Erebus* and the *Terror*, were both sturdy, former bomb vessels that had already been used successfully for exploration in ice. Both were refurbished to include such amenities as silver, crystal, and porcelain for the messrooms. Thus luxuriously equipped, the two ships sailed across the North Atlantic to Baffin Bay and their recorded 1845 encounter with the whaling ship.

When 1846 passed with no word from the expedition, no one was particularly concerned. Even into 1847 there was little official anxiety. Franklin was well supplied, and his previous land expeditions had given him valuable experience in Arctic conditions. Besides, when Sir John Ross had sailed into Arctic waters he had been caught by the ice for three consecutive winters, then trapped for a fourth after he had abandoned his ship—and he had survived for more than four years, losing only three men.

None the less it was Ross himself, then nearly 70 years old, who first publicly raised the alarm in the summer of 1847. The admiralty consulted with its experts and the consensus of opinion was that, although probably all was still well, there would be no

Above: life in the Arctic around 1800, not too long before Franklin's expedition sailed to look for the Northwest Passage. Here a group, probably of Europeans, hunts seals in Baffin Bay. Eskimos usually hunted alone, though different tribes had different techniques. The Mackenzie Bay people would crawl up pretending to be a seal and then capture their prey by surprise. The Victoria Island Eskimos would sit at seal holes for hours, waiting for the seal to come out.

Above: Lady Jane Franklin, wife of Sir John, who eventually became a popular heroine for her determination to find out what had happened to her husband.

harm·in making preparations for a rescue expedition the next year if there were still no word.

The months dragged by and still nothing was heard from the ships. Although she had been specifically warned by her husband not to worry if the expedition did not return within the three years, Lady Jane Franklin was troubled by the silence. In November 1847 the admiralty finally bowed to pressure and announced three relief expeditions. The first, by sea to Bering Strait, left in January 184 on the hopeful premise that Franklin would be intercepted as he completed the Passage. The second, led by Sir John Richardson, would go east overland from the mouth of the Mackenzie River, searching the oastline from there to the Coppermine River at Coronation Gulf—the very coastline that Richardson had surveyed with Franklin himself more than 20 years before. He was accompanied by Dr. John Rae of the Hudson Bay Company, who was known for his successful survival techniques, mainly derived from the Eskimo way of life. He had just returned from two years of living off the land while mapping Rae Isthmus and Committee Bay, southeast of Boothia.

The third expedition, commanded by James Clark Ross with Robert McClure and Francis Leopold McClintock as his first and second lieutenants, set off in June 1848 to retrace the route that Franklin had presumably followed. The ice was menacing that year, and the two relief ships had to circle far to the north to reach the now-familiar entrance to Lancaster Sound. As they sailed in past icy headlands, Ross fired guns, set off rockets, and dropped a daily cask filled with papers explaining what they were doing and where they were going. Foxes were captured, fitted with copper collars giving the position of the ships and supply depots, and set loose, on the supposition that Franklin's men would by now be hunting them for food. Winter came early, and the ships reached only as far as Somerset Island before they were iced in. But this rescue mission could not afford to wait passively for spring: every week counted if Franklin and his men were to be saved. As soon as the worst winter storms were over, sledge parties set out to hunt for wreckage or cairns that might contain records and to establish food depots for the missing men.

Sledging parties crossed Somerset Island and came to Peel Sound, a new southerly opening off Barrow Strait. They followed its easterly shore for miles, but there was no sign of life. The sledging parties went out throughout the spring and summer, but theirs was a new technique for polar exploration. In the event the sledges proved cumbersome and the men's rations insufficient to sustain them in the low temperatures to which they were exposed day and night, with the heavy labor of pulling massive sledges. All of the search parties returned weak and emaciated; seven men died.

They returned to England in 1849. They had explored Somerset Island and discovered Peel Sound, but they had not rescued Franklin and his men nor found any trace of them.

The overland expedition of Richardson and Rae was equally unsuccessful. They had followed the coastline from the Mackenzie to the Coppermine but had seen no ships. Eskimos living in the region told them there had been no ships the previous year either, nor had the expedition to Bering Strait found anything.

The Search for Sir John Begins

Left: Dr. John Rae (1813–1893), a Scot and the resident surgeon at the Hudson Bay Company's station at Moose Factory. He was a particularly successful Arctic traveler, borrowing from the early fur traders the habit of making his journeys with little equipment but in the company of natives of the region. He learned the skills they used to survive. He was a superb hunter and could build an igloo or a stone house if necessary.

It was as if Franklin's men—and his ships—had evaporated.

When the rescue expeditions returned with no news whatsoever public concern intensified at the grim picture of 100 or more men starving in the frozen Arctic wasteland. In 1850 12 ships set out from both sides of the Atlantic. One, the *Prince Albert*, was sponsored by Lady Franklin herself, whose determination to find her husband had made her a popular heroine. Two ships, the *Enterprise* under Richard Collinson and the *Investigator*, commanded by Robert McClure (barely returned from the fruitless Ross rescue expedition), were dispatched by way of Bering Strait to push east toward Melville Island. The main flotilla of six admiralty ships under Henry Austin went to Lancaster Sound, where they were joined by Lady Franklin's *Prince Albert*, the elderly Sir John Ross in the *Felix*, and two American brigantines which arrived later in the season to help in the search. It was the Americans who first discovered traces of the missing ships at Beechey Island, a tiny, rocky promontory at the southwest corner of Devon Island near the entrance to Wellington Channel. There were bits of rope and traces of a tent site, and after further search the graves of three of Franklin's men were discovered. No written record survived, but a pair of gloves were found that had

More Relief Expeditions

been left to dry in the sun, and a store of tinned meat left behind suggested the location of the expedition's winter harbor, from which the ships may have hastily departed.

Again the ice was hostile, and the fleet could not advance further than the eastern part of Barrow Strait. Sledging parties ventured out under McClintock, who had returned to the search in Austin's party. McClintock had greatly developed the techniques of sledging so that the men were less exhausted and could travel much further. He was able to explore new territory to the west and north. Lady Franklin's *Prince Albert* contributed the most important piece to the geographical puzzle by finding Bellot Strait, a narrow channel that cut Somerset Island off from Boothia Peninsula.

But when the Lancaster Sound contingent returned to their home ports only three of the 129 men who had originally sailed with Franklin were accounted for: the fate of the rest was as dark a mystery as ever. In addition, more men were now missing. Collinson and McClure had sailed in January 1850; by the winter of 1851 they seemed to have disappeared as completely as the ships they had gone to rescue. Faced with this melancholy situation the admiralty was disposed to give up the search, but the indomitable Lady Franklin was not. Thus in the spring of 1852, by which time Franklin and his men had been gone for nearly seven years and Collinson and McClure with their crews for over two, yet another relief expedition of four ships, under Edward Belcher, was dispatched to search for all the missing sailors.

Belcher divided his forces into two—one to search Wellington Channel, where traces of Franklin might reasonably be expected, and one to sail on to Melville Island, which McClure and Collinson had hoped to reach from the west. Henry Kellett in the *Resolute* went directly to Melville Island, arriving there in September. He investigated Parry's old base, Winter Harbor—and discovered a note from McClure, left there five months before.

McClure had taken his ship *Investigator* through Bering Strait in July 1850. He had followed the coastline east to Cape Bathurst, past the mouth of the Mackenzie River. Then, sighting land across the channel, he had discovered and crossed Prince of Wales Strait, which divided Banks and Victoria Islands. According to his message he had then sailed north up the strait until ice

Right: the departure of exploring parties from their ship once it has become frozen in the Arctic ice. Sledges pulled by men or dogs were the only means of covering large areas in the search for Franklin and his men.

blocked his way, only 30 miles from Melville Sound. Sledging parties reached the northeasternmost point of Banks Island, and from there McClure was able to see that Prince of Wales Strait flowed into Melville Sound. Across the ice-covered water to the north was Melville Island, which Parry had reached from the east 30 years before. This was the last link in the long-sought, mysterious Northwest Passage. All that remained was to wait for the next summer season when he would be able to sail the last 30 miles, and the Passage would be his.

That season had never come. The next year the last few miles were as impassable as before. Deciding to approach from a different direction, McClure sailed back south and west around Banks Island to try again. This time he became hopelessly locked in the polar ice pack off the northwest coast of the island. That winter he sledged across to Winter Harbor on Melville Island and left the message giving his ship's location and a report of what he had accomplished. Again the next summer—by now it was 1852—the ship remained icebound, and by winter, McClure's third, provisions were dangerously low and scurvy had taken hold of the crew. They could not all stay where they were: if they

Above: Robert McClure's ship the *Investigator*, frozen in the ice in the Prince of Wales Strait in 1850 during his search for Franklin. McClure continued eastward by sledge after his ship was imprisoned in the ice, and he reached Melville Sound. Earlier explorers coming from the east had managed to get as far as Melville Sound, so McClure can be given credit for discovering the first of what later turned out to be several northwest passages to the Pacific Ocean.

Below (top): the chronometer watch issued to the H.M.S. *Terror*, which McClintock found on the ship's boat.

Below (bottom): Sir John Franklin's own cutlery, bearing his crest, which Rae was given by Eskimos in 1854.

did they would starve. Therefore they would have to split into smaller groups and, weakened though they were, sledge out in hope of rescue, some southwest toward the Mackenzie River and others east toward Lancaster Sound where other ships might be sighted.

Eight days before the parties were due to leave, McClure and a lieutenant were walking on the ice outside the ship debating whether it would be possible to cut a grave for a member of the crew who had died the day before when they sighted a figure running toward them. At first they thought he was a fellow member of the *Investigator*'s crew, but his clothes were unfamiliar. They had started toward him half-fearfully when he threw up his arms and shouted, "I'm Lieutenant Pim, late of the *Herald* and now in the *Resolute*. Captain Kellett is in her at Dealy Island!"

Sick men on the ship scrambled out of their hammocks. The crew swarmed down on to the ice as Pim's accompanying sledge arrived, pulled by two seamen who were plainly appalled at the emaciation of the men they had come to save. In spite of

The Searchers Find Remains

McClure's protests—he wanted to try the Passage with any volunteers who would stay on until the next summer—the *Investigator* was abandoned on the grounds that the crew were too weak to sail her. The men were transferred to the *Resolute* and eventually returned to England in September 1854.

A year later Collinson and his men arrived home. Having reached the Arctic later than McClure, he had been unable to pass through Bering Strait until 1851. He had then followed McClure in the discovery of Prince of Wales Strait, finding a food cache and message left there by McClure. He then determined to round Banks Island to the west but the ice had closed in, and he spent the winter in Walker Bay. In 1852 he reached Cambridge Bay at the southeast corner of Victoria Island and spent the winter sledging along the east coast of the island. That summer, having found a door casing which he assumed had come from one of the Franklin ships, he started back west to Bering Strait but was iced in again short of Point Barrow in the Beaufort Sea and only reached ice-free waters in the summer of 1854.

Above left: drawing by Sir John Ross from the 1820s of an Eskimo village known as North Hendon, near Felix Harbor on the Boothia peninsula. It was from Eskimos on hunting trips away from villages like this that Rae received information about what had happened to Franklin's expedition.

Above: Cross of the Guelphic Order of Hanover, Franklin's medal, found by some Eskimos and given to Rae in 1854.

Above: the *Fox*, a small steamer which Lady Franklin purchased and equipped privately in 1857 for yet another search expedition. She obtained from the British navy the services of Sir Francis Leopold McClintock (1819–1907) as commander with the help of the personal intervention of Prince Albert.

But however remarkable the feats of endurance of the men who set out to find Franklin—and in spite of the fact that the Passage had been discovered, if not actually navigated—the question of what had happened to Franklin and his men remained unanswered. It was nine years since they had sailed, and in 1854 they were officially pronounced dead.

Ironically, it was only after the official search ended that the story began to emerge. In 1854 John Rae, who had searched the continental coastline fruitlessly with Richardson in 1847–9, was surveying the western coast of Boothia for the Hudson Bay Company when he encountered some Eskimos who had interesting information. They told him a party of white men had been seen, years before, dragging a boat southward over the ice near the north shore of King William's Land. All were thin and gaunt. Later another group of Eskimos had found 30 or so bodies in the area of Back River. Some had been buried, but evidence was found—the mutilated condition of some of the corpses and the contents of the kettles found with them—implying that the starving men had turned to cannibalism. As mute confirmation of their story the Eskimos offered a few relics, including a medal belonging to Sir John Franklin and silverware bearing the personal crest of several of his officers. At the time it seemed almost incidental that Rae had discovered the strait which separated King William Land from Boothia Peninsula. With his report, the pathetic relics, and his maps, Rae hurried back to England.

Lady Franklin was still not satisfied. Pointing out quite reasonably that now fewer than 40 men had been accounted for out of a total of 129, she still clung to a shred of hope that there might have been another party that had survived. In any case, no written records had yet been recovered to prove whether or not Franklin's men had succeeded in finding—if not navigating—a Northwest Passage several years before McClure. But by this time the admiralty were deeply involved in the Crimean War against Russia, and despite Lady Franklin they relied on the Hudson Bay Company, which sent its own expedition in 1855 to the mouth of the Back River. What they found confirmed Rae's information—stories of white men who had starved to death years before and tent poles, oars, and tools salvaged for Eskimo huts. Clearly at least a few survivors had reached Simpson Strait, between King William Land (now renamed King William Island) and the mainland, and by so doing part of the Franklin expedition had completed a Northwest Passage. They had been the first to solve the mystery but had paid for the solution with their lives.

Only Lady Franklin was still prepared to persevere. She had already spent half her fortune on the search, but in 1857, with the aid of a public appeal, she bought a pleasure steamer called the *Fox* and chose Sir Francis McClintock to sail it on a last search expedition. He left Aberdeen, Scotland, in July 1857, 12 years after John Franklin's departure, but again the ice was against them. The ship was caught in the Baffin Bay ice pack and carried remorselessly southward, until in the summer of 1858 they finally came free in very nearly the same position they had achieved the

Lady Franklin is Unconvinced

Below: Eskimos fishing through holes they have made in the ice. Many of the white men who died in the Arctic wilderness, such as those of the Franklin expedition, might have had a better chance of surviving the hostile conditions if they had learned to fish and hunt from the Eskimos they encountered.

The Tragedy Confirmed!

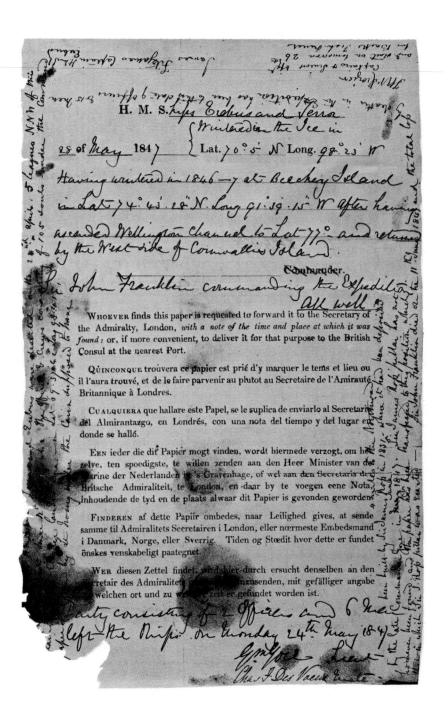

Right: the last message of the Franklin expedition, written on one of the official printed forms that discovery ships would throw overboard enclosed in bottles to prove the direction of ocean currents. The finder was requested to send it on to the admiralty with a note of the time and place it was found. This form was filled in twice, once by Lieutenant Gore in 1847 and again around the margins by Captains Crozier and Fitzjames in 1848.

year before. But during 1858 McClintock did manage to enter Lancaster Sound. Peel Sound was ice-choked, so McClintock went down Prince Regent Inlet east of Somerset Island, intending to reach the area north of King William Island by way of Bellot Strait. That strait was also impassable, so McClintock wintered just outside its eastern end. In early spring a new series of sledge journeys began, this time using dogs to draw them. On one journey McClintock met some Eskimos who told him of two ships that had been caught in the ice; one had sunk and the other been driven ashore, and the crews had left with their boats in the direction of Back River.

One search party, under McClintock, then followed the eastern

coastline of King William Island, while the second, under his lieutenant W. R. Hobson, combed the western shore. McClintock met an old Eskimo woman who told him that the white men had moved south, dropping one by one as they walked. He also found silver articles which the Eskimos said had been recovered from a wreck on the western shore. Continuing south, he searched the desolate lands around the Back River estuary and then crossed back to King William Island. He headed up the western coast to meet Hobson, and it was there that he found a skeleton face down on the beach. It was that of a young man, and beside it were a clothes brush and pocket comb. He had apparently fallen and died as he walked; by that time his companions must have been incapable of helping him or even of noticing that he was no longer shambling along beside them.

It was Hobson who finally found the long-sought written record. In a metal box under a cairn at Point Victory, on the northwest coast of King William Island, they found one of the printed forms usually supplied to discovery ships, filled in by Lieutenant Graham Gore. He had been leading a party of seven men from Franklin's two ships. Dated May 28, 1847, it gave the ships' position and stated that they had wintered in 1846–7 at Beechey Island north of Somerset Island, and had circumnavigated Cornwallis Island to the west. At that time all was well. But around the margin was a very different note. On April 22, 1848 Captains Crozier and Fitzjames reported that they were abandoning the ships, which had been beset for two winters. Franklin had died in June 1847, and in all 24 men had died. The 105 survivors were starting for Back River the next day.

The forlorn story was now complete. Franklin had apparently found Barrow Strait impassable and had turned north up Wel-

Above: the crew of the *Erebus* haul their boats onto an ice flow after the ship's progress was blocked in Lancaster Sound. Franklin's expedition eventually foundered at the entrance to an impassable channel, Victoria Strait.

Right: *The Death of Franklin* by W. Thomas Smith, painted in 1895. The record left by Crozier and Fitzjames stated clearly that Franklin had died before the ships were abandoned, but in this melodramatic version the bodies lie around the lifeboat with a noble Franklin the last man alive. The painting was widely exhibited in England, where the public was stunned by the 50-year-old disaster.

lington Channel, between Cornwallis and Beechey Islands, as per his instructions. Not finding any clear way west from north of Cornwallis Island, he came back south along its western side and wintered at Beechey Island. The next year he was able to move further—he discovered Peel Sound (as Ross' first relief expedition in 1848 was also to do) and sailed south through what is now known as Franklin Strait. There at its southern end, where the channel widens north of King William Island, Franklin made his fatal mistake. He headed around the western side of the island. In a sense, of course, he had had no choice, since back in 1830 James Clark Ross had reported that King William Island was connected to Boothia Peninsula. It was not until 1854 that Rae discovered that this was not so, seven years too late for Franklin.

Victoria Strait, the channel to the west of King William Island, was not—and is not now—navigable. The heavy polar pack ice, driven by the wind from the Beaufort Sea through McClure Strait and down McClintock Channel, forms a permanent, unyielding obstacle off the southeastern coast of Victoria Island. There Franklin's ships were hopelessly surrounded and there Franklin himself died. There also his expedition, begun with such bright hopes, came to an agonizing end, dogged by gnawing hunger, the deadly lassitude of scurvy, and the bitter pain of

A Fatal Error

Below: Roald Amundsen (1872–1928),
Norwegian explorer of both the Arctic and
Antarctic who first navigated the Northwest
Passage between 1903 and 1905. The son of
a shipowner, he deliberately trained himself
for polar exploration by studying navigation
and seamanship.

frostbite. Around them lay, as it lies even now, the implacable, impervious ice.

In the end it was a Norwegian who first navigated the Northwest Passage. Roald Amundsen left Norway in June 1903 with six companions in a small sloop called the *Gjöa*. They followed the route Franklin had pioneered, west through Lancaster Sound and Barrow Strait and south into Peel Sound. Fortune smiled— that year Franklin Strait was ice-free—and they were able to reach the sanctuary of the straits between King William Island and the Boothia Peninsula. The island itself protected them from the heavy polar ice. They spent two years on the island in a snug harbor they named Gjöa Haven, befriending the local Eskimos and living, like them, off the land while they made scientific observations. In 1905 the *Gjöa* continued west along the continental coastline, and in August 1905 Amundsen realized they had been successful when they met an American whaler which had come east through Bering Strait.

In comparison to the drama and tragedy of their 19th-century predecessors, the successful voyage was straightforward and uneventful. But the Arctic took its toll even on the calm, experienced Amundsen. Those who met him just after he had completed the Passage estimated his age at anywhere between 59 and 75; he was actually only 33 years old at the time.

Chapter 2
The North Pole Controversy

From the time people first realized that the world was round the idea of reaching the top of it—the North Pole—must have occurred to many of them. It certainly became an obsession with a few. What would it be like to stand on the spot from which all directions are south? A Norwegian explorer, Fridtjof Nansen, shrewdly speculated that the North Pole lay in a frozen polar sea. He hoped to reach it by letting his ship drift with the ice current. Then two Americans determined, separately, to challenge the icy wasteland—Dr. Cook and Commander Peary vied with each other for the long-sought prize of being the first person to stand at the top of the world.

Somewhere in the jumbled pack ice of the Arctic Ocean lies an imaginary point called the North Pole. It has no more physical reality than the invisible line called the equator which circles the earth: both are simply mathematical concepts. The Greeks theorized that the earth was a sphere and invented two imaginary lines, the equator and the axis (which runs through the center of the earth). The points where the axis pierces the surface of the sphere, north and south, they called poles.

In September 1909 two men announced within five days of each other that they had struggled across hundreds of miles of chaotic, drifting ice to the North Pole. Both were American. The first, Dr. Frederick Albert Cook, said that he had reached the pole on April 21, 1908, accompanied only by two Eskimos. The world was just beginning to honor Cook for his achievement when the second announcement came. Commander Robert Edwin Peary of the United States Navy had embarked, after President Theodore Roosevelt bade him a personal farewell, on his third attempt. He said he had reached the pole on April 6, 1909 with four Eskimos and his black manservant, Matthew Henson. He went on to insist furiously that Cook was lying, that he had not gone anywhere near the pole.

A tremendous controversy erupted as to which man had reached the pole which simmers on to this day. The fact that neither had seen any trace of the other proves nothing: the ice of the Arctic Ocean is in constant motion, drifting with the great

Opposite: Peary's expedition to the Arctic, painted as it moved across the ice by F. W. Stokes, a member of the team. The sledges had to travel across vast, featureless expanses, where each mile looked much like the last, with only the changing pattern of ice ridges or the challenge of the leads opening before them to break the monotonous sameness of the trek.

Early Failures -and Disasters

Opposite above: illustration of "Eskimaux Women of Igoolik," from *The Private Journal of Captain G. F. Lyon of H.M.S. Hecla During the Recent Voyage of Discovery Under Captain Parry*, published in London in 1824. This refers to one of Parry's earlier Arctic expeditions in search of the Northwest Passage.

Opposite below: Elisha Kent Kane (1820–1857), senior medical officer with the First Grinnell Expedition searching the Arctic for Sir John Franklin in 1850–51. He headed the Second Grinnell Expedition in 1853–55, which reached territory not previously discovered.

Below: map of the polar region, which drew explorers who were attracted by the challenge of an area as yet uncharted.

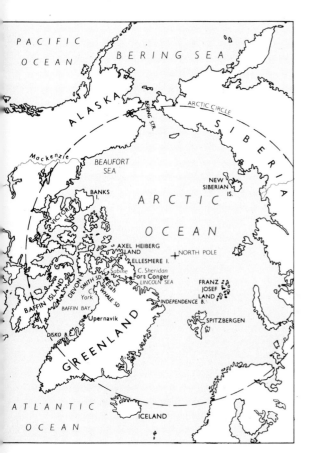

polar currents and blown by the wind. The ice that Cook stood on, if indeed he ever reached the pole, had long since drifted away by the time Peary arrived, if indeed he had reached the pole either. The pole, to the extent that it has any fixed location, exists on the Arctic Ocean seabed over 13,000 feet beneath the shifting ice. Was it Cook who reached the ice drifting above that elusive spot—ice which drifted on even as he made his observations? Or was it Peary who first stood triumphantly at the point from which all directions are south?

Whoever it was had achieved the culmination of centuries of effort. Initially the North Pole was merely a possible way across the Arctic, not a destination in itself. Among the first seekers of a Northwest Passage were several who believed that going over the North Pole would lead straight to Cathay, and that the North Pole lay within an iceless Arctic Sea. Sea ice forms first near land. Therefore geographers theorized that arctic ice formed only where fresh water mixed with the salt water—near land. The idea was that, if you could just get far enough away from the land so that the proportion of fresh water became insignificant, the sea would obviously be ice-free. Until late in the 19th century, when reports by explorers made it plain that the profound cold of the Arctic froze even salt water, navigators continued to set out hopefully, convinced that once past the ice barrier they would reach clear sailing.

Sir William E. Parry, the British explorer, had set off northward in 1827 with a new idea. He proposed to "reach the North Pole by means of traveling with sledge boats over the ice, or through any spaces of water that might occur." The ship was thus to be a floating base camp, transporting the expedition to the farthest possible point north, and sledges would take the men from there. His ship, the *Hecla*, reached the north coast of Spitzbergen in June. Leaving the *Hecla* with 27 men and two wooden boats equipped with steel runners, Parry set off for the pole. For the pioneer sledging teams, grappling with unwieldy boats and melting ice, it was an agonizing experience. Tormented by summer fog and wet snow, they inched northward. Water lay over the top of the ice, too shallow to float the boats but too deep to cross without getting soaked. In spite of all they could do, Parry's observations showed they hardly moved north at all. After 61 days of back-breaking effort, Parry returned to the *Hecla*. They had walked nearly a thousand miles, but at most they had been only 172 miles from the ship. They had encountered the powerful polar current sweeping down the eastern coast of Greenland, so for 12 hours each day Parry's men had struggled northward, and as they slept, completely spent, the current had carried them back south. They were on a giant treadmill. Even so, they had reached 82° 45′N.

The British were not inclined to attempt the polar ice again. Lancaster Sound appeared to be the most promising gate to a Northwest Passage and so the Franklin expedition went that way in 1845. Its disappearance and the subsequent rescue operations completely absorbed the attention of arctic explorers for the next two decades. Even so, the idea of a north polar route persisted. Another concept was also taking shape—that the pole itself was a splendid geographical prize.

Dr. Elisha Kent Kane, a member of a private United States rescue expedition in search of Franklin, probed the icebound channels between Greenland and Ellesmere Island, north of Devon Island, in the early 1850s. Kane thought the most probable route to the North Pole was through Smith Sound, but he himself was unable to get further than the upper end of the sound.

A disaster that opened the way for the eventual conquest of the North Pole was set in motion in 1879 when Lieutenant George Washington De Long of the United States Navy set off from San Francisco in the *Jeannette*, probably for the North Pole. By winter the ship was frozen fast in the ice, and the following June the ship was crushed north of the New Siberian Islands. The crew fled south over the ice to Siberia, but De Long and all but two of the crew died of starvation and cold before rescue could reach them.

But wreckage from the ship drifted on. Three years later clothing from the *Jeannette* was found by an Eskimo on the southwest coast of Greenland. The mystery of how it had reached Greenland from Siberia tantalized a young Norwegian explorer, Fridtjof Nansen. The New Siberian Islands and Greenland lie almost directly across the pole from each other. Was it possible that the wreckage had been carried across the pole by the currents? The *Jeannette* was no isolated fluke: Greenland Eskimos from time immemorial had fashioned their boats and sledges from driftwood, some of which was Siberian larch.

Nansen decided to use that current to carry him across the

Right: the discovery of the bodies of the crew of the *Jeannette*, commanded by Lieutenant George Washington DeLong of the U.S. navy. All but two of the crew died after the ship was wrecked north of Siberia.

polar basin. It might not take him directly across the pole itself, but it should be close enough. He designed a ship called the *Fram* ("Forward") to withstand the ice. It was small and short with rounded sides so that it would rise as the ice pressed in. With 11 companions, Nansen sailed from Norway on June 24, 1893. By September, northwest of the New Siberian Islands, the *Fram* was safely frozen into the ice.

However, the ice drift was not carrying them over the pole. The *Fram* reached about 84°N., but then the current took it west. The pole was 350 miles away, and the *Fram* was clearly going to get no closer. Nansen decided to try for the pole on foot, with sledges and dog teams. Taking one of the *Fram*'s officers, Hjalmar Johansen, Nansen started out for the pole on March 14, 1895. The first few days Nansen and Johansen skimmed easily across flat, smooth ice. The prize appeared to be there for the taking. But then they learned what the polar pack ice could be like—huge hummocks of jumbled ice, leads of open water thickly clouded with frost smoke, and pressure ridges where wind-driven ice floes had collided. Floes rafted up on each other, forming massive heaps of tumbled blocks over which dogs and men had to drag heavy sledges. Twenty-four days after they had set out they were still 270 miles from their goal. Nansen's diary records drearily, "Ridge after ridge . . . stretching as far as the horizon. There is not much sense in keeping on longer; we are sacrificing valuable time and doing little."

On April 8 they turned southward and after a long and difficult trek arrived at the group of islands east of Spitzbergen called Franz Josef Land, where they encountered another expedition. They returned to Norway in August 1896, the same month that the *Fram* arrived, finally broken out of the ice after 35 months and with all its crew aboard.

Nansen's observations and the information gained by the drifting *Fram* provided the first solid data about the polar region. It had been conclusively proven that the Arctic Ocean was a frozen sea. And Nansen's method of crossing it—with dogs and sledges—appeared to be the most promising.

Meanwhile, in the United States, Peary and Cook were growing into adulthood during this great period of Arctic exploration. Peary was born in Pennsylvania in 1856 and Cook in New York in 1865; both lost their fathers early and both were restless children, fascinated by tales of the faraway northern world. In Peary's papers is a Sunday School newspaper account of the work of Elisha Kent Kane in the Arctic, clearly treasured by the then 6-year-old Bertie Peary. Cook wrote as an adult of the "innate and abnormal desire for exploration" he had felt as a child.

Peary, the older of the two, was the first to see the Arctic. He joined the United States Navy as a civil engineer. He was tall, lean, athletic, and very conscious of himself. He was absolutely determined to be famous and decided to achieve that fame by conquering the North Pole. He read all the first-person accounts of Arctic explorers that he could find, and his diary for 1885 shows his thinking. Ten years before Nansen's voyage he wrote, "I do not believe in a perennial open polar sea . . . but I do believe that the unknown sea is like Kane Basin or Smith Sound." He added, "Smith Sound is preeminently the American route . . . let the English, the Germans, the Austrians have . . . all the other routes, but let us stick to Smith Sound . . ."

In 1886 he obtained six months' leave from the Navy, borrowed $500 from his mother, and went north to Greenland. He said not a word about the North Pole.

Nansen's Attempt

Below: Nansen and Johansen after leaving the *Fram*. At first they traveled by dog team, but conditions became so desperate that they had to kill their dogs one by one for food. They carried kayaks on their sledges, and once they reached open water they lashed the two kayaks together, rigged a sail, and set off across the water.

Peary and Cook

His scientific objectives in Greenland were not modest. He intended to find out if Greenland were an island or part of a continent; he wanted to discover the extent and nature of the icecap (at that time no one had crossed it); and he wanted to check out his arctic equipment.

He arrived in Disko Bay on the west coast in June 1886, where he joined forces with a young Dane, Christian Maigaard. The two set off to challenge the icecap—1500 miles long, 900 miles wide, rising to an altitude of 8000 feet, and featureless from coast to coast. Peary described the view across the icecap as composed of three elements only, "the infinite expanse of the frozen plain, the infinite dome of the cold blue sky, and the cold white sun— nothing but these." The glare of the sun on the white snow presented a constant threat of snowblindness, an agonizing condition that begins with the sensation of sand under the eyelids and turns into a painful temporary blindness. Only heavily smoked glasses can protect against it. Overcast days offered a different challenge, for when everything is white, white is invisible. Peary walked, able to feel the snow crunching under his snowshoes but unable to see it.

Peary and Maigaard had managed to cover about 100 miles

Left: the Greenland icecap—1500 miles long by 900 miles wide and rising to an altitude of 8000 feet. Peary attempted to cross the icecap in 1886 but only managed to cover about 100 miles. Fridtjof Nansen was the first to complete the crossing in 1888.

of the icecap by July 19. They had only six days' food left, and it was time to turn back. Peary had accomplished one of his dreams: he had seen places no other man had seen before him. He had not discovered much about the geography of Greenland, nor about the extent of the icecap, but at least he had started.

While Peary was testing himself against the Greenland ice, Frederick Cook was working as a milkman in Manhattan to finance his medical education. He graduated in 1890 and set up practice. That year his wife, whom he had only married the year before, died in childbirth with their baby. Cook sat in his lonely office and obsessively read books about exploration and travel.

Peary did not consider his road to fame particularly smooth. In 1888 Fridtjof Nansen achieved the first crossing of the Greenland icecap, and Peary was devastated. It was a feat he had marked out for himself. He wrote his mother sulkily, "Nansen profited much by my experience," and he mulled over plans to travel into northeast Greenland, the then-unmapped territory. But how was he to pay for it? During the winter of 1890 he managed to raise the finance—some of it from individuals who proposed to join the expedition—and in 1891 an advertisement for expedition members appeared in the Brooklyn *Standard*

Above: Dr. Frederick A. Cook (1865–
1940), Peary's rival to the honor of being
the first man at the North Pole. He was the
author of *Through the First Antarctic Night
1898-9* (1900), *To the Top of the Continent*
(1908), and *My Attainment of the Pole*
(1909).

Union. Cook promptly replied, was interviewed by Peary, and
became the first official member of the expedition, serving as the
surgeon and ethnologist without pay.

It was to be a small expedition, including no more than six.
One of these was Matt Henson, Peary's black personal servant,
who had been with him in Nicaragua on a Navy surveying
expedition.

They sailed on July 6, 1891, and on July 11—by this time off
Greenland—Peary broke his leg while navigating through ice.
Cook was able to set it and, although Peary had to be unloaded
from the ship strapped to a board, his iron constitution and
determination had him walking again within weeks. During the
winter Peary worked with the local Eskimos learning how to
build snowhouses, how to handle a team of dogs, and how to
use Eskimo fur clothing. By spring the expedition was ready to
set out. There were only four men in the traveling party, two of
whom would turn back after providing early support. Cook was
to be one of these. Peary and Eivind Astrup, a young Norwegian,
pressed on toward the northeast. After six weeks of struggle
across ice and snow, they reached a spectacular cliff almost 4000
feet high. Peary named it Navy Cliff and was sure the cleft beyond
it was a channel. He was thus convinced he had proved the in-
sularity of Greenland. He was wrong: the cleft is not a channel,
and the northern coast of Greenland lies a hundred miles further
on. He and Astrup turned back and reached the opposite coast
in August.

When they returned Peary began planning another expedition
for 1893. He wanted Cook to come with him again, and Cook
agreed. Unfortunately their continued collaboration foundered
on Cook's intention to publish in a medical journal some of the
ethnological information he had gathered. Peary considered that
all publication of any kind arising out of his expeditions should
be under his name and the proceeds devoted to his future polar
work—and thus the two parted. Peary asked Cook to give medical examinations to the members of his 1893 team, and Cook
obligingly did so, but when the ship sailed Cook was not aboard.

Nevertheless, Cook was determined to return to the north, and
in the summers of 1893 and 1894 he managed to get to Greenland. His finances allowed only modest journeys, and neither
was really satisfactory. In 1893 he chartered a yacht, but the
captain refused to sail to Cape York, and Cook had to be satisfied with studies of the Eskimo way of life near Upernavik, much
further south along the western Greenland coast. The next year
was even less successful. Cook's ship, the *Miranda*, collided with
an iceberg off Labrador and then rammed a submerged rock
coming into its Greenland harbor. Cook had to pilot a small
boat 90 miles northward to get the aid of a fishing boat, which
eventually evacuated the luckless *Miranda*.

Peary's enterprises were on a grander scale but not much more
productive. The dual problems of obtaining both leave from the
Navy and sufficient finance absorbed him through the winter and
spring of 1892–3, but the first was eventually resolved by the
intervention of an influential supporter; lectures, which grew increasingly theatrical, provided the money. Peary's Second North
Greenland Expedition sailed in July 1893. The expedition team

The Partners Become Rivals

Left: Robert E. Peary (1856–1920), who claimed to have reached the North Pole on April 6, 1909, here in his North Pole costume. He wrote *Northward over the Great Ice* (1898), *Nearest the Pole* (1907), and *The North Pole* (1910), and this illustration appeared in the last of these. His wife Josephine accompanied him on two of his expeditions, and his daughter was born on the second.

this time was expanded: there were 12 members, among them Astrup and Henson.

In the spring the first attempt was made on the icecap with the intention of reaching Independence Bay and moving northward, perhaps even to the North Pole. But the weather was not like that of 1892. The party was ravaged by blizzards, in the end equipment had to be abandoned, and to save themselves the exhausted men raced for home. The next spring, of 1895, Peary set out again with six companions (four of them Eskimos) and six sledges. But bad weather dogged them again. One Eskimo deserted with his team and the other three had to be sent back when the food supply dwindled dangerously, while Peary with Henson and Hugh J. Lee, a young American, pushed on for Independence Bay. They reached it but found little game, and with nine dying

The Rivalry Continues

dogs and rations for only 14 days they turned back desperately for home. They reached Whale Sound after a series of 25 forced marches, sick with exhaustion. They had accomplished nothing that Peary had not already done, with much less effort, in 1892.

Peary left for the south with the stubborn determination to succeed in his main objective. He would push through Smith Sound—marked out so long ago as his route to the pole—and establish a base at the tip of Greenland or Ellesmere Island for the final assault. He would waste no further time on the icecap. But first he must—again—arrange for time and money. For this attempt, he decided, he must plan on taking five years, so that if he failed one year he could try the next, and the next, and if necessary the year after that.

Cook's career was taking an unexpected turn. In 1897 a Belgian expedition headed by Adrien de Gerlache was organized to locate the magnetic South Pole. The ship's doctor resigned at the last moment, and when Cook read about it he immediately cabled de

Above: photograph of an iceberg at the edge of the pack ice, about 120 feet high, from Frederick Cook's book *Through the First Antarctic Night 1898-9*, which describes the voyage of the *Belgica*.

Right: the interior of a hut built by explorers in the Antarctic nearly 15 years after Cook and de Gerlache ventured there in the *Belgica*. Unless a building is heated, even the moisture in exhaled breath produces frozen condensation, which hangs from the ceiling like stalactites.

Gerlache, volunteering his services without pay. His offer was accepted, and Cook met the ship that autumn in Rio de Janeiro, Argentina. In the crew was Roald Amundsen, the young Norwegian. De Gerlache decided to map the coastline of Tierra del Fuego on the way south. By the time the mapping was finished the Antarctic exploring season was nearly over, but de Gerlache decided that his ship, the *Belgica*, would attempt to break the record for reaching the furthest south. The *Belgica* was soon surrounded by giant icebergs, and de Gerlache lost control of the ship. Storms drove her further south until she was hopelessly ice-bound inside the Antarctic Circle. It was the first ship to be thus trapped in the Antarctic ice, and the expedition was totally unprepared. Morale on the ship came near to absolute collapse, and Amundsen reported later that Cook was "the one man of unfaltering courage, unfailing hope, endless cheerfulness, and unwearied kindness." It was Cook who, in the spring, figured out the way to free the ship: under his direction, the crew cut a

Below: "Sunrise and Sunset Together, over the Eastern Shore of Belgica Strait," a photograph from Frederick Cook's book about his Antarctic voyage.

Right: Otto Sverdrup (1855–1930), Nansen's captain on the *Fram*, from a photograph taken in 1895 and reproduced in Nansen's book *Farthest North*, published in 1897.

channel through the ice to a small basin of melting ice and then towed the *Belgica* into the basin. After weeks of anxious waiting, the ice between the basin and the open sea cracked and a narrow passage to freedom was created.

By the time Cook returned to New York Peary was back in the Arctic. His money problems had been solved by a group of wealthy businessmen who eventually formed themselves into the Peary Arctic Club. Each man who joined was expected to contribute $1000 for each year of a Peary expedition and to "stand behind him." Five years' leave from the Navy was arranged by President William McKinley himself at the request of a Peary supporter who also happened to be a loyal and influential Republican. A ship, the *Windward*, was provided by another Peary admirer, Lord Northcliffe, the British newspaper magnate. But before the *Windward* arrived from England Peary received what he chose to interpret as disturbing news.

Otto Sverdrup, Nansen's captain, who had remained with the

A New Contender?

Left: the *Windward* leaving Tromso, Norway. This ship was provided for Peary by Lord Northcliffe, a powerful British newspaper magnate.

Fram during its entire drift across the Arctic Ocean, was bringing his ship into the same area Peary expected to visit. Peary was instantly convinced that Sverdrup intended to "poach" the North Pole. He chartered another boat, the *Hope*, and on July 3, 1898 he raced off, accompanied only by Henson and a doctor, T. S. Dedrick. Ice stopped them at Cape D'Urville, far south of the position Peary had hoped to attain. He had meant to use Fort Conger, but that was still 250 miles away, and his supplies could not be sledged north until colder weather thickened the ice. Restlessly Peary spent the summer exploring the east coast of Ellesmere Island. During this time he happened upon the camp of his supposed rival, Sverdrup. Sverdrup himself had no plans to try for the pole. He intended to cross Ellesmere Island to the west to survey and map the area west of Greenland, which is in fact what he did. Peary was not mollified. He clearly considered Sverdrup an intruder in his private territory, and he refused to stay at his camp even for a cup of coffee. Sverdrup wrote, "We were glad to have shaken hands with the great explorer even though we scarcely had time to take off our mittens before he was gone."

On the way back to his camp Peary brooded over the threat presented by Sverdrup's position and, according to Henson, came to the remarkable conclusion that Sverdrup intended to reach Fort Conger before Peary could get there. "I'll get to Conger before Sverdrup if it kills me!" Henson quoted Peary as saying.

It very nearly did. Peary, Henson, and Dedrick set out in late December in the middle of the Arctic night, traveling in temperatures as low as −63°F. On the way Peary's feet froze, and when Henson took off his boots for him when they reached Conger, several of his toes snapped off. Dedrick amputated parts of seven toes, and for six weeks Peary lay helplessly on his back. Storms, snow, and the Arctic night pinned them down. It was clearly necessary to return to the ship: Peary's stumps were agonizingly painful and required a more sophisticated operation than was possible at Fort Conger if he were to be able to walk again. Clearer weather conditions and the dim light of February finally

Below: the Arctic ice, over which Peary, Henson and Dedrick set out to reach Fort Conger. Temperatures dropped as low as −63°F, and Peary's feet froze.

made it possible to move, and Dedrick and Henson strapped Peary to a sledge and dragged him over the ice back to the ship. It must have been a nightmare journey, with his tender stumps jolted and jarred as the sledge bounced over the rough ice. Back at the ship Peary underwent another set of amputations. By summer he was walking, but he was never completely self-sufficient again. Matt Henson became more and more essential to him, and Peary later would frequently ride on a sledge, wrapped in warm furs, instead of walking alongside. But he did not admit this to his public.

In April 1900 Peary and Henson set out on a surveying trip and reached the northernmost point of Greenland. In 1901 he and Henson started out hopefully over the pack ice—so much more rugged than the glacial ice they were accustomed to—but turned back after eight days. Peary returned to Cape Sabine where he met the *Windward*, which had returned north on a relief expedition which included his wife and Dr. Frederick Cook. Cook had been asked by the Peary Arctic Club to come along and undertake a rescue operation if necessary. Once there, Peary was persuaded to let Cook examine him. Cook found him to be suffering

Peary Defeated

Left: Matthew Henson, Peary's faithful companion on his Arctic voyages, from Peary's book *Nearest the Pole* (1907).

Above: "the party of 1903," the team assembled for conquering Mount McKinley. Frederick Cook is second from the right.

from the early symptoms of anemia and, in view of his crippled feet, recommended that he should return home on the *Windward*. Peary refused the advice.

In 1902 Peary and Henson left Fort Conger for a direct assault on the North Pole. It lasted only 15 days, long agonizing days in which they zigzagged across the pack ice to get clear of open water, hacked their way through pressure ridges with pickaxes, and encountered the eerie elasticity of young ice, which quivered underfoot as they inched their way across. Once a lead of young ice collapsed under them—Peary's sledge crashed through and was nearly lost. They made a new record for reaching the furthest north, 84°16′27″, still 343 miles from the pole. But it was impossible to continue. When Peary returned to Conger he wrote gloomily in his diary, "Forty-six. Too old for this kind of work."

However, his optimism and determination returned when he got back to the United States. In October 1902 his feet were operated on to improve his walking. He then devoted his energy to arranging for a ship to be built, to his own specifications, capable of reaching the Arctic Ocean.

Cook in the meantime had his own project. He had experimented with lightweight equipment with Amundsen in the Antarctic, and he decided to try out his ideas on the newly discovered Mount McKinley in Alaska, the highest mountain in North America. In May 1903 he set out with a party of four. The territory around Mount McKinley was indeed forbidding. During 54 days of incessant rain Cook and his men stumbled through marshes, icy glacier-fed streams, and endless underbrush. He did reach a height of 11,200 feet on the southwest ridge of McKinley but was stopped by impassable granite cliffs. Winter was closing in, and the expedition turned back.

In 1906 he tried again, and after some initial failures—the weather was even worse that year than in 1903—he made one last attempt with a packhorseman from Montana, Edward Barrill. They reached 12,000 feet on the northeast ridge, at which point Cook had intended to stop after leaving a cache of supplies for a future attempt. But the going was easier than they had expected, and they pushed on. At 18,000 feet they were beginning to suffer seriously from the altitude, but the summit was within reach, and on September 16, 1906, Barrill and Cook at last achieved their aim when they arrived there.

Cook Climbs Mt.McKinley

Left: summit of Mount McKinley, the highest mountain in North America with an altitude of 20,390 feet. The photograph was published in Cook's book *The Top of the Continent*.

Peary Tries for the Pole Again

Or so they said. Alaskans were deeply skeptical, and they doubted that an outsider could conquer McKinley. One vociferous critic, Hudson Stuck, declared, "It is going to take a better man than [Cook] to reach the top of that mountain." In 1913 Stuck announced that he had done it himself. Although he noted that the major earthquake of 1912 had shaken the mountain, Stuck disregarded any possible changes between 1906 and 1913 in the northeast ridge, which he also followed, and triumphantly reported that Cook's description of his route could not be retraced. He thus "proved" what he had already decided—that Cook was a liar.

Meanwhile Peary took his new ship, the *Roosevelt*, to the Arctic. In 1905 the sturdy craft, specially designed for ice, crept through Smith Sound and headed northward past Kane Basin, past Fort Conger (inland to the west), and finally reached Cape Sheridan in Lincoln Sea, part of the Arctic Ocean itself.

They had to wait until winter to set off across the ice. By now Peary knew the Arctic well enough to recognize that only when the pack ice was at its most solid was it possible for men to travel over it. The assault on the pole had to be delicately timed: the dark Arctic night must be nearly over so that there would be light enough to see, but the return to base had to be completed before the summer thaw.

In late February 1906 they began to push across the ice. Small groups were to move onto the sea ice and station themselves 50 miles apart. Then the first group would return to base, take another load of supplies along for 50 miles, and pass it on to the next group. Peary's main party would thus be saved for the final

Below: Peary's sledges stored on board the *Roosevelt*.

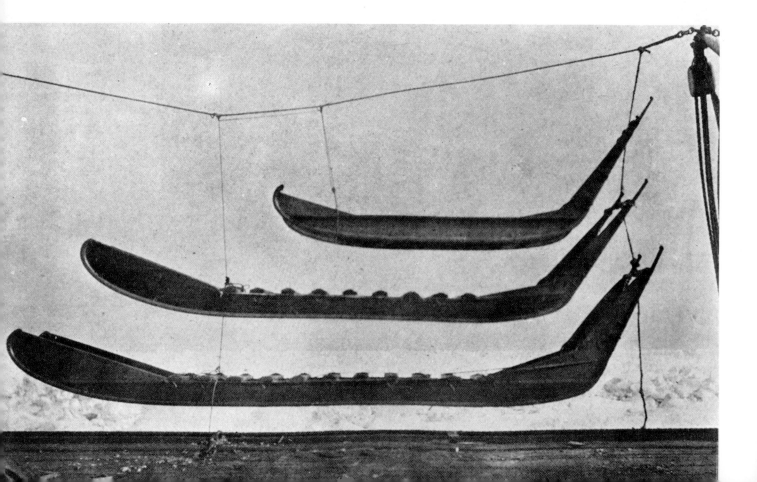

dash, picking up supplies as it moved down the line to the pole.

It was a fine idea, but a neat long trail across drifting polar ice was impossible to maintain. Parties stacked up at leads of open water, and the depots drifted steadily eastward. Finally Peary's division caught up with three other groups marooned on the south side of the "Big Lead," a wide stretch of murky water that seemed a semipermanent feature of the area around the 84th parallel. After six long days young ice finally formed, but it was too late. They had drifted too far east. Peary and Henson crossed the Big Lead and reached 87°6', but then they turned back.

Peary's report presented a few unanswered questions. As Henson had not taken any observations of position, only Peary knew where they were. Although the ice was drifting at a rate Peary estimated as 4.5 miles per day, and although Peary apparently took few longitudinal readings, he was still able to return in a straight line to a camp he had left 15 days earlier. This camp had apparently drifted from the 60th meridian to a position on the 50th meridian, in the line of Peary's return, and it had supposedly stopped there rather than continuing to drift. In addition, Peary's speed had increased phenomenally. Although on the earlier stages of the march he had averaged about six miles per march, once he and Henson were alone with their Eskimos they claimed to have made 20 miles on each march.

Above: deck scene on Peary's ship, the *Roosevelt*.

Cook-First at the North Pole?

In any case, they had not reached the pole. He took a brief survey trip westward across Grant Land in the north of Ellesmere Island, during which he was a victim of an Arctic mirage and "discovered" Crocker Land lying north of Axel Heiberg Land. It has never been seen since. In July 1906 Peary left what he grandly described as "my new domain" and went south again.

He was determined to try again in 1907, but repairs to the *Roosevelt* took longer than expected. During the summer of 1907 he heard disquieting news: apparently one man, at least, did not consider the far north to be exclusively Peary's domain. Frederick Cook had sailed from Massachusetts on July 3, 1907 on the yacht *John R. Bradley*, named for its owner, a wealthy gambler. Bradley and Cook had originally intended just to go north on a hunting trip, but Cook, like Peary, felt the North Pole beckon. He had thought of a new route up the western side of Ellesmere Island, through Nansen Sound and then north across the ice to the pole. He left the yacht at Etah, Greenland, 700 miles from the pole, and in February 1908 set off with nine Eskimos, heading northwest to the tip of Axel Heiberg Land. On March 18 Cook moved out over the pack ice and sent back five of the Eskimos.

At first, Cook wrote later, the going was relatively easy. The ice close to shore was reasonably smooth and glacierlike. But after three days he hit the jumbled, drifting offshore ice, and two more Eskimos returned to shore, leaving their supplies with the men on the ice. Cook was now on his own with Etukishook and Ahwehlah, both only 20 years old. They were by this time nearly 100 miles from the coast, and the Big Lead loomed ahead. Like Peary he had to stop and wait for young ice to form a temporary bridge, but Cook was luckier—overnight a fragile connection formed between the southern edge of the lead and some of the larger ice floes so that they could creep across on snowshoes, a lifeline strung between them. Cook wrote, "We rocked and heaved on the ice as a boat on waves of water." But they got to the other side.

Below: ice flows at Kap Dan, Greenland, the largest island in the world. The greater part of it lies within the Arctic Circle. Cook set out from Etah to try to reach the North Pole.

Cook looked for Peary's Crocker Land but, not surprisingly, saw no sign of it. However, he experienced a mirage of his own further north at 85°50'—"land" lying to the west that he named Bradley Land. By this time he was relieved to see any sort of land at all. His Eskimos were increasingly uneasy at being so far out on the ice, and Cook used the landlike appearance of fog along the horizon to reassure them. On April 13 both young men were completely dispirited, and Cook only managed to rally them with the promise that they would reach the pole after five sleeps.

It actually took longer. It was not until April 21, 1908 that he reached the North Pole. He stayed there, taking observations every six hours, from noon on the 21st to midnight on the 22nd. Having fixed his position with what he described as "reasonable certainty," he buried in the snow a note and a small American flag protected by a metal tube and turned back for home.

Peary, meanwhile, had not yet left New York. He had heard by then of Cook's intentions and of the rumors from Alaska that Cook's ascent of Mount McKinley had been a fake. At first he

Above: Dr. Frederick Cook, medical doctor, explorer, and mountaineer, in the Arctic. Cook always insisted that he had reached the North Pole.

brushed aside predictions that Cook would try to fake the North Pole, too, saying, "Cook is an honorable man." The more he thought about it, however—and the delays allowed him plenty of time to think — the more it upset him. Whatever could the man be up to?

In July 1908, one year later, the *Roosevelt* sailed. In Etah Peary met Rudolph Franke, a German steward from the *Bradley*, who had been left behind by Cook to look after various pieces of equipment as well as a box of furs and ivory horns. Franke had injured his leg and was ill with scurvy, and he wanted to leave Etah. At first Peary refused to have anything to do with Franke or to let the ship's surgeon treat him, but when Franke appealed directly to Peary himself he relented and allowed Franke to return south on his auxiliary supply ship. Either as a condition or as payment for the trip (accounts vary), Peary took possession of the box of furs and ivory. He also placed a guard over the shack which held the rest of Cook's equipment and left a curt notice that read, "This house belongs to Dr. F. A. Cook, but Cook is long ago dead and there was no use to search for him. Therefore I, Commander Robert E. Peary, install my boatswain in this deserted house."

Creeping northward through the ice, the *Roosevelt* reached

Below: the *Roosevelt* in Arctic winter quarters on a moonlit night. The ice pressure was such that the ship was nearly pinched between the floes.

Peary Sets Out

Left: Peary's photograph of "five flags at the Pole." Matthew Henson (center) holds the "polar flag" he and Peary had carried for 15 years. The four Eskimos hold the flags of various organizations that had supported Peary's attempts.

Cape Sheridan on September 5, and Peary's party moved out onto the ice on February 28, 1909. There were seven men in all, including the faithful Henson and Robert Bartlett, master of the *Roosevelt.* The Big Lead yawned open when Peary reached it, and the wind continually shifted the edges so that young ice which might have formed within 24 hours did not form for five days. On the sixth day they crept across and, as planned, one by one the supporting parties passed over supplies and turned back. The last, led by Bartlett, pushed on to 87°46′ before returning. Peary, with Henson and four Eskimos, had only 133 miles left to go.

He covered the distance in five forced marches. On April 6

Peary at the North Pole

they reached 89°57′, about three miles from the pole. He wrote in his diary, "The Pole at last!!! . . . It all seems so simple and commonplace." That evening he sledged with two of the Eskimos to a point 10 miles further on where he took a midnight reading which showed him to be beyond the pole. He returned, sledged eight miles toward the sun, and then came back again for more observations. By this time, although he had at no time on the approach figured his longitude (relying on his watch and his sense of direction), he was convinced he had crossed the pole. He lined his men up for a photograph. Then he wrapped two notes reporting his success in a diagonal strip cut from a silk flag made for him by his wife, and he buried the entire package in a glass jar in the ice.

While Peary had been en route to his triumph Cook was in the final stages of his return to civilization. On leaving the pole, the westerly drift of the ice carried them out of range of their food depot. Thick fog enveloped them, and by the time Cook was able to fix their position they were west of Axel Heiberg Land and much further south. They headed east along Jones Sound, hampered in finding food by a lack of ammunition. Winter overtook them 300 miles from Annoatok, the nearest settlement, and they took shelter in an abandoned stone Eskimo house. In February 1909, with the return of the sun, they started north for Annoatok, near Etah. The last two months were terrible: their food ran out and there was no game. At last, weak, gaunt, and

Below: Captain Robert Bartlett (right) and his party. Peary set up small teams like this to transport supplies during his attempt to reach the North Pole. Tents were used for shelter during hunting expeditions in early autumn and for moving supplies. Igloos were used in winter during sledge journeys.

exhausted, they crept within range of rescue from Annoatok. Harry Whitney, an American big-game hunter who had come north with Peary's supply ship, was in Annoatok at the time, and he described Cook when he was found as the dirtiest white man he had ever seen. He helped Cook clean himself up, and Cook told him of his achievement.

After resting for only a few days Cook decided to sledge south to Upernavik, where he would be able to get a boat for Canada or Denmark. As he could not take all his possessions with him on the sledge, he left those of his instruments which might get damaged and his original work sheets with Whitney. He took his record of his trip, with the results of his observations—but not the original data itself—south with him. Cook reached Upernavik in May, and in August he sailed to Copenhagen. The government of Denmark was notified by telegram from the ship that Cook had reached the North Pole.

In many ways, Peary's own return march from the pole was like his return in 1906. Once again he and Henson apparently marched in a straight line, in spite of the drift of the ice which had so hampered Cook, and also in spite of the fact that Peary did not check their longitude. Once again they managed pheno-

Above: characteristic view of Peary's expedition on the march in fine weather. The men walked in single file in order to save their strength and that of the dogs and also to accentuate the trail. The passage of each sledge made the trail easier for those behind.

menal speeds once they had left the others, achieving an average of over 35 miles per day (before they left Bartlett they were averaging about 13.3 miles per day). In fact, they arrived back at the *Roosevelt* only two days after Bartlett did, having gone at least 266 miles further.

It was not until the *Roosevelt* was heading southward down the Greenland coast that Peary heard that Cook had returned. In Etah he was told, to his increasing fury, that Cook had told the Eskimos he had reached the North Pole. Peary had Etukishook and Ahwehlah interrogated, and in spite of considerable translation problems—Peary never did learn to speak Eskimo properly, and he and his assistants used a kind of rough pidgin— he extracted the information that they had never been out of sight of land.

Continuing south on the *Roosevelt*, Peary stopped at the first telegraph station in Labrador and fired off a telegram, "Stars and Stripes nailed to the Pole." He was astonished to discover that Cook had made his announcement five days earlier and was even then being feted as the man who discovered the North Pole. Enraged, Peary sent off further telegrams denouncing Cook as a liar, basing his evaluation on the interview with Etukishook and Ahwehlah.

Unfortunately for Peary at the time, Cook had been taking a far more gentlemanly line. When, still in Denmark, he heard of Peary's triumph, he sent off a letter of congratulation. "Kindly convey to Mr. Peary my hearty congratulations upon his success . . . I am glad he has won, as two records are better than one." The public, having begun to embrace Cook as a hero, was at first disinclined to take the word of a rival that he was lying.

Cook arrived back in the United States on September 21; Peary got there a few days later. Whitney had returned south on the *Roosevelt*, but without Cook's instruments and records because Peary had forbidden him to bring anything on board that belonged to Cook. Cook therefore had nothing but his manuscript to prove he had been to the pole.

At first it seemed that this might be enough. But the massive support which Peary had built up over his long years of polar exploration swung into action, and charges of fraud began to fly. The Peary Arctic Club located Barrill, Cook's climbing partner, and Barrill swore an affidavit that the only peak they had reached was a much smaller summit 20 miles away from McKinley, and that that was where the alleged summit picture of Mount McKinley had been taken. Cook went to Montana to confront Barrill in a public meeting and was appalled to discover that Barrill stuck to his story. Cook was challenged to produce his original polar worknotes and explained that he had left them with Whitney. Whitney replied that all he had been given was the instruments and then, clearly distressed by the uproar, he refused to say anything further at all.

Cook's report of the food he and his Eskimos had taken with them was analyzed and reported to be inadequate. His photographs were challenged. Some, Cook admitted unperturbed, had been taken earlier and were only used for illustrative purposes. The date Cook had first recorded the midnight sun was challenged. Cook said the sky had been overcast and he had recorded

Did Cook Really Reach the Pole?

Left: Frederick Cook being questioned about the details of his claim to have reached the North Pole by a gathering of journalists and explorers at Copenhagen, Denmark.

the time of his first sighting, although it might have been visible sooner in theory.

The hubbub grew daily. In November Cook sailed anonymously for Europe and dropped out of the public eye for a year. Peary's claim gradually gained strength. With Cook unavailable, the spotlight rested on the commander. His story was examined, but more sympathetically than Cook's, as he had established a well-known record in the Arctic. The National Geographic Society "investigated," but it was later revealed that their only examination of his instruments took place in a railway depot and that some were not even lifted out of their trunk. Besides, as the Society had contributed to his expedition it was hardly unexpected that they should come to a favorable conclusion. The speeds at which Peary claimed to have traveled were questioned —no other polar explorer, north or south, had come near them —but the conclusion seemed to be that for anyone else they would

be incredible, but for Peary they were possible. When his navigation was queried he retorted that longitudinal observations were
a waste of time.

Peary's ordeal came to a climax with a series of American
Congressional hearings on a bill to promote him to rear admiral
in the Navy, effective April 6, 1909, the day he had reached the
pole. During the hearings his work was challenged by Congress-
men, some of whom knew little about geography let alone the
Arctic. After long days of questions covering everything from
the shadows in his photographs of the pole to the curious gaps

in his log—there were no entries for April 7th or 8th—the chairman concluded, "We have your word for it, and we have these observations to show you were at the North Pole . . . as a member of this committee, I accept your word; but your proofs I know nothing about at all."

There was one last word from Cook, a letter supporting the Peary promotion bill. "From various sources I am informed that my prior claim stands as a bar to Mr. Peary's demand for national honor. My object in writing you is to clear the way for Mr. Peary," he wrote. "My claim of the attainment of the Pole is a personal one. I was not in the government pay, nor has the government or any private society advanced my cause in any way . . . Give Mr. Peary the honors—the retirement with increased pay. His long effort in a thankless task is worthy of such recognition. My reward will come with the reward that our children's children will give."

The bill was passed in March 1911, but the controversy simmered on. In 1917 Peary was diagnosed as having pernicious anemia (just as Cook had suggested 16 years earlier, at Cape Sabine), a condition that was then incurable. He fought courageously against physical deterioration until he died on February 20, 1920.

Cook lived until 1940. He lectured for several years on the polar triumph he still claimed, sustained by a hard core of supporters. In 1923 he made the headlines again when he was brought to trial for using the mails to defraud, as a result of his involvement with an oil promotion scheme. By all accounts the judge was deeply prejudiced against Cook, and at the end of the trial delivered a scathing denunciation of the man and sentenced him to 14 years in prison, by far the heaviest penalty given to any of the 14 codefendants. Cook was sent to Leavenworth, Kansas, where he was a model prisoner. In 1926 an old shipmate from the *Belgica* visited him—Roald Amundsen, who by then had conquered the South Pole. Afterward he said that Cook was the finest traveler he ever knew. "Dr. Cook may not have discovered the Pole," the *New York Times* quoted Amundsen as saying, "but Commander Peary also may not have, and the former has as good a claim as the latter."

Cook was granted parole in 1930. A supporter and biographer of Peary tried to organize a protest to prevent his release, but Cook, by then 65 years old, was set free. On his deathbed 10 years later he was granted a full pardon by President Franklin D. Roosevelt. He died still insisting he had reached the pole.

In the end, who can know which man stood on the fatal spot? Neither of them had reliable witnesses to check their positions. Each story included improbabilities and inconsistencies. Each man set out onto the shifting, jumbled pack ice and came back with a story of success. Up until this episode an explorer's word had always been enough. It was Peary who first accused Cook of being a liar, so it is ironic that now supporters of Cook claim it was actually Peary who lied, that he and Matt Henson had never reached the pole and, given Peary's inadequate navigation, wouldn't have known it even if they had. Did they? Didn't they? The mystery, like the drifting ice of the frozen Arctic Sea, still remains impossible to pin down once and for all.

An Unresolved Controversy

Above: Peary's signature. The Arctic explorer, who died in 1920, has become a folk hero for his achievements.

Opposite: front page of *The New York Herald* of September 7, 1909 reporting that Peary had reached the North Pole. The news did not reach the United States until five months after the event.

Chapter 3
The Unknown Southern Land

About 150 A.D. the Greek geographer Ptolemy drew a map of the world, and when he did not know something he guessed. At the bottom of his map, connecting the continents of Africa and Asia, he drew an area which he called Terra Incognita—the Unknown Land. Logic seemed to demand its existence, and for centuries people set out across the vast trackless expanse of the Pacific Ocean in search of it. Legend grew upon legend of the fantastic plant and mineral wealth to be claimed by the first nation to set foot on its shores. The Portuguese, Dutch, Spanish, and British all sought the elusive continent, some to make Christian converts or initiate trade, others for purely scientific motives. What did they actually discover?

Like most rumored but unseen places, the "Unknown Southern Land" glittered with promise. The Greeks had suggested its existence on their maps, and by the 16th century it carried a definite aura of reality. For one thing, voyages by the Portuguese and Spanish had established that the world was round, as knowledgeable men had long been aware from the traditions of antiquity. And, as the great 16th-century Flemish mapmaker Gerardus Mercator argued, the symmetry of the earth required a mass of land in the southern hemisphere to balance the immensity of land known to exist in the north; otherwise the world would topple over to destruction amid the stars.

For another thing, the previously unknown continent of America had been proved to exist: was it not reasonable to believe that another continent was waiting to be found? There was even space for it in a southern sea of unknown dimensions. The Portuguese, traveling east around Africa, reached the Spice Islands—the Moluccas—and looked out to the east over what we now call the Pacific Ocean in 1511. Only two years later, Vasco Núñez de Balboa was taken by his Indian guide to a mountaintop in Panama where he could look out at the same ocean, stretching endlessly to the west. No one could more than guess at the distance between the two points, but it was certainly big enough to contain an Unknown Southern Land—*Terra Australis Incognita*.

One small, rather undistinguished-looking man was convinced the distance was not overly large. His name was Fernão de

Opposite: clouds over the Pacific Ocean, for centuries a vast trackless expanse in which an undiscovered continent was thought to be located.

Magellan-First Pacific Explorer

Magalhães, better known in its anglicized form of Ferdinand Magellan. Magellan had an idea and an ambition. His idea was that it was possible to sail west past newly discovered America and reach the Moluccas. His ambition was that he would be the man to do it.

Although Magellan had spent long years in the service of the king of Portugal (he limped due to a wound received in Morocco), Don Manuel, strangely enough, did not like him. In 1512 he refused Magellan further employment, and, insultingly, told him he was free to enter any other service he chose. Magellan went to Spain.

This was to be unfortunate for Don Manuel. Back in 1493, just after Columbus' momentous voyage, Ferdinand and Isabella of Spain had asked the pope for his agreement to their monopoly over their new western possessions. At that time the pope divided the undiscovered world into two portions: all discoveries made to the west of the Cape Verde Islands belonged to Spain, and all to the east were the province of Portugal, which had pioneered the route around the tip of Africa to India. The Portuguese were not entirely happy with this arrangement, and after a year of negotiations the Treaty of Tordesillas was drawn up between Spain and Portugal, adjusting the line to some 340 miles west of the Cape Verde Islands. The problem then became how this affected the other side of the world. There was then no method of determining longitude at sea—a navigator simply guessed, based on his speed and latitude, his likely east/west position—so an absolutely accurate computation of location was impossible. In which half of the world did the Moluccas fall? Magellan was willing to support the Spanish argument that the Pacific was narrow enough for the islands to lie in their half, and to sail west to reach them.

He set out in September 1519 with a little fleet of five ships. "Very old and patched," the Portuguese ambassador reported

Right: a fleet of Portuguese carracks such as those sailed by Magellan in 1519 when he set off across the Atlantic.

Left: a 16th-century portrait of Magellan, born in Portugal about 1480. In 1519 he set out with five ships and 268 officers and men on a voyage around the world in the service of Charles V of Spain. Only one of the ships ever returned to Spain.

Below: 16th-century map, which shows the Strait of Magellan seemingly open and free of the many small islands now known to exist.

scornfully to his king, who by this time was seriously alarmed at the course events were taking. He ordered out his own ships to stop the traitor at the Cape of Good Hope, but Magellan had already sailed, and his route was not to be around Africa.

He spent the first winter—from March to October in the southern hemisphere—off the coast of South America, where he had to quell an incipient mutiny. In late October he sailed south and after only four days entered a bay which proved to open into a strait. Luck was with him: in only 38 days he managed to thread his way through the strait now named for him, avoiding the innumerable possible dead ends among the lacework of islands that lie off the southern tip of South America. On November 28, 1520 he sailed into what he named the Pacific Ocean, up to then simply called the South Sea.

But by this time he had lost two ships. One was wrecked during the winter; another deserted in the strait and fled back to Spain. The three survivors steered northward for the latitude of the Moluccas. It was an unfortunate route: on that course they missed most of the main archipelagoes of Pacific islands, and for 98 terrible days they sailed without touching land. The heat was

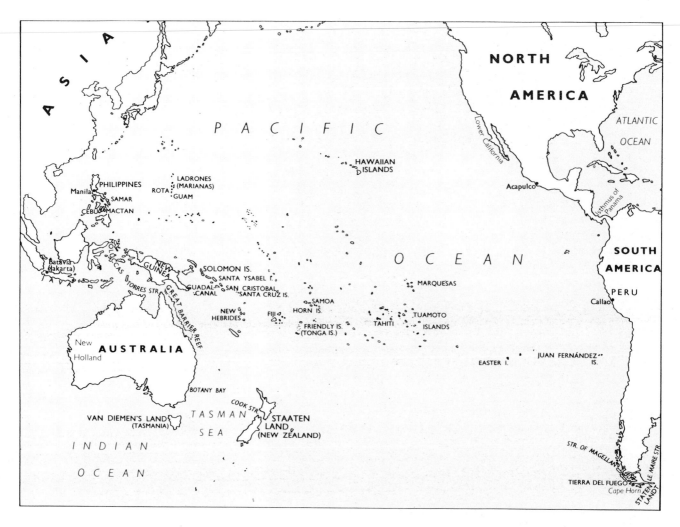

Above: map of the Pacific area in which many explorers sought the Unknown Southern Land.

blistering; food ran out; the water was foul and stinking. Rats were auctioned off between hungry men, but there were not enough. Scurvy, the terrible scourge of the sea, swept the crew.

In March 1521 they finally reached an island where they could anchor. The natives, fascinated by their unprecedented visitors, stole everything they could lay their hands on, and Magellan named the two islands in the group they sighted that day the Ladrones, or Thieves. (They were Guam and Rota, in the group now called the Marianas.) Refreshed by the fruit and fresh food, Magellan and his men sailed on to what is now the Philippines, first to Samar, then Cebu. On April 27, 1521, Magellan undertook to aid his new Christian convert, the chief of Cebu, on a raid against a rebel in neighboring Mactan. For all his Christian valor the battle went badly, and Magellan was covering the retreat of his men when he was speared and stabbed to death.

Without their commander, the surviving crew members sank one ship—there were too few of them left to man all three—and careered about the islands for seven months before they reached the Moluccas. Only the *Victoria* managed to return to Spain, arriving on September 6, 1522 by way of the Cape of Good Hope. She had a cargo of 26 tons of cloves. There were only 31 men left of the 170 who had set out, but those 31 were the first men to circle the globe.

They had also proved that the Pacific Ocean was far wider than anyone had previously suspected, and the passage across it was more terrible. To modern eyes the difficulties they faced were appalling. Their ships were tiny and incapable of sailing close to the wind, and as a result they were completely dependent on the winds and the currents. They were made of wood, and in tropical waters the *Teredo navalis* (shipworm) was fearfully active. It was imperative every few weeks to find a beach or creek where the ship could be hauled up for careening and patching. On shipboard the men ate salted meat and biscuit, and the dreaded scurvy raged. The cause was then unknown (scurvy is now recognized as the inevitable result of a Vitamin C deficiency); seamen usually relied on the pragmatic remedy of fresh food, which again required that land be found. As it often was not, it was considered inevitable that a substantial percentage of an average crew would perish.

Navigation was such an imperfect science that ships were unable to determine accurately either where they were or where such land they did discover was, so that relocating previously charted islands was alarmingly haphazard. There were gifted pilots and navigators, and their successes are all the more remarkable considering the unreliability of their instruments. The crews, however, were less admirable. Often they were the dregs of piracy, prison, and the taverns of the world's ports. Mutiny runs like a black thread through the fabric of Pacific exploration.

Whatever the rigors, however, there was the temptation of immeasurable riches. A Spaniard in Peru, Don Pedro Sarmiento de Gamboa, used the customary barbaric methods of inquisition on the natives and heard of an Inca tradition—marvelously wealthy islands that were supposed to lie to the west. It sounded promising enough to warrant an exploratory expedition, and in 1567 one was planned. Sarmiento, however, was not given command. Instead a young man in his 20s, Álvaro de Mendaña, the nephew of the viceroy, was appointed. Sarmiento was named as captain of the smaller of the two ships.

They sailed from Callao in Peru in November 1567 with 150 men, expecting to find land (according to Sarmiento's information) within 600 miles. They covered nearer 7000. For 80 days they saw only endless water. On February 7, 1568 an island was sighted and named for Santa Ysabel, their patron saint. The islanders were initially friendly but were unwilling to provide food for two boatloads of hungry strangers. When human meat was provided—the arm and shoulder of a young boy—the Spanish were revolted and felt justified in savage retribution on such unnatural heathens. Misunderstandings fueled ambushes, villages were burned, and the Spanish moved southward to two other islands, Guadalcanal and San Cristóbal. The same melancholy sequence of events was played out again, and it was on a lonely beach on San Cristóbal, watched by hostile islanders lurking in the surrounding undergrowth, that Mendaña had the ships careened and cleaned while they decided what to do next.

Mendaña and Sarmiento had already quarreled; now Sarmiento wanted to remain in the islands and establish a settlement while Mendaña thought it wisest to return to Peru. It was true that the ships were worn and leaky; it was also true that ammuni-

The Amazing Circumnavigation

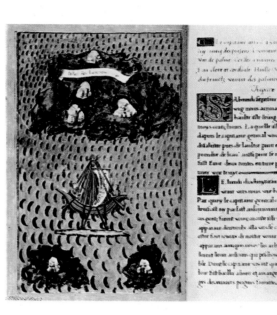

Above: illustration showing the Ladrones Islands, now called the Marianas, from the *Relation*. This was an account of Magellan's circumnavigation, written in 1524 by Antonio Pigafetta, a volunteer on Magellan's flagship.

Searching for a Continent

tion was low, and without it settlers would probably be massacred. The decision was that the sea offered less danger, and they set sail to return. The wind was against them, and it was seven days before the islands disappeared behind them. It would be two centuries before these lands were rediscovered.

The return journey was a nightmare. The ships were badly provisioned, the captains and pilots argued constantly about the course so that the ships veered indecisively back and forth, and in the end Sarmiento either fell behind or deliberately deserted. Lashed by hurricanes, they crept east across the vast expanse of sea. Their water turned putrid, the biscuit was rotten, and the inevitable scurvy ravaged the crew. Bodies were thrown over-

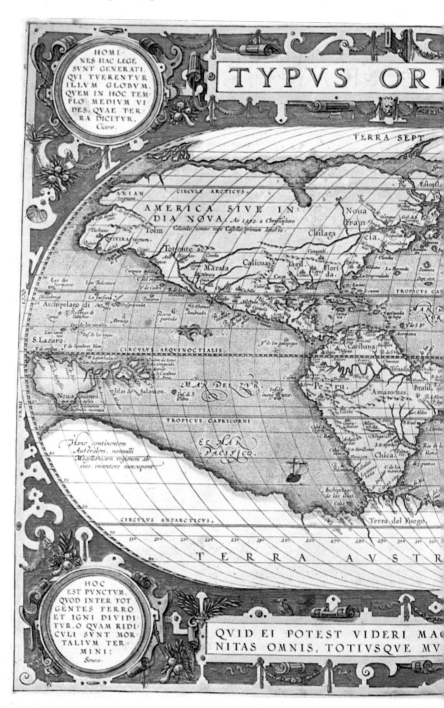

board daily. Mutiny was threatened, but at the point of crisis Mendaña prevailed, and at last Lower California was sighted on December 19, 1568. Sarmiento's ship, equally enfeebled, crept into the bay of Colima to the same harbor the next day.

The Spanish authorities viewed the results of the expedition with little enthusiasm. Mendaña had found some islands but no gold, silver or spices, and the inhabitants were naked cannibals. It was not, by any stretch of the imagination, *Terra Australis* and, taken altogether, not particularly promising. Mendaña, understandably enough, did not see it that way. True, he had not reached the mysterious continent, but these could well be outlying islands. After all, the islands Columbus had reached were

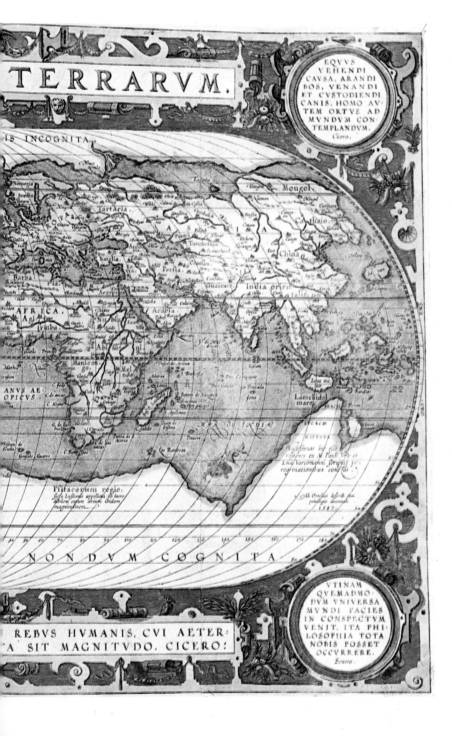

Left: map drawn by Ortelius in 1570 showing the "southern land not yet known." Tierra del Fuego was discovered by Magellan when he sailed through the strait now named after him. The rest of the coastline follows the outline of what cartographers thought should be there, and in one place it reaches almost to the equator.

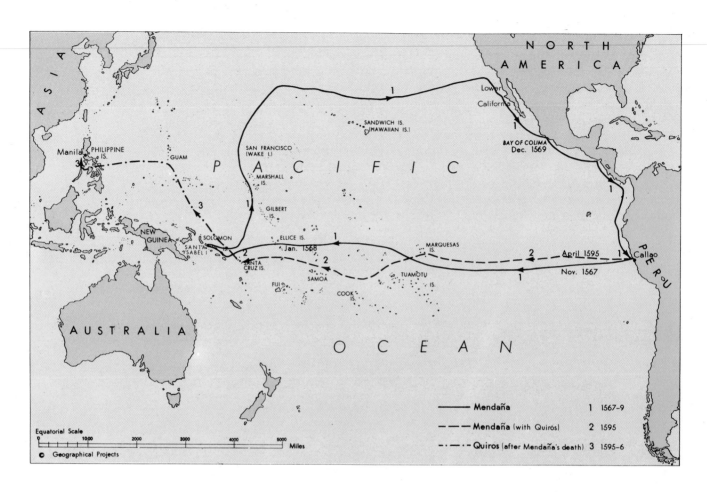

Above: map showing the voyages of
Mendaña and Quiros in the Pacific Ocean
during the 16th century.

poor enough, yet the gold and silver of America were indisputable. He was determined to return.

He surely did not anticipate that he would have to wait 27 years. It was not until April 1595 that Mendaña sailed from Callao again to colonize his discovery, now known as the Solomon Islands. In the years since they had been sighted their attractions had been magnified greatly, and on his four ships Mendaña carried 378 men, women, and children to settle there. His colonists were a mixed lot: there were many unemployed adventurers, prostitutes, and soldiers as well as respectable married couples. Mendaña's wife, a disagreeable woman, also insisted on accompanying him. Only in his chief pilot, Pedro Fernandez de Quiros, was Mendaña fortunate.

The entire expedition was a disaster. In the first place, Mendaña did not know where his Solomons were—he anticipated finding them within 4500 miles of Peru. Twice he thought he'd found them: the first time was when they reached what he named the Marquesas, the second time at the Santa Cruz islands. In both places the relationship with initially friendly islanders became unmanageable. Soldiers restless for action after months at sea attacked at random. Quiros estimated that 200 Marquesans were left dead when the ships sailed away. At Santa Cruz, further west, expedition members turned on each other as well. At his wife's urging Mendaña agreed reluctantly to the murder of his willful camp master, and this led to general slaughter on all sides. In the frenzy the local chief, Malope, was pointlessly shot down in cold blood. Malaria swept the ranks of the survivors, and Mendaña himself was one of the many who died. The dreaded Doña Ysabel, his wife, took command, and with Quiros as pilot undertook to sail the tattered remnants of the fleet to the Philippines. She would not permit the smaller ships to be abandoned and the decimated, fever-ridden crews combined (one ship was lost and eventually discovered with sails set and all hands dead). She washed her clothes in the desperately short supply of drinking water. She sat in her cabin, praying and playing with the keys to the supply room in which she hoarded food, while those around her starved. Quiros' accurate navigation did in the end bring one ship into port at Manila on February 11, 1596. On that ship alone 50 had died since they left Santa Cruz. Doña Ysabel complained bitterly about the survivors to a local magistrate.

In spite of it all, Quiros was confident that he now knew where the southern continent lay. He was convinced that the Santa Cruz islands, Mendaña's lost Solomons, and New Guinea (known to lie east of the Moluccas) were all close together, and that nearby was the unknown continent where an innumerable multitude of heathen waited to be saved. His mind became more and more fixed upon his missionary task. He petitioned steadily for nearly 10 years: finally at the end of 1605 he was given a fleet of three small ships, and he set out from Peru on a holy crusade. He would convert the inhabitants of *Terra Australis*. His second-in-command was Luis Vaez de Torres, a gifted navigator in his own right.

Quiros had already proved himself an exceptional seaman. He was, however, no leader of men, and as the months passed his crews became more and more restive. The ships passed many uninhabited atolls and stopped at three islands while sailing for Santa Cruz; at the third they were told of a large land to the south. Full of joy, Quiros sailed to find it, and on May 1, 1606 he entered a wide bay—"big enough for all the fleets in the world," Torres said. As they approached there seemed to be land to the south and southwest as far as the eye could see, and Quiros was convinced that he had found the southern continent at last. He named the river that flowed into the bay the Jordan and declared he would found a city there called New Jerusalem.

The natives did not appear to welcome their salvation. In the first encounters between them and the Spaniards several natives died, and after three weeks spent exploring, planting seeds, and building a church of branches, Quiros abruptly decided to explore the land to windward. The ships set off, but after a night of squalls Quiros' ship was blown out to sea and did not return. Quiros hoped to meet the other ships at the Santa Cruz islands, but as he was unable to locate either the islands or the ships he eventually sailed for Acapulco, which he reached in November 1606.

Torres, left behind with the ships near land, woke to find Quiros gone. He searched for wreckage far enough along the coast to confirm what some had already suspected: Quiros' new land was not the southern continent at all, but merely another group of islands. Three overlapping islands, in a group now known as the New Hebrides, had been mistaken for continuous coast. Torres searched as far south as 21° latitude looking for

Mendaña's Return

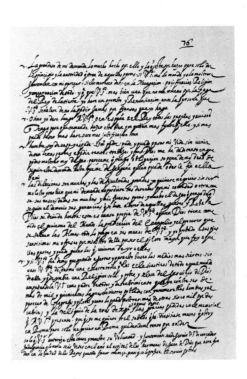

Above: Quiros' memorial to Pope Clement VIII requesting his support for a voyage of religious conversion to the Pacific. The pope readily approved the enterprise, and Quiros was deeply convinced of the spiritual necessity of his mission.

The Dutch in the Pacific

new land, but finding none he decided to reach the Philippines via the north coast of New Guinea. But, he observed simply, "I could not weather the east point, so I coasted along to the westward on the south side." By passing through the strait now named after him which separates New Guinea from Australia, Torres settled a major geographical question of the 17th century: New Guinea was not a projection of *Terra Australis*, but an island.

At the time no one recognized the significance. Torres reached Manila in May 1607, and from then on nothing more is known of him. His report was filed and forgotten.

Quiros reached Peru and eventually returned to Spain. His many petitions to return to his southern land were an embarrassment to Spain, whose colonial fortunes were waning. At length he was allowed to return to Peru to organize an expedition; simultaneously, orders were given to the viceroy to keep him quiet with empty promises. Quiros died in Panama in 1615, unaware of this final betrayal.

As Spain yielded up her ambitions—her treasury was exhausted and her manpower depleted by the continuous demands of her empire—a new power was moving into the Pacific. In 1581 the Netherlands had declared its independence of the Spanish crown. By 1600 Dutch ships—sturdy, efficient ships in which the crews were not crowded and where standards of diet and cleanliness were remarkably high for the time—were sailing around the Cape of Good Hope to a profitable trade in Java. First the Portuguese and then the English were driven out of the East Indies, and after 1623 Dutch supremacy was assured.

But the Dutch were traders whose first priority was trade, not the elusive promise of exploration. The rumored riches of *Terra Australis* were less productive than the certain returns to be made from Java. Such discoveries as were made tended to be accidental. From time to time ships sailing to Batavia (now Jakarta, Indonesia) went further than they intended and came up against the west coast of Australia—New Holland, they called it. The west and part of the north coast were gradually charted, but more pressing concerns kept the East India Company from investigating what lay inland of those coasts; the few reports they had were not encouraging.

One notable Dutch voyage into the Pacific was made during those early years, but it was not under the auspices of the East India Company. It was, in fact, in defiance of the company. A long-time critic, an Amsterdam merchant named Isaac Le Maire, succeeded in obtaining permission from the Dutch government to trade in *Terra Australis* and the islands of the South Sea—but he was barred from using either the passage around Africa or the Strait of Magellan. Le Maire consulted with an eminent navigator, Willem Cornelis Schouten, who believed that Tierra del Fuego, which lay south of Magellan's strait, was an island. In 1615 two ships set out to investigate, with Isaac's son Jakob Le Maire as commander and Schouten himself as navigator. By the next January the expedition—reduced to one ship, the *Eendracht*, after the other had burned at Port Desire in Patagonia—passed the opening of the Strait of Magellan. They coasted Tierra del Fuego and, to their satisfaction, came to the end of it. There was

Opposite below: Jakob Le Maire and Willem Schouten sighted the Horn Islands in 1616. Their ship, the *Eendracht*, anchored in the bay and, after their men had scared the islanders by firing their guns, the sailors and natives became friendly. No blood was shed during the visit. The Dutch explored the islands but reported no signs of cultivation.

land to the east, but with a channel about eight miles wide between the headlands. They named the eastern coast Staten Landt (perhaps it was the southern continent?) and within five days found themselves in the Pacific. They had made the passage. They named the southernmost extremity of the American continent, then to the north of them, Cape Hoorn after their native town in Holland.

Their passage across the Pacific was competent and unremarkable. They passed through the Tuamotu archipelago, faring no better than the Spanish in their encounters with the islanders. In late May, however, they reached Futuna and Alofi, now known as the Horn Islands, and there they spent two weeks with hospitable natives. Le Maire thought these islands might be the Solomons, but they were actually between the groups now known as Fiji and Samoa. Le Maire wanted to sail west to reach the continent he was sure lay near at hand; Schouten was apprehensive of the unknown south side of New Guinea (Torres' report lay buried in Spanish files, inaccessible to foreigners) and felt it prudent to bear northwest around the more familiar north coast. Schouten's view prevailed, and after two months' sailing along the coast of New Guinea they reached the Moluccas, less than 17 months after leaving Holland.

Above: Jakob Le Maire (1585–1616), who set out under his father's charter to trade in the Pacific. He made his way around the southern tip of South America (without using the Strait of Magellan) and then sailed to Java across the Pacific Ocean.

Right: Abel Tasman (1603–1659), seen here with his wife and daughter. In 1642 he was commissioned by the Dutch governor general to explore the seas to the south of New Holland (western Australia) and to take possession of "all continents and islands which [they should] discover, touch, and set foot on" in the name of the Netherlands.

Below: Tasman's drawing of the events in Golden Bay north of New Zealand's South Island, when the ship was attacked by Maoris. His own ships (A) are the *Heemskerck* and *Zeehaen*. Native canoes (B) come alongside the Dutch ships, and a boat returning to the *Zeehaen* (C) is attacked. A Maori canoe (D) is shown in detail. Other Dutch ships (E) sail out to sea while nearby a pinnace (F) tows a Dutch boat and casualties back to the ships. This drawing is from Tasman's journal of the 1642–43 voyage. He called the area Murderers' Bay.

The aftermath of the voyage was not happy. The East India Company refused to believe Le Maire and Schouten's account of the new strait and confiscated their ship and all their goods on the grounds that they had infringed the Company's monopoly. Jakob Le Maire died on the melancholy return to the Nether-

An Elusive Goal

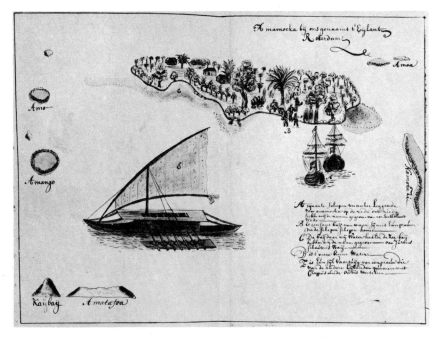

lands, and Isaac Le Maire, infuriated, sued the Company. After two years of wrangling he finally succeeded in recovering ship, cargo, and all costs with interest from the date of seizure. The Le Maire Strait was established beyond doubt.

Schouten and Le Maire had not, however, been any more successful than their predecessors in pinning down the elusive southern continent. In 1642 the East India Company itself undertook the project of investigation. The then governor general, Anthony van Diemen, wanted to discover the relationship between the vaguely known coast of New Holland and whatever lay south and east of it. With the advice of one of the ablest Dutch navigators of the time, Franz Jacobszoon Visscher, plans were drawn up for a voyage under the command of Abel Janszoon Tasman, on which Visscher would accompany him.

In August 1642 they left the Netherlands, stopping at Mauritius in the Indian Ocean. From there their instructions were to sail south to latitude 54° unless they encountered the unknown southland before that. By 49°4′ they had sighted no land, but the cold was so intense that they returned to 44° and sailed east; toward the end of November they sighted land to the north. They named it Van Diemen's Land—it is now Tasmania. They followed the coastline until it fell away to the northwest and then sailed east across what is now the Tasman Sea.

Two days later they saw more land, an inhospitable rocky shore which rose through forests to cloud-covered summits. The local inhabitants were no more welcoming than usual: when the ships approached the coast the Maoris attacked from their canoes and left four men dead. Tasman and Visscher scurried off to the north. As they coasted along, they named their discovery Staten Landt, believing it might be the western coast of the land Le Maire and Schouten had seen as they rounded Cape Horn. It was actually the south island of what is now New Zealand. Tasman and Visscher missed the strait between the islands and

Above left: another drawing from Tasman's journal illustrating the discovery of "Anamocka, by us named the island Roterdam." Here the ships took on fresh water. They saw many wild ducks, "which were not in the least shy or afraid of no people"; the inhabitants "brought various coconuts and calabashes with water to the ships, also some fruit and pigs." The annotation refers to the Dutch ships at anchor (A); the sandy bay (B) from which the natives came in their canoes; the bay from which the Dutch got their water (C); a body of fresh inland water (D); and a sailing craft (E) from another island which had brought coconuts and yams.

There Must be a Southern Land!

Below: an illustration from John Hawkesworth's *Account of the Voyages for Making Discoveries in the Southern Hemisphere*, published in 1773. It is "a representation of the attack of Captain Wallis in the *Dolphin* by the natives of Otaheite," which resulted in the surrender of the island's queen, Oberea.

so charted them as a continuous coast with a deep bay.

Leaving the coast at the northern tip, the wind carried them northeast until they encountered the Tonga Islands. Here the islanders were cordial—Cook later renamed them the Friendly Islands—and Tasman was able to get badly needed water and fresh food. From there, Tasman and Visscher faced exactly the same problem Le Maire and Schouten had: should they sail west, which offered the possibility of new discovery but also the danger of unknown shoals, or should they vote for safety and sail along the known north coast of New Guinea? The weather was bad and, like their predecessors, they chose the familiar course. Using Schouten's charts, they followed the entire north coast of New Guinea. From there they sailed straight for Java through the Moluccas. They arrived in June 1643. They had managed to circumnavigate Australia without ever once catching even a glimpse of the continent.

The company was not particularly pleased with their results.

One of the discoveries hoped for had been a passage through to the South Sea whereby the Dutch could sail to Chile and perhaps plunder their old enemies, the Spanish. Although there might be such a passage north of Tasman's Staten Landt, it was not proven. Nonetheless, Tasman and Visscher were sent out again in 1644 to investigate whether there was a passage south of New Guinea. No detailed account survives, but apparently they missed Torres Strait and so reported that New Guinea was connected to the land to the south. It was the last of Tasman's long voyages and was no more enthusiastically received by the company than the other. The Amsterdam managers decided they had had enough of expensive and profitless exploration. The East Indies they already knew about possessed gold and silver enough, and the vision of a Dutch Pacific faded.

By the beginning of the 18th century the search for *Terra Australis* had primarily succeeded in mapping large areas where it was *not* to be found. The Spanish voyages had discovered nothing but open ocean and scattered island groups north of the Tropic of Capricorn. Schouten and Le Maire had eliminated the possibility that Tierra del Fuego was a projection of the southern continent by sailing south of it; in 1643 Henrik Brouwer found that Le Maire's Staten Landt was only a small island. Tasman's voyage had proved that New Guinea, even assuming it was connected to the land to the south, did not extend further south than Van Diemen's Land, and the existence of the Tasman Sea proved that New Holland (western Australia) did not stretch as far east as Tasman's Staten Landt (New Zealand).

Curiously, as the southern continent was shown not to exist in more and more places, it was argued more fiercely than ever that it must exist somewhere else. In 1697 William Dampier, an English buccaneer, published his journals as *A New Voyage Around the World*, in which he mentioned that another English pirate, Captain Edward Davis, had told him of sighting land in 1687 about 1500 miles west of Chile in latitude 27°20'. The general public, fascinated by Dampier's tales of the Pacific, was intrigued, and in 1721 the Dutch explorer Jacob Roggeveen set off to find it. *Terra Australis* remained elusive, but he did find Easter Island, with its mysterious giant carved statues and friendly inhabitants.

He was followed by the Englishmen Samuel Wallis and Philip Carteret in 1766, who were no more successful. Like all the other sailing ships entering the Pacific around the tip of South America, their ships were forced by the strong winds and storms of the "roaring forties" to head north before turning west. Carteret's course was the most southerly so far achieved, and he became convinced that Davis Land did not exist; Wallis discovered Tahiti, an earthly paradise of beautiful scenery and complaisant island women.

None of this discouraged Alexander Dalrymple, an English geographer who had worked for the East India Company. He was inspired by the exploits of the Spaniard Quiros and echoed his conviction of the existence of the southern continent. Studying the writings of the Pacific explorers, Dalrymple decided that the coast of *Terra Australis* ran north (slightly west of the usual route from South America to the Juan Fernandez Islands) turned

Above: William Dampier, pirate and author of *A New Voyage Around the World*, is the first Englishman known to have landed on the coast of Australia.

west at latitude 28°, joined the land Quiros had seen, and then probably extended south to the coast Tasman had charted (of New Zealand). The continent was thus "of a greater extent than the whole civilized part of Asia, from Turkey eastward to the extremity of China," he wrote enthusiastically in 1767.

A British expedition was being planned at that very time. The transit of Venus between the earth and the sun was to take place on June 3, 1769 and would be best visible from the southern hemisphere. Wallis' Tahiti was selected as the most suitable location for observation; and such an expedition to the South Seas would clearly also be able to search for the southern continent. Dalrymple himself hoped to lead the expedition, but he insisted on entire control of the ship, and his seagoing experience was limited. The admiralty insisted on the prerogatives of the navy, and so in the end the command was given to a Yorkshire-born lieutenant who had risen through the ranks, James Cook.

Cook's ship, the *Endeavour*, sailed from Plymouth in August 1768, and after a smooth journey around Cape Horn it reached Tahiti the following April. Her men were physically in very good condition: Cook had a passion for maintaining the cleanliness and proper diet of his crew, on the sensible grounds that only with a healthy crew could the ship follow the course she had been given. They spent three months in Tahiti, making observations of Venus as directed and enjoying the land and its people, whose charm was only exceeded by their expertise in thievery. They even stole Cook's stockings from under his pillow. Cook surveyed Tahiti and the neighboring islands, reprovisioned the ship, and on August 9, 1769 the *Endeavour* sailed off to fulfill the second, and secret, part of its orders.

Cook had been instructed to proceed south to 40° and then west. He did so, thus sailing through what Dalrymple had claimed was the western part of *Terra Australia*. His crew saw no land until October 6, when they sighted the north island of New Zealand. Cook then proceeded methodically around the coastline, mapping as he went. He paused in the deep bay Tasman had seen to clean and repair the ship, and he thus discovered the

Captain Cook's First Voyage

Opposite: model of Captain Cook's 368-ton ship, the *Endeavour*. Originally named the *Earl of Pembroke*, it was used to carry coal to Scandinavia. Four years later it was refitted for Cook, and new cabins were built, the rig was replaced, the underplanking was reinforced to protect it from shipworm, and it was armed with 22 guns.

Above: Wedgwood portrait medallion of Captain James Cook. Cook's superb navigational abilities and gifts of leadership attracted great respect.

Left: a member of the *Endeavour* crew bartering with a Maori for a lobster in what is now New Zealand.

An Astonishing Achievement

Below: drawing by a ship's artist, John Webber, of Captain Cook (right) watching a ceremony of human sacrifice in Tahiti. Beside him are two boys flaying a pig. The priests, or *arioi*, are sitting in front of two men beating tall drums. The sacrifice is a middle-aged man who had been clubbed to death the day before. On the platform behind the two gravediggers Cook estimated there were 49 skulls of previous victims.

strait that separated the two islands. Sailing through, he continued surveying around the south island.

When all 2400 miles of coast had been charted—in less than six months—he turned west in the hope of encountering New Holland's unknown eastern coast. He landed near what is now Botany Bay and worked his way northward up the coast, until to his dismay he discovered himself within the Great Barrier Reef. The ship struck a coral reef of terrifying sharpness and remained impaled on it. All hands turned to the pumps and the ship's gear, and after 23 hours the *Endeavour* was heaved off into deep water. A makeshift plug held the water out until the ship could be safely beached. Cook, usually moderate in his praise as in all else, said that no men had ever behaved better than his ship's company had done in that crisis.

The ship repaired, Cook managed by luck and superb navigation to work his way painstakingly west through the reefs and shoals to a passage between small islands, and so past the south shore of New Guinea. He had proved again that New Guinea and New Holland were separated, 160 years after Torres.

When Cook returned to England the admiralty was astounded at his achievement. He had charted 5000 miles of coastline; he had fixed the position of that coastline with a precision not yet achieved in most of the civilized world; and until he reached Batavia, with its malaria and dysentery, not a single man had been lost through sickness. He had not discovered the southern continent, but his work made most men wonder if it existed to be discovered. Dalrymple's huge continent was disintegrating.

Above: the Tahitians preparing for war against a neighboring island at the time of Cook's second voyage in search of the Southern Continent. After exploring the Antarctic the *Resolution* put in at Tahiti for reprovisioning. Over 300 canoes took part in the preparations for war, and nearly 8000 men were required to man them. This painting is by a young artist, William Hodges.

Cook's second voyage, in the *Resolution* and the *Adventure*, began in 1772 and lasted three years, and with it the dream of an unknown southern continent was finally destroyed. From the Cape of Good Hope Cook turned south, searching for any indication of land. There was nothing but ice fields as they worked further south than anyone had been before, crossing the Antarctic Circle for the first time. They continued in the high southern latitudes until they came to the longitude of New Zealand, when they turned north. After a brief pause near Cook Strait between the north and south islands, Cook moved off to the east.

Approaching from the west, Cook was able to use the winds that had for so long pushed other ships north. Through June, July, and part of August he searched fruitlessly between latitudes 41° and 46°. After a pause in Tahiti, he returned to New Zealand to refit the *Resolution* for another plunge into the Antarctic. Leaving in late November 1773, Cook soon found himself among icebergs. Once again he dipped below the Antarctic Circle, sailing further south than the previous summer. The cold was frightful—the ship was encased in ice and the men covered in frozen snow. Cook zigzagged back and forth until, at 71°10′S., their progress was absolutely stopped by the ice. There was no land.

Right: Cook's ships, the *Resolution* and the *Adventure*, collecting water by taking on ice at latitude 61° south, in a watercolor by William Hodges, an artist traveling with the expedition. Cook's second voyage, which lasted three years, proved at last that the mysterious *Terra Australis Incognita* simply did not exist.

He found no land to the northeast either, except for Rogge-veen's Easter Island. After a final sweep through latitudes 54° to 55° on his way home past Cape Horn, when they spent Christmas in a cove off Tierra del Fuego, Cook gave up the search. Back in England after his three-year voyage he wrote, "I have now done with the Southern Pacific Continent, and flatter myself that no one will think that I have left it unexplored."

The unavoidable conclusion was that there was no *Terra Australis*—at least not the continent the ancients had postulated and generations of men had hoped to find. The land of milk and honey, gold and silver, and jewels and spices simply did not exist. At the southernmost extremity of the world lay only frozen, ice-bound Antarctica. Across the rest of the vast expanse that European geographers had thought must be land spread the shimmering waters of the Pacific Ocean, broken only by occasional islands. Across that emptiness had sailed dreamers, villains, mystics, and fortune hunters. One by one the islands were charted and the routes marked, often by men who were dying of thirst or hunger or trembling with the enfeebling curse of scurvy. In the end, with the ease of genius, Cook made it all look easy. The quest was over, and the mysterious *Terra Australis Incognita* slipped into history.

Cook Solves the Pacific Puzzle

Chapter 4
Secrets of the Silk Road

The burning, dry heat of the Gobi desert preserves not only the ruins of buildings and the marks of roads but even manuscripts and works of art, which were once housed in the traditional stopping places of the caravan route between northwest China and the Mediterranean Sea. From about a century before Christ until the 6th century, caravans of mules and camels followed the Silk Road over its 6000 miles, bringing to the West the coveted luxury of silk fabrics. Each ruler or chieftain along the way charged a sizeable tariff for the privilege of crossing his territory. What has become of their fabled cities? How did they falter and decay? What other mysteries do the shifting sands conceal?

It had once been a quiet country lane, curving between rush fences. Even now rustling dead leaves from the poplar and fruit trees that had once flourished on either side, desiccated by the harsh desert wind, were caught at the foot of the fences. Between the fences the wind had swept parts of the ground clear, so that pieces of charcoal and pottery—debris left by the last inhabitants —were clearly visible. A black and white fox terrier crossed and recrossed the roadway, sniffing with interest. His owner, a small, methodical man, poked curiously with his walking stick at withered tree stumps which had once been peach, apricot, plum, and mulberry trees. Straightening up, he looked around at his surroundings thoughtfully. Once this had been a pleasant rural orchard with ripe fruit hanging among green leaves. But the last of that fruit had been picked 16 centuries before, and during the intervening years the wind and sand of the Taklamakan Desert, in the heart of central Asia, had torn at both the orchard and the big house nearby until only timber posts, rush fences, and shriveled stumps remained. Sir Aurel Stein, a noted British archaeologist, called to his dog and turned back to the house where his diggers were working. It was then a bitterly cold day in January 1901. The house had been abandoned to the desert sometime around 300 A.D.

All around him, heaped in smooth, wind-shaped dunes, lay the yellow sand. Here and there a bleached tree trunk protruded. A mound surmounted by rows of timber posts marked where the

Opposite: the Gobi Desert. Called the *Han Hai* (dry sea) in Chinese, it is today sparsely inhabited by Mongolian nomads and crossed by the Kalgan-Ulan Bator highway. During the heyday of the Silk Road the region's varied cultures met through the activities of trade and commerce.

Above: photograph taken by Sir Aurel Stein during his excavations in Khotan. Here local workmen are shown in the emerging ruins.

house had once stood and indicated what the ground level had been before centuries of erosion wore it down into undulating dunes. It was the sort of desert any schoolchild would visualize, endless sand, endless sun, and a silence broken only by the roar of the buran—the violent windstorm which abruptly sweeps out of nowhere, tormenting the desert traveler with a lacerating rush of flying sand that tears at exposed flesh, blows under clothing, and penetrates the most carefully sealed containers. This was pure, uninhabitable desert. No nomad tribes wandered from well to well across it, because in the heart of the desert there are no wells. Only at the edges, where oases have developed near mountain-fed rivers, can man survive.

The house had been part of such an oasis, known as Niya. Niya had once formed a patch of brilliant green in the yellow sand; it had been a resting and watering spot for the weary traders and travelers of the camel caravans that followed the Silk Road—the trade route that connected China and the West. It was nearly midway between Lop to the east and Khotan to the west on the arm of the road that bypassed the Taklamakan to the south. Documents found in the excavated houses indicated the

Sir Aurel Stein Traces the Road

Above: Sir Aurel Stein (1862–1943), a quiet, unassuming man who took great pains to record all his archaeological discoveries carefully. He took many thousands of photographs and wrote numerous books about his amazing finds.

official business transacted there: payments and requisitions made, laborers listed, orders for safe conduct or arrests issued, and so forth. It must have been a bustling place when the caravans were passing through, heading west laden with bright silks and eastbound carrying jade, wool, and precious stones, but most of all gold—Roman gold to pay for Chinese silk, a continual drain of Roman wealth into Asia. With the noise of the animals, the gabble of voices, and the creaking and groaning of carts, Niya must have been a sharp contrast for the travelers to the enveloping silence of the desert track.

Another arm of the Silk Road skirted the Taklamakan, but to the north. On either route more than 800 long miles had to be covered by caravans moving slowly from one oasis well to another. The wells carried evocative names such as One Cup Well, where the bitter water accumulated so slowly that the first driver to reach it could water his animals, but the person following him had to wait until more trickled between the stones at the bottom of the well; Gates of Sand, the last well before a long waterless stretch of track; and Inexhaustible Spring Halt, where the traveler could drink long and deeply of fresh, sweet water

Early Travelers

after eight stages in which only bitter water was available.

All the thousands who over the centuries traveled the desert road had one thing in common: all of them were thirsty. Never was there enough water to satisfy the body's relentless demand for moisture, and what there was frequently was bitter or brackish. Walking or riding, under the glaring hot daytime sun or the freezing cold of night, each traveler knew the feeling of cracked lips and dry throat and found his thoughts during the long marches turning more and more often to water—the feel, the sound, and the shimmering wetness of water.

Enclosing this great desert basin are the most immense mountains on earth. To the south lie the Kunlun Shan range of Tibet, Karakorum, Himalayas (which include Mount Everest), and the Hindu Kush, which converge on the Pamirs, the mountain gateway lying just west of the Taklamakan. To the north are the Tien Shan mountains. Marco Polo called the Pamirs "the roof of the world," taking that name from the Kirgiz shepherds who fattened their flocks on the remote mountain plateaus. From the Pamirs the road descended following the Oxus River (now called Amu Darya), bearing ever westward across what we know now as the U.S.S.R., Iran, and Iraq, and then split into two branches, one dipping southward toward Egypt, the other crossing through Syria and Turkey to ships sailing for Rome. Few men made the entire trip from the Jade Gate of the Great Wall of China all the way to Rome. The goods traveled in stages,

each caravan transferring its cargo to the next at the main stopping places on the road. Each trader took his profit, and thus the price of the silk rapidly escalated. It took a year for silk to reach Rome, and by then its price had been doubled and redoubled several times.

Oddly enough, the man who first opened up the way from China to the West had no particular interest in introducing silk to outsiders. His name was Chang Ch'ien, and he was a military officer during the reign of the Han emperor Wu Ti, who ruled from 141 to 87 B.C. The Chinese were then being challenged by the Hsiung-nu (the early Huns), who were menacing China's Great Wall frontier. Wu Ti wanted to develop tribal alliances among the people living west of the Great Wall, so Chang Ch'ien was sent to make contact with the Yüeh-Chih, a tribe which had been driven from its traditional homeland on China's northwestern border by the Hsiung-nu. Wu Ti hoped they would be willing to return to their original territory under Chinese protection and that together they might crush their common enemy.

Chang Ch'ien set out accompanied by about 100 men, including a Hsiung-nu slave, Kan-fu, who had presumably been captured in a border skirmish. The entire party was seized almost immediately by the Huns, and Chang Ch'ien was forced to remain in their hands for over 10 years. His captivity does not seem to have been overly rigorous: he was given a Hsiung-nu

Below: camels in the Gobi Desert. The total area is about 500,000 square miles, but only certain parts of this are covered solely by sand. Much of it is rocky, with sparse vegetation and occasional grassland watered by seasonal streams.

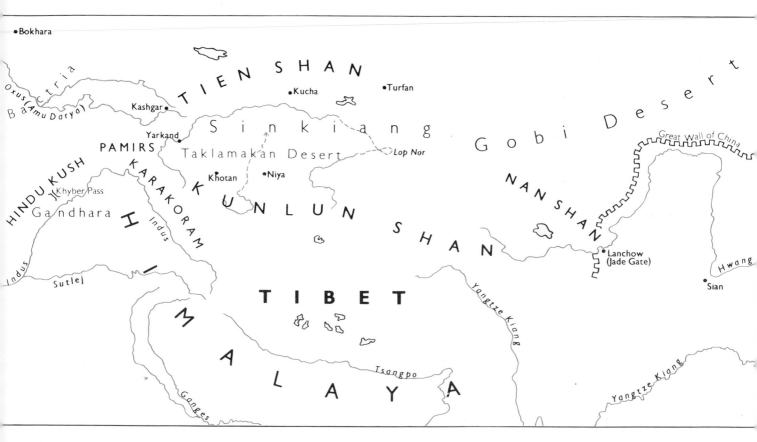

• Bokhara

B a c t r i a

Oxus (Amu Darya)

Kashgar •

Yarkand •

PAMIRS

HINDU KUSH

Khyber Pass

Gandhara

KARAKORAM

Indus

Indus

Sutlej

H I M A L A Y A

Ganges

T I E N   S H A N

•Kucha   •Turfan

S i n k i a n g

Taklamakan Desert

Khotan •   • Niya

K U N L U N   S H A N

T I B E T

Tsangpo

• Lop Nor

G o b i   D e s e r t

Great Wall of China

N A N S H A N

• Lanchow
  (Jade Gate)

Yangtze Kiang

Yangtze Kiang

Hwang

• Sian

Above: map showing the areas crossed by the Silk Road.

Right: the ramparts of Bactria, capital of the ancient land of Bactria in what is now Afghanistan. The city was later renamed Wazirabad and was one of the main centers for the silk trade. It was also a stopping place on the Silk Road between the Pamirs and Merv, an oasis city near the present-day border between the U.S.S.R. and Iran. This part of the Silk Road was controlled by the Yüeh-Chih in Chang Ch'ien's time.

wife, who bore him a son. Finally, a Chinese historian records, when "he had lived in Hsiung-nu territory for some time and was less closely watched than at first," he managed to escape with his barbarian wife and Kan-fu. They made their way west, encountering other friendly tribes, and at last found the Yüeh-Chih, who had settled in Bactria (now northern Afghanistan).

Chang Ch'ien was greeted with respect, but he quickly discovered that circumstances had changed. The old king had died, and his son found Bactria a rich and fertile place. The Chinese

Chang Ch'ien the Pioneer

Left: the Chinese emperor Wu Ti of the Han dynasty, who sent Chang Ch'ien on a mission to make an alliance with the Yüeh-Chih. Chang was away from Wu Ti's capital for 12 years, but he came back with priceless information about the peoples and lands to the west and their desire for silk. (Museum of Fine Arts, Boston)

were now too far away to bother about, and the new king had no particular wish to avenge his father's death. He did not intend to return, either. Accepting the failure of his mission, Chang Ch'ien tried to go back by a southerly route, but he was again captured by the Hsiung-nu. This time Chang Ch'ien was able after only a year to slip away with his wife and Kan-fu and return to China. He had been gone for 12 years.

In spite of his failure with the Yüeh-Chih, the emperor Wu Ti welcomed him back with honor. Chang Ch'ien was made a palace counselor, and the former slave Kan-fu was given the title "Lord Who Carries Out His Mission." They had returned with unique information about the peoples and unknown territories to the west. Chang Ch'ien had discovered that silk, used within China for more than 2000 years, was highly prized by foreign "barbarians"—and he had pioneered a trade route. Rulers of the central Asian kingdoms and leaders of nomadic tribes to the west of the Great Wall quickly appreciated that a silk trade would be profitable and therefore worth protecting, and the Silk Road came into existence.

Of course, it was never what we now think of as a road. In most places it was merely a track, barely perceptible except to those who were familiar with the route. But within a few years of Chang Ch'ien's journey, caravans of mules and camels were journeying from northwest China to the West. The silk they brought to Rome became the height of fashion, a symbol of

Impossible Demand

wealth and position, and thus a necessity for aristocratic ladies. Gauzy, semitransparent silk clothed the nobility, and its suppliers built up thriving businesses. Seneca wrote, "I see silken clothes that in no degree afford protection either to the body or modesty of the wearer, and clad in which no woman could honestly swear she is not naked."

Some goods traveled the other way, but the balance of trade was always in favor of the self-sufficient Chinese, who considered themselves uniquely civilized and did not believe any imports from the barbarians beyond their borders were necessary. Gold, however, was always useful, so gold from the Roman treasury flowed out to China. So great a drain was the cost of silk on the Roman economy that official measures were taken to restrict the import of silk along with other expensive and exotic goods. The emperor Marcus Aurelius tried to cut back the increasing Roman addiction to silk by refusing to wear it himself and forbidding his wife to do so, but little came of his gesture of renunciation (or his wife's: all the other noble Roman ladies continued to drape themselves in silken luxury).

In 166 A.D., when war with Parthia (now a territory divided between Iran and Iraq) had disrupted the western sections of the road, some Roman merchants succeeded in reaching China by sea in an attempt to bypass both the dangers and the proliferating middlemen of the overland route. But the sea route was hazard-

Left: Chinese ladies preparing a length of newly woven silk. Silk was one of the Romans' most sought after luxuries, but the Chinese held a monopoly on its manufacture for over 3000 years. This painting is actually done on silk and dates from the period 1082–1135; it is based on an even earlier work by Chang Hsuan, a court painter active from 713 to 742. (Museum of Fine Arts, Boston)

ous and uncertain, considering the frailty of the vessels, and the pirates of the coasts were as ruthless as the bandits of the interior. The price of silk remained high, and no regular sea trade was established. The Silk Road was still the only practical route to China.

More than luxury goods traveled over the road. Gossip and rumors, idle chatter and extravagant reports of the wonders to be encountered further on, enlivened conversation in the towns and stopping places along the route. Traveling artists and artisans carried with them the styles with which they were familiar, thus producing a rich blend of cultural influences. Ideas traveled the road as well. Buddhism was spreading during the same centuries as the infant religion of Christianity moved outward from Judea. In both the East and West the established order was crumbling. In China the Han empire collapsed, fatally shaken by successive peasant rebellions, and the country disintegrated into a quarrelsome collection of kingdoms whose frontiers constantly shifted. In the West the Roman empire fell into pieces under the onslaught of barbarian invaders from the north.

Both civilizations were open to new ideas. Buddhism spread north and westward from India into Bactria and Parthia and then followed the Silk Road east, through the oasis towns of the desert, into China. There Indian Buddhism was absorbed and made Chinese. Knowing themselves to be far from the sources of

Opposite: the Vicus Tuscus, the silk market near the Forum in Rome. Here the silk imported from China was eventually sold, but by this time its price had been forced up by the numerous middlemen who had each taken their profit as it was carried west along the Silk Road.

their faith, Chinese Buddhists began to make pilgrimages—even as Christian pilgrims, far to the west, traveled to the holy places of their religion.

The earliest on record is that of the Chinese monk Fa-Hsien, who set out westward in the last year of the 4th century to study Buddhist doctrine in India. Traveling with three companions, he followed the Silk Road as far as Kashgar and left such clear accounts of the towns and monasteries on the way that Sir Aurel Stein was able to use his writings as a guide 1500 years later for locating promising archaeological sites. Then the pilgrims turned southward through the precipitous cliffs and gorges of the region where the massive Kunlun and Himalaya mountain ranges meet. It took them six years to reach central India, and a further six years were spent in study and travel—they went as far as Ceylon (Sri Lanka)—before they returned to China by sea.

The missionaries and pilgrims added another colorful thread to the continually shifting tapestry of the Silk Road. During these centuries, however, the road dwindled in importance. Without the stability of central government, the irrigation canals which sustained some of the towns were allowed to run dry, and without water the settlements quickly reverted to lifeless desert. It was during this period that Niya was abandoned. Wave after wave of nomadic horsemen swept in to raid towns in the territories the road traversed. Frequently the invaders would settle and discover the pleasures of peace and relative prosperity, before

Below: travelers at a wayside inn. This Chinese painting is full of action and indicates that, although on many occasions the early travelers had to sleep in the open, they sometimes found lodgings for the night. Missionaries and pilgrims jostled with the traders at the oasis towns along the Silk Road.

being invaded in their turn by the next wave of covetous nomads. During these periods of turmoil and disorder, often lasting for many years, trading centers would be either destroyed by ruthless invaders or abandoned by their inhabitants. But the silk trade was sufficiently valuable to insure that some caravans were always kept moving.

In 540 Justinian—ruler of the eastern half of what had been the Roman empire—made another attempt to stop the drain of Roman gold into China. He fixed the price of silk at a level he considered appropriate. But the Persians, who by then controlled the long length of the Silk Road that stretched westward from the Pamirs and sold the silk directly to the Romans, were not impressed. They simply refused to deal at the Roman figure. Faced with the possibility of being unable to obtain any silk at all, the Romans decided to smuggle the secret of silk cultivation out of China so that they would be able to produce it themselves.

By this time the Western world had some idea of how silk was produced, although even the most knowledgeable were vague about the details. It had not always been so. Pliny, the learned natural historian who lived from 23 to 79 A.D., wrote that silk was a pale floss that grew on leaves. Later some had become aware that it was spun by insects, but as late as 380 A.D. Pliny's theory was still considered generally accurate.

The story of how the secret of silk—and the first silkworms—reached the West has become surrounded by a variety of colorful

Missionaries and Pilgrims

How the Silk Trade Began

legends. Procopius, the 6th-century historian, wrote that certain monks who had been living in India came to Justinian and told him that silk was produced by caterpillars. They offered, for a sufficient reward, to go into China and bring back some silkworm eggs. These eggs, once smuggled out to the West, could be hatched by covering them with dung, which produced sufficient heat for incubation. Justinian agreed, and the monks left Byzantium only to reappear after many long months with a supply of eggs. (Another version of the story specifies that they presented him with precisely 550 eggs.) The eggs were duly hatched, the caterpillars were fed on mulberry leaves, they spun their silken cocoons, and silk culture was duly established in Roman territory.

Theophanes, another 6th-century historian living in Byzantium, claimed it was a Persian who smuggled the eggs out of China concealed in a walking stick and brought them safely to Byzantium. When Sir Aurel Stein was excavating at Khotan, one of the oasis towns on the arm of the Silk Road bypassing the

Below: Nestorian priests. One of the stories relating to the introduction of silk production to the West suggests that two Nestorian monks smuggled silkworm eggs out of China in bamboo canes.

Above: a silk moth. Silk was an important commodity from the beginning of the Christian era, and the Chinese monopoly was due to their exclusive knowledge of how silkworms produced silk.

Left: the Byzantine emperor Justinian, who tried to control the problem of the drain on Roman gold to the East by fixing the price of silk in 540 A.D. But the Persians, who had a virtual monopoly on the trade due to their position as middlemen on the Silk Road, refused to sell at the Roman figure, so the Romans were forced to consider new ways of obtaining sufficient supplies of silk.

Taklamakan to the south, he uncovered a painted tablet showing a Chinese princess. According to some sources she was the first to smuggle silkworm eggs out of China and established a silk production center at Khotan itself—and the town was indeed a silk center from the 6th century onward. On the tablet one of her attendants points to the diadem worn by the noble lady, under which the eggs were concealed.

But whoever it was—monk, Persian, or princess—it seems certain that the Chinese monopoly was broken during the 6th century and with it much of the power of the kingdoms along the Silk Road. They became progressively less able to pay for protection for the traders, and inevitably the rapacious nomad tribes, their subsidies dwindling, turned to plunder. The Turks threatened the eastern provinces of Byzantium as well as southern Russia; the Arabs, new masters of the Middle East, created a wedge between East and West, becoming familiar with both

Above: Hsüan-Tsang, the young Chinese Buddhist who traveled to India in the 7th century to learn more about his faith. His arduous journey lasted 16 years, some of which time was spent studying in various Indian monasteries.

while cutting off China and what had been Rome from further contact with or knowledge of each other.

In China, however, the long years of disunity and internecine warfare were drawing to a close. When the T'ang dynasty began in 618 a young Buddhist monk named Hsüan-Tsang was studying in a monastery at Sian, the Chinese city at the end of the Silk Road. He was only 15 years old but was already recognized by his fellow monks as wise and learned far beyond his years. Disturbed by constant disputes on matters of theology, Hsüan-Tsang conceived the bold plan of going to India—he would bring back a library of sacred books and firsthand interpretations of the points most under discussion at the time. He sent a petition to the newly installed emperor asking to leave China by the northwest frontier, but permission was denied: central Asia was still in a state of turmoil. Hsüan-Tsang was determined to begin his pilgrimage nonetheless.

Until he left Lanchow on the Silk Road to Sinkiang, Hsüan-Tsang was disobeying no order, but from that point on he had to travel secretly. His journey demanded great physical courage and spiritual dedication, for it was quite possible that both the journey and his life would be ended at any moment by murderous bandits, false guides, or the terrifying natural hazards of desert and mountains. Abandoned by one guide, he found his own way by following the tracks of camels and other pack animals which were faintly discernible in the yellow sand. At one point he stumbled along for five long days without water. At another, totally lost, he could only attempt to orient himself by the line of his own shadow.

At long last he reached Turfan, then a powerful city on the northern arm of the old Silk Road, where the ruler greeted him respectfully and supplied him with an escort of men to accompany him on the next stage of his journey. He continued through Kucha, the next main trading center, to the icebound Tien Shan mountains north of the Pamirs. His crossing of the mountain range was fraught with hardship, and 13 of his men perished. He then reached the Great Khan of the western Turks, who arranged for his onward journey to Gandhara, an ancient region of India whose main city is now Peshawar in Pakistan and which was then a great center of Buddhist worship and learning. Even then the journey was not easy. He crossed the Oxus into Bactria, came through the Khyber Pass, and then crossed the gorges of the Indus, using rope bridges that swung sickeningly over chasms and roads that clung to the very edges of precipices.

Eventually he reached India, where he traveled around gradually assembling the books which were to become the foundation of authoritative Buddhist teaching in China. When at length he was ready to return to his home monastery he went by way of the Pamirs and Kashgar. His former protector, the ruler of Turfan, was by this time dead, so he took the southern arm of the Silk Road around the Taklamakan. Again he found royal support: the king of Khotan came out to meet him and escort him into his city. Beyond Khotan the passage across the desert was a frightening experience—Hsüan-Tsang wrote feelingly of "drifting sand without water or vegetation, burning hot and the haunt of poisonous fiends and imps."

The Travels of Hsüan-Tsang

In spite of his obvious disobedience—which by this time was 16 years in the past—the emperor gave him an honorable reception at court when he reached China. When he asked the monk about that long-ago defiance, Hsüan-Tsang replied tactfully, "I did indeed request your gracious permit three times over, but, receiving no favorable answer and knowing myself to be so insignificant a subject, I could not suppose that you even knew of my request." The emperor graciously accepted this elegant evasion, and Hsüan-Tsang retired to his monastery. There he revised and enlarged the record of his long years of pilgrimage, which also saw the decline of the Silk Road. He wrote of abandoned towns and deserted temples and provided clear descriptions of the still-powerful cities and their rulers along the route. He had made careful note of the estimated distances between towns and stopping places; he reported the weather, the names and sizes of settlements, and the customs, clothing, and character of the people he encountered. Much of what he wrote was overlaid with superstition and fable, but the factual basis was sound, and the work of Hsüan-Tsang remains an eerily accurate guide to the geography of central Asia and an invaluable record of the life, politics, industries, and religion of its people.

The 9th and 10th centuries marked the decline and dissolution of the T'ang dynasty, which ended in a welter of blood. China was not reunified until 50 years later, in 960 A.D., under the Sung dynasty. Weaker than the T'ang had been, the Sung was under continual attack from barbarians. Her wealth and civilization were a rich lure to the nomadic tribes of the sparse, ill-watered grasslands of the Gobi desert. The northern provinces had already fallen: in 937 the Kitan tribes took northern China, founded the Liao dynasty, and gave their name, anglicized as Cathay, to the country. They were succeeded by the Juchen of Manchuria, who established the Chin dynasty which ruled

Above left: the Buddhist *Diamond Sutra*, the world's oldest surviving printed book. Made in 868 A.D., its printed sheets pasted end to end make a scroll 16 feet long. Buddhist books collected by Hsüan-Tsang in India had become the foundation of authoritative religious teaching in China by this time.

The Mongols and the Silk Road

Above: Ghengis Khan as portrayed in a miniature from a 15th-century Persian manuscript.

northern China from 1125 while the Sung controlled the south. This pattern might have continued for centuries but for the birth around 1162 of one of the most influential men in human history: a Mongol chieftan's son who grew up to become the ruthless and barbarous conqueror, Genghis Khan.

Genghis Khan was a military and political genius, and Asia and the eastern reaches of Europe literally ran red with the blood spilled by his ravaging horsemen. He welded together the scattered tribes of Mongol nomads into a massive, invincible army and then flung that army at the world. His first victim was the unfortunate Chin dynasty—by 1215 most of the Chin cities were under Mongol control. He turned west when a Muslim sultan in Persia committed the fatal error of murdering several hundred Mongol merchants who had traveled along the Silk Road to trade. At Herat in present-day Afghanistan, only one of the hundreds of cities devastated, the vengeful warriors with Genghis Khan at their head carried on their looting and destruction for a full week, and when they swept west to further conquest 1.5 million corpses lay rotting in the ruins behind them.

By the time Genghis Khan died in 1227 his forces had overwhelmed the Muslim states of central Asia and were ravaging Russia. His successors penetrated as far west as modern East Germany, Czechoslovakia, and Yugoslavia—and they only stopped there when a dispute arose over the succession upon the death in 1241 of Ogotai Khan, the son and heir of Genghis. The Mongol horsemen had proved themselves invincible against the weak and divided Europe of the early Middle Ages.

Cut off from the East by the Arab presence, Europe had had no inkling of the Mongols' spectacular rise to power until, as if by sorcery, the terrible hordes appeared on its eastern flank. Then, when total destruction appeared imminent, their progress (equally inexplicably) was halted and the threat withdrawn.

Left: Mongol cavalry as they looked at the time of the Polos. This illustration shows Mahmud ibn Sebuktegin defeating his opponent Baktuzun in 999 and comes from the *World History* of Rashid al-Din, a Mongol manuscript of 1307.

Christian Europeans, still largely ignorant of the danger they had so narrowly escaped, made a few attempts to learn something about the Mongols from missionary envoys. One interesting fact very soon became obvious—the Mongols favored trade more strongly than most Chinese dynasties—so the old trading routes began to be revived.

The devastation of the Mongol invasion had been appalling, but in its wake came the advantages of central control by a strong power. The cities along the old Silk Road once again sheltered and supplied caravans moving between East and West. The Chinese no longer held a monopoly on silk production, but their silks were still exquisite and greatly in demand in the West. With the silk came porcelain, spices, and precious jewels. In return the Chinese wanted Western glass, dyes, lead, and woolens. The oasis towns along the edge of the Taklamakan desert stirred back into life, military posts were reestablished to protect traveling merchants, and regular police patrols controlled the activities of bandits. In the more fertile areas trees were planted along the roads so that people could find their way more easily. It was during this period that the saying arose that it was safe for a maiden to walk the roads with a golden tray on her head.

Given this promising state of affairs, it is hardly surprising that two Venetian merchants, Nicolò and Maffeo Polo, set out eastward in 1260. They did not begin with the precise intention of reaching Cathay: they had spent several years trading in Constantinople and when unrest threatened they had moved further east in stages, fully intending to return to Venice as soon as it was safe to do so. They had gone as far as Bokhara when they received an amazing invitation from the Great Khan himself— Kublai Khan, who was then lord of all the Mongols but had taken the eastern section of his vast empire to rule himself. Kublai Khan, having heard of the presence in Bokhara of two

Below: the nearest to an authentic portrait of the Polos in existence, detail of a 14th-century Italian fresco by Andrea di Buonaiuto da Firenze in the Spanish Chapel of the Church of Santa Maria Novella in Florence. The Polos are thought to be the figures facing forward in the center row. From left to right they are Maffeo (in dark Eastern clothing), Nicolò (with white beard), and Marco (holding the book).

From Venice to the Great Khan

Above: depiction of Kublai Khan painted in 1291, his official Mongol portrait.

Opposite: view of Venice from a 1338 French manuscript of Marco Polo's book, showing the Church of St. Mark and the Doge's palace. St. Mark's was originally the private chapel of the Doge and is richly decorated with Eastern materials.

men from the far west who by then had mastered the Mongol language, invited the Polos to come to his capital.

The Venetians were not slow to grasp the opportunity. They reached the court of Kublai Khan in 1266, traveling in relative comfort along the northern arm of the old Silk Road. They were greeted with courtesy and graciousness, and the khan questioned them closely about the West's political organization and religion. Clearly interested by their replies, Kublai Khan decided with the approval of his nobles to use the Polo brothers to take a letter to the pope requesting him to send 100 learned men to present the case for Christianity to Kublai's court and his people. He supplied the brothers with the Mongol equivalent of a passport for their journey—a golden tablet bearing his seal, which declared that the bearers were his personal envoys.

Even protected by the golden tablet it took them three years to reach Venice. When they arrived there in 1269 they discovered that the pope had recently died and his successor had not yet been elected. They waited for two years, but still no choice had been made. Fearful of waiting longer lest the Great Khan be displeased with them, the Polo brothers decided to set off regardless —but this time they took with them Nicolò's young son Marco. Born after his father's first departure from Venice, Marco was then 17 years old.

The three Polos went first to Acre in what is now Israel, then the gateway port to the East. There they discussed their problem with the resident papal legate, who sympathized but was unable to do much officially. After the Polos had set out on their way eastward the legate himself was elected pope and became Gregory X, and he called the Polos back and gave them letters and gifts for the Great Khan. The learned men requested by Kublai seem to have been in short supply, because Gregory sent only two, and those two may have been learned but they were certainly not brave. At the first rumor of danger they handed over to the Polos all their privileges, papers, and letters and fled back to Acre.

The Polos continued, carrying with them the golden tablet of the Great Khan. They apparently passed through what is now Turkey and then worked their way down to Hormuz on the Persian Gulf with the idea of continuing their journey by sea. After one look at the flimsy, unseaworthy boats in which they would have had to travel, they changed their minds and returned northward through what is now Iran to the Pamirs. Marco Polo believed these mountains to be the highest in the world, and he remarked with wonder that fire did not burn so brightly there, nor did food cook as easily.

From there they followed the familiar trail of the Silk Road through Kashgar, Yarkand (where Marco Polo noticed the prevalence of the condition of goiter, which he suggested was due to the quality of the drinking water), Khotan, Lop (Niya, between them, had long since been covered by sand), and the sparse oases and wells along the edge of the desert. Their caravan, like so many others, inched along the yellow dunes continually watching for signs of water and never finding enough. Indeed, Marco Polo was told that it was unwise to travel with more than 50 people as there was not sufficient water to supply a larger group. At last the Polos and their caravan reached the end of their journey across

the plains, mountains, and deserts of Asia—the summer palace
of the Great Khan. It had taken three and a half years.

Marco Polo found great favor with Kublai Khan, and the three
Polos spent the next 17 years with him. Marco became a trusted
civil servant and traveled widely throughout the empire. He
covered greater distances and saw more of the world than any
European had ever done. At last an opportunity arose for them
to return to the West and the three Polos went home, by sea this
time, accompanying a Mongol princess who was to be married to
a Persian khan. At Hormuz the princess was duly handed over,
and the Polos then made their way overland by way of Constantinople to Venice, to family and friends, to fame, and to disbelief.

It was Marco Polo's account of the geography and wonders of
the East—as told to a writer in a Genoese prison where both were
incarcerated years later—which brought to European attention
the existence of a fabulously rich and sophisticated society, a
spectacular Cathay hitherto the subject only of vague rumors. So
unprecedented was his report that for many it was literally un-
believable. Marco Polo became known as *Il Milione*—the teller
of a million tall tales. It took the passage of centuries and the

reports of countless others to establish that most of what he reported was absolutely true. He always insisted that he did not write half of what he saw.

What the Polos had no way of knowing was that what they had seen was the brilliant high noon of the Mongol empire. The empire lasted less than a century, and the Ming dynasty which overthrew it was antiforeign. The trade routes again became the prey of raiding bandits. Merchants and pilgrims could no longer travel in safety, and trade with the Far East faltered and died. In the West ordinary people forgot Marco Polo and the world he had revealed, while princes and navigators tried to find a new route to the riches of Cathay. Ship design was slowly improved, navigation far from shore developed into more of a science and less of a guess, and captains and pilots began to creep down the coast of Africa and then—daringly—westward into the uncharted ocean searching for a sea route to Asia.

Lying forgotten behind their ring of mountains were the cities which had for so long seen the riches of East and West carried past by the slow-moving caravans. Little by little the desert reclaimed them, until in the end there were only small, ragged villages where great cities ruled by great kings had been. The road itself carried only local trade. Finally after many centuries came the archaeologist Sir Aurel Stein, who poked with his

Below: the Polos crossing the Balacian river on their way to China in 1271, from a medieval manuscript illumination.

stick and carefully uncovered traces of the bustling world that had once existed where only silent sand dunes lay.

Over the centuries since Chang Ch'ien first pioneered the route, the fortunes of the old Silk Road have waxed and waned. Stein reported with satisfaction in 1906 that some parts of the route Hsüan-Tsang and Marco Polo had followed were gradually being opened up again, and traders were passing through yearly. During World War II parts of the northern arm of the road were paved in order to transport munitions from the Siberian railhead. The ancient road was still the most direct route. What it is like now is a subject for the guesswork of China-watchers, for the Taklamakan lies deep in the heart of a China which is only now beginning to open up again, cautiously, to outsiders.

The old Silk Road and its merchants belong to the past. East–West encounters now take place in different settings, different places. Only tattered relics remain: in an ancient burial ground in the Lop salt desert, stretching east from the Taklamakan, Stein found scraps of fabric. Pieces of brightly colored patterned silk lay beside fragments of exquisitely worked wool tapestries in the Greek style. For all those centuries these bits of East and West have lain in the forgotten desert side by side, silent witnesses to the mingling of cultures that once took place along the old Silk Road.

End of the Road

Left: a village in modern Afghanistan near the Silk Road. The houses are typically dome-shaped. Merchant caravans passed regularly through this rugged country, as did the Mongol warriors from the East. The Polos traveled through the Hindu Kush and the Pamirs, which Marco called the "roof of the world."

Chapter 5 The Search for the Nile's Source

Since time immemorial the lower part of the Nile river has flooded annually, depositing rich soil along the banks of the river and making the Nile valley one of the most fertile in the world. But where does this river, so beneficial to humans, begin life? The problem has been particularly complicated because there are actually not one but two Niles, the Blue and the White, which unite at Khartoum. Flamboyant, highly individual characters set out, separately or in pairs, stubbornly to pit their determination and endurance against the perils of the African interior. Their claims and counterclaims were tossed back and forth across Europe. Who finally settled the question? How long did it take to solve the mystery?

The Nile begins in mountain rivulets which cascade white plumes down green equatorial mountains. It ends in a tan blur that pours into the metallic blue of the Mediterranean Sea, by which time it has traveled over 4000 miles across some of the most forbidding desert territory in the world. It is the longest and most powerful river of them all: 40,000,000 people depend upon it for life itself. Every year between June and October the silt-laden river overflows its banks in the Nile Valley, bringing life to the arid waste on either side. For well over 5000 years civilization has existed in the valley, dependent upon the annual flood. There is no record of the river ever having failed entirely, although a "low Nile"—a flood of less than average volume—is a disaster that has always meant famine. Through the ages the great brown river has seemed as much a part of the eternal order of things as the sun that continues to rise and set overhead.

Curiously, all of the recorded attempts to discover where the river comes from have been made by foreigners. It is as if only outsiders recognized how extraordinary the river was, were curious about its origins, and wondered how it happened that every year it suddenly rose up out of its banks and poured over the land. The ancient Egyptians certainly knew about the six *cataracts* (or, more properly, rapids, produced by ribs of rock rising up from the desert floor) that occur between Aswan and what is now Khartoum. The dominion of the pharaohs once stretched as far as the Fourth Cataract, which lies in the Nubian

Opposite: the Victoria Falls on the Zambezi River. The Africans called the falls "smoke that thunders," but David Livingstone, who was the first European to see them on November 17, 1855, named them after Queen Victoria. He wrote, "Scenes so lovely must have been gazed upon by angels in their flight." He calculated that "the depth down which the river leaps without a break is 310 feet, or, if I remember correctly, double the depth of Niagara." His measurements have since been proved nearly accurate.

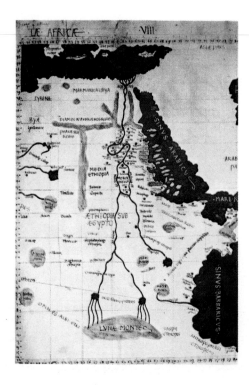

Above: map of southeastern Africa dating from the 15th century, showing Ptolemy's "Mountains of the Moon" as the source of the Nile. The river also appears to rise from three lakes, two of which are the sources of the White Nile and the other of the Blue Nile.

Right: map of eastern Africa, showing the regions crossed by the various Europeans who searched for the source of the Nile.

Opposite: James Bruce of Kinnaird, Scotland (1730–1794). He spent six years tracking down the source of the Blue Nile, which is actually only a tributary of the main White Nile.

The Earliest Speculations

desert. But the earliest speculation about the source of the river was offered by Herodotus in the 5th century B.C., who wrote that it originated in a bottomless lake. Another Greek of that time suggested a mountain source: Aeschylus said the Nile was "nurtured by the snow" of mountains in the interior. Around 150 B.C. Ptolemy, the great geographer, summed up what was then known about the Nile: he said it extended directly southward to the equator, where it rose from two round lakes. The lakes themselves took their water from what he called the *Lunae Montes*, the "Mountains of the Moon."

In the 1st century A.D. the Roman emperor Nero sent two centurions on an expedition to discover what they could learn, but they returned after being blocked by an impenetrable swamp, presumably the Sudd, a kind of landlocked Sargasso Sea of papyrus plants, elephant grass, and other floating plants that lies in the southern Sudan. The mystery was heightened by a persistent legend of a 1st-century Greek merchant, Diogenes, who was supposed to have gone inland from the Indian Ocean and arrived in the vicinity of two great lakes and a snowy range of mountains from "whence the Nile draws its twin sources." But as the geography of the whole of inner Africa was an enigma, Ptolemy's map, though questioned, was never refuted, and there the matter rested for 16 centuries.

It was a bluff Scotsman, James Bruce, who in 1768 set out to challenge the mystery. For his day he was huge—6 foot 4 inches tall. He was intelligent, rich, strong, very brave, and very determined. When his young wife died of tuberculosis only nine months after their marriage Bruce eased his grief with travel. He spent 14 years wandering through Europe and the Mediterranean countries, gradually becoming fixed on the idea of determining the source of the Nile. In 1768, by then in Cairo, he decided to search for the original spring itself.

There was one major complication in his search. In the upper reaches south of Khartoum there is not one Nile but two. What is called the Blue Nile originates in Ethiopia; the White Nile is much longer and its source is over 1000 miles further south, so in a sense the Blue Nile is a tributary. Bruce was convinced, however, that the Blue Nile was "the" Nile and the White Nile only a tributary. He was therefore pursuing the wrong river from the beginning.

He set out with Luigi Balugani, a young Italian he had hired as a secretary and artist, and they eventually reached the Ethiopian port of Massawa on the Red Sea. In November 1769 Bruce and Balugani turned inland from Massawa to Gondar, then the national capital. Ethiopia—then generally known as Abyssinia—was not completely unknown to Europeans. Seventy years before Bruce a French doctor, Jacques Charles Poncet, had traveled up the Blue Nile to Gondar; 80 years before Poncet a group of Portuguese Jesuit priests had reached Ethiopia from the Indian Ocean, and they had briefly converted the court from their ancient Coptic Christianity to Roman Catholicism. But apart from their reports (short, and by then decades old) nothing was known of the country.

Bruce learned a lot for himself almost immediately. He found people imprisoned in cages who were held until their families

James Bruce Begins the Search

Above: engraving after a drawing by Henry Salt titled "The Residence of the Ras at Antelow," as seen about 30 years after Bruce's arrival by another European traveler.

Opposite: Tisisat Falls, 20 miles below Lake Tana on the Blue Nile. The river approaches gently and then suddenly vanishes in a tremendous, foaming downpour of water. From above it appears to be a narrow gorge through which water races with terrifying turmoil. It remains a spectacular sight to this day; for Bruce it must have been overpowering.

could buy their release. He saw men throw a live cow to the ground and cut two bleeding steaks off her flanks, which they ate raw and warm. The skin was then pinned back over the wound, and the cow was driven on. At Gondar, which he reached in January, he first met the young 15-year-old king and his vizier Ras Michael—the real ruler of the country—when they were putting out the eyes of recent captives; 44 chiefs, taken in battle, were thus mutilated and turned out into the fields to die. Bloody horror was piled upon horror as Bruce discovered that violence and savagery were inherent parts of the life of this society. He was treated well himself, though, for however brutal Ras Michael was he was not unintelligent, and he obviously saw Bruce as a man who could be useful. Thus Bruce accompanied the royal forces on their next expedition to subdue a rebellion south of Lake Tana.

Lake Tana was the lake from which the Blue Nile issued, and Bruce was able not only to see the river close to its outflow from the lake, but to stand at Tisisat Falls, a splendid cascade of foaming, thundering water. He returned with the army to Gondar, but in October 1770 he set out again with Balugani around the west side of Lake Tana. He was taken to the marsh where, his guides told him, the ultimate source of the Nile lay. Bruce flung off his shoes and ran rapturously to the spring, convinced that he had solved a centuries-old puzzle.

He was wrong, of course. He had found only the source of the Blue Nile, and even that had been visited previously by Pedro Páez, one of the Jesuits, in 1618. Bruce knew of Páez but, unfairly, claimed that his account was based on hearsay. Still, Bruce was undoubtedly the first to fix the spring's position.

Having achieved his goal, however, it took him over a year to get out of Ethiopia. Civil war broke out; Bruce suffered with malaria; Balugani died of dysentery. At last, in December 1771, Bruce received permission to leave and set out to cross the Sudan deserts and then follow the Nile Valley to Cairo.

It took him four months to reach Sennar, during which he narrowly escaped death at the hands of desert marauders. In Sennar Bruce was safe from bandits but was at the mercy of a petulant young ruler who refused to let him leave. Tormented by unremitting heat, Bruce bartered almost everything he had for food before he was able to escape. At Abu Hamed he avoided the great western loop of the Nile by striking out overland to Aswan, but he very nearly died in the sands. The camels did perish, but he struggled on, walking, and he had to abandon all his instruments and painfully gathered notes. Eventually, after 18 agonizing days, Bruce dragged himself into Aswan. Exhausted and ill as he was, he immediately set out on a camel to retrace his steps and recover his baggage. He found it again, untouched. From Aswan he sailed down the Nile to Cairo.

He had expected acclamation when he returned to England in 1774, but he was disappointed. Fashionable London found the tall, noisy Scot with the preposterous stories simply too amusing for words. Steaks cut from living cows, barbarous emperors, fat princesses with gold rings in their noses—it was all too incredible. The great Dr. Samuel Johnson, who had written a novel set in a fictional Ethiopia that had nothing in common with Bruce's

reports, said that he did not believe Bruce had ever been there at all. Overcome with anger and indignation, Bruce retreated to his estates in Scotland. Only after 16 years did he publish the report of his journey, which was then greeted with fascination by the general public. But Bruce did not have long to enjoy his popular success. In 1794, when he was 64, he fell down a staircase and died.

There was a lull in activity after Bruce. Egypt was rocked by successive political convulsions, and exploration along the Nile would have been suicidal. By 1850 the situation had stabilized, and Turkish rule from Cairo extended into the Sudan. Several Europeans reached Khartoum, where the Blue Nile and the White Nile join. The Turks themselves dispatched three expeditions to explore the river, but the first stopped at the floating swamp of the Sudd, and the other two only reached the area near the present-day town of Juba, 750 miles south of Khartoum, still nowhere near the source of the White Nile.

The mystery itself persisted as a challenge to the world, and in 1856 two Englishmen set off for Africa to take it up. They were

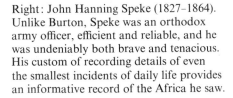

Right: John Hanning Speke (1827–1864). Unlike Burton, Speke was an orthodox army officer, efficient and reliable, and he was undeniably both brave and tenacious. His custom of recording details of even the smallest incidents of daily life provides an informative record of the Africa he saw.

Burton and Speke

complete opposites: Richard Francis Burton, aged 35, was an accomplished linguist and flamboyant romantic. John Hanning Speke, six years younger, was calm and methodical, the model of a Victorian gentleman. He was a passionate hunter, and one of his goals was to build up a natural history museum using the specimens he collected. Both men were officers in the Indian Army. Burton had served in the intelligence unit. When he left India he had continued to exploit his flair for disguise and his thorough knowledge of Islam—he had entered Mecca dressed as a Muslim holy man. He had gone on later to Harar, the forbidden Ethiopian city holy to Muslim Somalis. It was on the Harar expedition that Burton and Speke first traveled together (although Burton went into the city alone), and both men were wounded when their party was attacked at night. Back in England, Burton planned to return to Africa and strike inland from Zanzibar to find the "Coy Fountains" of the Nile, and it was natural that he should ask Speke to join him. Speke immediately agreed.

They sailed from Zanzibar in June 1857 after collecting supplies and porters on the island. Zanzibar was then one of the "last outposts" of the known world and the center for the East African slave trade. Although the export of slaves was made illegal in 1845, slavery within the sultan's dominions was still permitted. Between 20,000 and 40,000 slaves were brought to Zanzibar from Africa each year, and of them about two-thirds were illegally exported. To the extent that the mainland west of the island was known by any but the native Africans, it was familiar only to Arab slave traders.

Burton and Speke came ashore at Bagamoyo in what is now Tanzania and set out westward along the slavers' route. They were only able to travel in the early morning until the intense midday heat forced them to stop and make camp. Their progress was slow and painful: both men were racked by fever, and it took them nearly five months to cover some 500 miles. At Kazé, near

Above left: Richard Burton (1821–1890), by Frederick Leighton in 1876. With his flair for languages and enthusiasm for blending into an exotic and dangerous environment, Burton was one of the most flamboyant of the African explorers.

Below: a gang of African captives on their way to be sold as slaves. A European observer noted wryly that the black drivers, who carried muskets, seemed to feel that "they were doing a very noble thing, and might proudly march with an air of triumph." The island of Zanzibar was an established center for the extensive East African slave trade.

Karagwe-the Amazing Kingdom

Below: James Augustus Grant (1827–1892) in the clothes he wore in Africa. Grant recorded many of the sights of his journey with Speke in watercolors and sketches. The two men, both army officers, got along very well.

present-day Tabora, they met Arab slave traders who used the settlement as a base of operations, and the two Englishmen were given a gracious welcome and considerable information. After two months Burton and Speke set off again, almost due west, until they came upon Lake Tanganyika. Burton hoped this lake might be the source of the Nile, but he was told (to his disappointment) that the river at the north flowed *into* the lake, not out. Both men were then at a low ebb physically—Burton was semiparalyzed with malaria and his mouth was horribly ulcerated; Speke was so blind from ophthalmia that he could barely see the lake and was almost deaf from abscesses in his ears. They managed to return to Kazé where Speke, the younger man, recovered more quickly than Burton. They had heard rumors of a great lake lying to the north, so while Burton, still feeble, stayed with his Arab friends to refit the caravan and compile his notes, Speke went north on his own to investigate. After only 16 days Speke found himself on the shore of a vast inland sea with sandy beaches and wooded slopes. Instantly, in a flash of inspiration, he decided that he had found the source of the Nile. He hurried back to Kazé to tell Burton that the quest was at an end.

Burton was not impressed. He pointed out that Speke had seen a lake but no sign of a river. Speke remained convinced that his lake, which he named for Queen Victoria, was indeed the source. In the face of such complete disagreement both men avoided the subject. The silence between them, however, was hardly harmonious. The trip back to Zanzibar was as slow and tortuous as the march inland—both men collapsed almost at once and had to be carried. They reached Zanzibar on March 4, 1859, nearly two years after they had left. Again Speke recuperated more rapidly, and as he was impatient to be home, in mid-April he went on ahead. According to Burton, Speke's last words were a promise to wait until Burton arrived in London before putting their claim to the Royal Geographical Society.

Burton arrived in England only 12 days after Speke, but he discovered to his fury that Speke had already announced his discovery of Lake Victoria, lectured on their expedition to the Royal Geographical Society, and was even then organizing a new attempt to find the Nile's outlet from the lake and follow it downstream to Egypt. Burton was not to be included in the new expedition, nor was anyone particularly interested in his discovery of Lake Tanganyika.

Speke was the man of the hour, and in 1860 he hurried back to Africa, this time with James Augustus Grant, a modest, self-effacing man who was devoted to Speke. During their expedition, Grant wrote later, "not a shade of jealousy or distrust or even ill-temper came between us." They chose almost exactly the same route inland from Zanzibar as Speke had followed earlier with Burton, and the perfect harmony between the explorers did not spare them from a repetition of most of the same misfortunes. Porters deserted, local chieftains demanded rich payment for allowing them to travel unhindered through their territories, and Grant became ill with malaria. It took them over a year to reach Karagwe, the territory west of Lake Victoria.

Karagwe was one of three amazing kingdoms in the heart of central Africa. Totally untouched by the outside world, Karagwe,

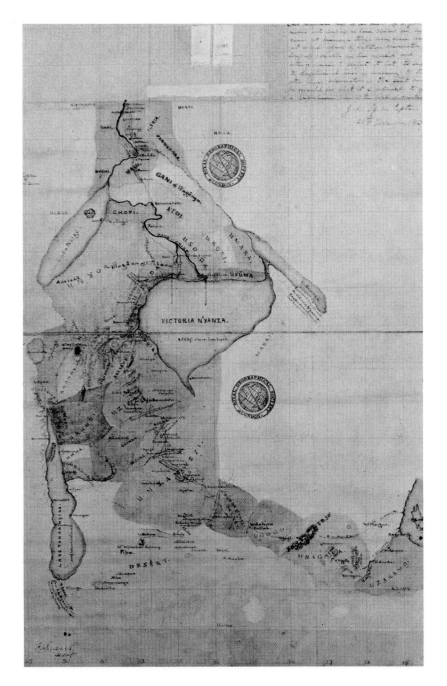

Left: Grant's map of the African territory
he and Speke covered in search of the Nile's
source. Speke's note added, "This miniature
map is the result of a foot march with
compass in hand . . . compass variation has
been regarded and nothing remains to
perfect it but to shift the longitudinal line
if necessary to the other lunar observations."

Bunyoro (north of Lake Victoria), and Buganda (between
Karagwe and Bunyoro) had evolved a curious state of semi-
civilization. Their systems of government were well developed,
each having a king and court, but the kings had absolute power
and ruled with barbaric cruelty according to their own whims.
They knew nothing of the world outside their kingdoms, and
the rest of the world had no idea that they existed.

Speke and Grant's arrival, therefore, was unprecedented. The
first of the monarchs they encountered was Rumanika, the tall
and handsome king of Karagwe. He was fascinated with their
tales of the wonders of Europe. Speke enjoyed his company
greatly. Rumanika had his own wonders to show, primarily his
fat harem. His wives and daughters were so obese that they could

Right: drawing by Speke of Ripon Falls,
which he labels with the African name.
When he first saw the falls he was surprised
to find that they were only about 12 feet
high.

not stand upright but lay like seals on the floors of their huts.

Forewarned by Rumanika, Speke and Grant waited in Karagwe until Mutesa, the young king of Buganda, had been informed of their arrival and could invite them to enter his territory. The two Englishmen waited a month for the invitation, and by then Grant was bedridden with an abscessed leg. Under the circumstances, it seemed advisable for Speke to proceed on his own. During his march north to Mutesa's capital, on a hill-top not far from modern Kampala, he finally caught a glimpse of Lake Victoria and was more convinced than ever that he was looking at the source of the Nile. However, the immediate task was to establish good relations with Mutesa, so he turned his back on the lake and continued north.

Mutesa's palace turned out to be a collection of grass huts encircled by a tall fence of yellow reeds. Within its precincts lived Mutesa, his nobles, his pages, and his wives—200 or so of them. Etiquette was elaborate, and any breach was punished by instant execution. When Mutesa spoke his entire court fell to the ground, crying out in admiration. He affected a curious stiff-legged walk which was meant to show his similarity to a lion, and when he walked the court followed dutifully behind. Life was cheap, and execution by decapitation, burning, or burial alive was an every-day occurrence. The king was greatly impressed by Speke's gift of several rifles, one of which he immediately had put to use by telling a page to go and shoot someone in the outer court. The page obeyed and scampered back full of delight in his successful feat. Speke wrote, "I never heard, and there appeared no curiosity to know, what individual human being the urchin had deprived of life."

Speke remained at Mutesa's court for three months before Grant was well enough to join him and for another two months before Mutesa would permit them to leave. By that time they had heard of a river that emerged from Lake Victoria very near

Opposite: Sir Samuel and Lady Florence
Baker. Samuel Baker's character could be
summed up by his own words: "I could not
conceive that anything in this world had
power to resist a determined will, so long as
health and life remained." However he also
wrote, during a spate of particularly awful
misfortune, "I shall be truly thankful to
quit this abominable land."

them to the east, which they were determined to find and then follow it downstream wherever it went. Eventually, on July 7, 1862, Mutesa let them go, and they started off together. But Grant's leg was still hindering him, and Speke was desperately impatient. Thus Grant was left to make his way slowly toward the court of Kamrasi, king of Bunyoro—the third of the kingdoms—while Speke made a quick march to the river. He reached a point about 40 miles downstream from the lake on July 21. A week later he reached a spectacularly wide waterfall where the great stream poured out northward from the lake. Speke named it Ripon Falls after the president of the Royal Geographical Society. Contentedly he surveyed the scene—fish leaping, crocodiles basking in the sun, and native fishermen in boats. For him the mystery was now solved, and all that remained was to get home to tell others about it.

But even that was a frustratingly slow business. Kamrasi arrogantly commandeered almost everything the explorers possessed before he would let them continue down the river, and by then it was the flood season so that they had to march overland in order to make any progress. It was not until they reached Gondokoro, near present-day Juba in the southern Sudan, that they rejoined the Nile. There, on February 13, 1863, to their immense relief, they met the British sportsman Samuel Baker and his wife. Speke was now lean and worn, Grant's clothes were in rags, but their ordeal was over. They sailed north on Baker's boat, cabling triumphantly to London, "All is well . . . and the Nile is settled."

It was not, of course. For one thing, Richard Burton had several difficult questions to put to his old companion when he returned in triumph. Speke was challenged for proof of his assertions: he had seen a river flowing out of Lake Victoria to the north, but how could he be sure it was the Nile? He had neither followed the shoreline of the lake nor sailed across it— how could he be sure it was even the same lake he had seen in 1858? He had made no investigations into what other streams or rivers might have flowed in or out of it—how could he conclude that he had settled anything? For Burton, it was the same old Speke guesswork all over again.

The whole controversy was to be brought to a head in September 1864 when the British Association for the Advancement of Science arranged a meeting which both Burton and Speke promised to attend. Burton was prepared not only to demolish Speke's theory but to propose that Lake Tanganyika and its feeder streams were the true headwaters of the Nile, and that he and Speke had both been misled—both of them had certainly been ill at the time—into the erroneous belief that the Ruzizi river at its northern tip flowed *into* the lake. They had not seen the river themselves; they had relied upon the reports of the local Africans. From all accounts, Speke was equally determined to insist that the Nile did flow out of Lake Victoria, and that the falls he had seen were its headwaters.

On September 15, the day before the great debate was scheduled to take place, Burton and Speke encountered each other at a preliminary session. Each man looked at the other and moved past without a word. The next morning a note was handed around

The Burton-Speke Confrontation

Samuel Baker's Nile Expedition

in silence. John Speke had died the afternoon before in a shooting accident. Burton, visibly shocked, sank into a chair on the platform and exclaimed, "By God, he's killed himself!" But the verdict at the inquest was accidental death—apparently Speke's shotgun went off as he was lifting it over a wall.

The answer to the question of which man was right clearly lay in Africa, and while it was debated in London an extraordinary couple were still investigating in central Africa. Samuel Baker, then 38, and his second wife Florence, a blond Hungarian girl 15 years younger, had set off from Khartoum in December 1862 to discover the sources of the Nile. Their expedition was well provisioned (Baker was a wealthy man) with three boats and nearly a hundred men. For 500 miles their journey was straightforward. Then, a short distance north of what is now Malakal, the river turned west and everything had changed. From being a broad and well-defined river, the Nile abruptly became a floating quagmire. The boats had to be hauled along on ropes through the Sudd by men who stood on solid chunks, sometimes 20 feet thick, of rotting vegetation. Crocodiles and hippopotamuses sur-

rounded them; the air was thick with mosquitoes and other insects. It had taken them 40 days to make the journey from Khartoum to Gondokoro, and they had been there less than two weeks when Speke and Grant arrived from Bunyoro with their announcement that the Nile puzzle had been solved.

Baker managed to conceal his disappointment—surely there was now no reason for his expedition?—but then the two exhausted explorers made a tantalizing suggestion. At Bunyoro they had heard of another lake a short distance to the west, the Luta Ngizé, and it seemed possible that this might be a second source of the Nile. But they had been too near the end of their resources to investigate. They gave a map of their route to the Bakers, and when Speke and Grant continued north to Khartoum the Bakers went south toward the lake.

It was the rainy season, and their journey became a torment. They fell victim to malaria, their baggage animals died, and smallpox broke out among the porters. In late January 1864 they at last reached Bunyoro, where Baker was accepted as "Speke's brother." Kamrasi countered Baker's requests for guides to the

Left: the Bakers' boat being hauled through the Sudd, a huge mass of decaying vegetation that is mostly matted grass and papyrus from the surrounding swamps. The Sudd formed an obstacle big enough to defeat many early efforts to trace the Nile to its source. When the thick mass reaches the main channel of the river it forms a dam extending up to 25 miles long and 20 feet deep.

Above: the sandy spit where the White Nile enters Lake Albert (Luta Ngizé). When Baker discovered the lake he was certain that he had found a source of the Nile, but Lake Albert is no longer regarded as a true source since the river flows in and out again at the lake's northern tip.

western lake with demands for Baker's watch, his compass, his gun, and finally his wife. He was quite willing to provide one of his own wives in exchange. Baker indignantly pointed his pistol at the king (later he wrote, "If this were to be the end of the expedition I resolved that it should also be the end of Kamrasi") and Florence Baker flew at him with a furious speech in Arabic, not a word of which the king understood. But he got the message, and the following day porters were provided.

They followed the general line of the Kafu river southwest. Florence Baker collapsed with sunstroke, and for three days she was carried along unconscious. For the next week she raved deliriously, and after seven days a half-starved Baker collapsed at her side. He awoke to a miracle—Florence was sleeping naturally, and when she awoke she was herself again, her eyes calm and clear. They moved on, and on March 14 climbed a low hill from which they could see the lake before them. Baker renamed Luta Ngizé Lake Albert after Queen Victoria's beloved husband

"The Two Sources of the Nile..."

Left: Samuel Baker meeting with local chiefs on entering Bunyoro. They decided that he was "Speke's brother." This illustration is from Baker's book *The Albert N'Yanza*, published in 1866.

Below: elaborate ceremonial form of the African wooden stool, used by Baker during his exploration in central Africa. It was probably a gift from one of the many local chiefs he met.

and consort who had recently died, so that "the Victoria and the Albert are the two sources of the Nile." (In fact Lake Albert is no longer regarded as an actual source, since the river runs in and out of the lake at its northern tip). They headed north until they reached the point where the Nile entered and, continuing up the river, discovered another magnificent waterfall where the full volume of the river burst through a narrow ravine only 20 feet across. They named it Murchison Falls for the then president of the Royal Geographical Society.

The next problem was how to get home. The situation was aggravated by a civil war in Bunyoro, and with villages depopulated and guides nonexistent it took the Bakers, both of them weak with starvation, two months to get back to Kamrasi. Here they discovered a different man—the earlier Kamrasi had not been the king at all but a younger brother. The real Kamrasi was no less acquisitive than the pseudo-Kamrasi had been, and he set about relieving the Bakers of their last possessions. Had a

Livingstone and the Nile Problem

slave caravan not providentially arrived with supplies for the Bakers they might never have been able to leave. It was a long slow journey back to Gondokoro, and when they arrived in February 1865, after two years away, they discovered that they had been given up for dead. No supplies awaited them. They hired a boat to return to Khartoum, but the Sudd blocked them for many weeks, and the plague broke out on board. One of their faithful servants went mad and died almost within sight of Khartoum. From there they went on to Cairo and eventually back to England to enthusiastic acclaim.

Baker now believed that he had settled the source of the Nile. But, like Speke, he had simply seen a lake which he had not circumnavigated. He had proved that Speke's river ran into his lake and then out of it to the north. But he had not proved that this was the Nile, for he had not followed the river to Gondokoro. And if Speke's Lake Victoria and Baker's Lake Albert both

Above: drawing of his exit from Bunyoro by Samuel Baker. After Baker pointed his pistol at Kamrasi and refused to swap wives with him, he and his wife were finally allowed to leave; they bade the king "a very cold adieu," and out rushed their escort—about 600 men, dancing and yelling, dressed in leopard skins with antelope horns strapped to their heads.

fed the Nile, which was the true source? Even before the Bakers reached England Sir Roderick Murchison had announced that the most famous of all African explorers, Dr. David Livingstone, had undertaken to resolve the thorny problem of the watersheds of central Africa. He was to look south of Lake Tanganyika (where Livingstone himself believed the source would be found) and then proceed to the lake itself to discover if the Ruzizi flowed into the lake (as Burton had first reported) or out of it (as Burton

Left: David Livingstone in 1864, painted by General Need. Livingstone's self-reliant determination was acknowledged by all who met him. A friend said of him, "One trait in his character was to do exactly what he set his mind on . . . without feeling himself bound to give any reason."

Below: Livingstone reading the Bible aloud. It was the cornerstone of his life, and he read it constantly for comfort and inspiration. He often compared his own difficulties with those he found in the Scriptures, and he gave talks on Christianity to the natives wherever he stopped.

by then was inclined to believe). By the end of January 1866 Livingstone was in Zanzibar.

David Livingstone was completely unlike any of the other men who made their names in Africa. Born in Glasgow, at the age of 10 he was working 14 hours a day in a cotton mill, six days a week. Possessed of a deep and abiding religious faith, he managed against all the odds to gain an education, and in 1840 he first arrived in Africa as a medical missionary. He went to Cape Town and from there into the interior. Although he always saw himself as foremost a missionary, the world came to know him as an indefatigable explorer. On his first journeys he had explored much of southern Africa. From 1858 to 1864 he ascended the Zambezi river to the Victoria Falls (which he named) and discovered Lake Nyasa. At the same time he identified one of the principal slave routes from the interior to the coast. Deeply sympathetic to Africans, Livingstone hated slavery with all his heart, knowing intimately the horrors inseparable from the trade.

On this expedition he planned to stay well south of the usual caravan routes, so with his men (none of them European) he sailed down the east coast of Africa from Zanzibar to the mouth of the Rovuma river, now the border between Mozambique and Tanzania. Arab slavers had plundered the countryside, and the ravaged land offered little food. His pack animals died, his men collapsed with illness or deserted—even his medicine chest was lost, taken by two runaway porters. After nearly a year of exhausting effort, Livingstone struggled up to the southern end of Lake Tanganyika. He was virtually penniless, starving, and de-

Above: the Victoria Falls, painted by Thomas Baines, who accompanied Livingstone, in 1863.

Right: a massacre of Africans by Arabs. Livingstone saw many such senseless killings, but the worst took place one hot, sultry day when nerves were taut and tempers strained. Three men carrying guns in a crowded market haggled about the price of a chicken, two guns went off, and the slaughter began. Panicking people ran in all directions, some jumping into the river and drowning, while shot after shot cracked out into the helpless mob.

bilitated by rheumatic fever and dysentery. Ironically, he was rescued by a party of Arab slavers, who fed him, nursed him, gave him clothing, and resupplied him with beads to use in trading. He then went west, adding Lake Mweru to the map and ruling it out as part of the Nile drainage system. He went south to Lake Bangweulu, but again he found himself without sufficient supplies to obtain guides and had no alternative but to return to the Arabs.

In March 1869 he was in Ujiji. It was on a well-trodden caravan route, so he expected to find medicines, supplies, and letters. But in fact there was hardly anything—his supplies had been looted on their way upcountry. Nevertheless, he pushed on westward toward a river, the Lualaba, which he was beginning to believe might be the Nile. He reached Nyangwe on the banks of the river and was there on the morning of July 15, 1871 when a party of Arabs, haggling over the price of a chicken at the busy market, suddenly began firing at random, gunning down helpless men, women, and children. Some jumped into the river to escape the bullets and were drowned—in all about 400 people

A Massacre by Arab Slavers

Above: Livingstone's sextant, which he used in mapping much of southern Africa. His most precious possessions were his scientific and medical instruments, his journal, a magic lantern, and his Bible.

"Not all pleasure, this exploration"

were killed. After this there was no hope of obtaining men or boats to follow the river. Livingstone struggled back to Ujiji, destitute. He faced the choice of starving or begging from the Arabs.

It was at this providential moment in October 1871 that Henry Stanley, an American journalist born in Wales, came marching into Ujiji at the head of a caravan. He had been sent by his newspaper to find Livingstone. Unsure of his welcome, since friends of Livingstone in Zanzibar had suggested he might be less than enthusiastic to discover a reporter hot on his trail, Stanley approached him, took off his hat, and said, "Dr. Livingstone, I presume?"

Dr. Livingstone was in fact profoundly grateful to see him. The two men, as different as night and day, remained together for five months. For Stanley the meeting was a turning point in his life: he had never met anyone like Livingstone before, and he developed a respect for the missionary amounting to hero worship.

As Livingstone recovered his health, it seemed natural to suggest that they should explore the northerly end of Lake Tanganyika together to settle the question of Burton's Ruzizi. They discovered once and for all that the river flowed southward into the lake, not out of it. Livingstone was thus encouraged in his growing conviction that the Lualaba was indeed the Nile and that it should be his next goal. Stanley wanted him to return to Zanzibar to resupply, but Livingstone said he would not leave until his work was finished. In March 1872 Stanley left for the coast alone, promising to send supplies and porters. When they arrived five months later Livingstone set off again, this time for Lake Bangweulu and the fountains of the Nile he expected to find beyond it. He wrote of one apprehension: what if the Lualaba turned out not to be the Nile at all, but the Congo?

He was never to find out. At the end of April 1873 he was working his way around the southern end of Lake Bangweulu hunting for a feeder stream which would flow through the lake

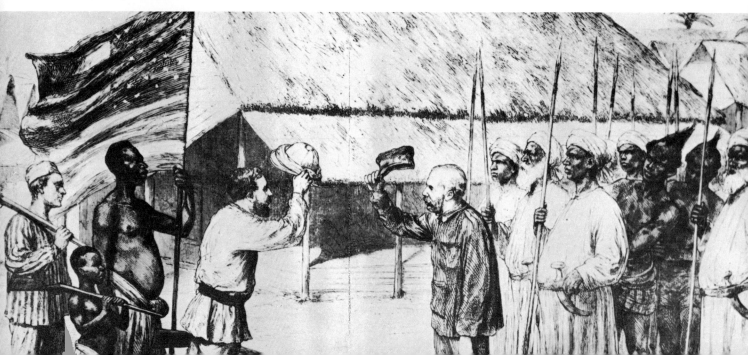

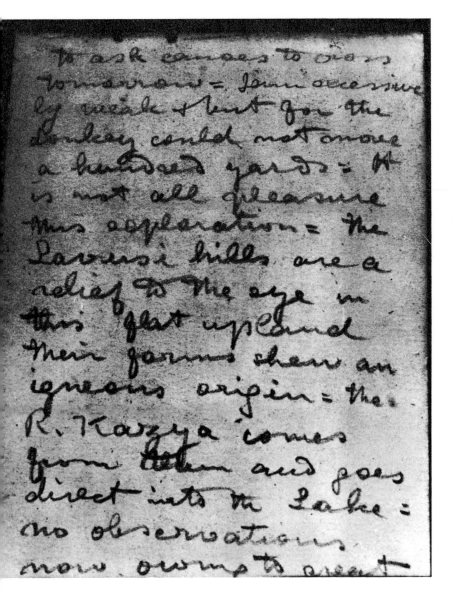

Left: Livingstone's last diary entry, of April 19, 1873. Until then he had kept up his scientific notes in spite of severe pain. That day he wrote, "No observations now . . . I can scarcely hold the pencil."

Opposite above: Henry Morton Stanley (1841–1904) in a photograph taken just before he left on his seven-month search for David Livingstone. He was passionately interested in many things and, somewhat surprisingly, was extremely impressed by the character of the man he went to find.

Opposite below: contemporary newspaper illustration of the famous meeting between Livingstone and Stanley in Ujiji on October 28, 1871.

Below: Stanley as a pallbearer at Livingstone's funeral in England, where his body was eventually buried.

into the Lualaba. He was plagued with fever and dysentery which his medicines could not control. Finally he became so weak he had to be carried in a hammock. His devoted men, Susi and Chuma, went on with him, even when it was clearly hopeless. On May 1, 1873, close to the village of a chieftain named Chitambo in what is now Zambia, the end came. In a last dogged effort, Livingstone struggled up to pray. His men found him, dead, kneeling across his bed.

His body now lies in Westminster Abbey in London. Susi and Chuma cut out his heart and viscera and buried them under a tree. They embalmed his body with raw salt, dried it in the sun, and then wrapped it in cloth and bark and lashed it to a pole. For eight months they carried it through swamp and forest, over lake and mountain, to deliver it to the Zanzibar authorities with his journals and notes. Livingstone's body at last came home to England, but his heart remained, as it had always been, in Africa.

In 1874 Henry Stanley returned to Africa. His first task, as he saw it, was to circumnavigate Speke's Lake Victoria (which had

Above: Stanley's portable barge, the *Lady Alice*, showing how it could be carried in sections overland by porters and then be reassembled.

been almost entirely ignored in the effort to map the lakes to the south and west) and verify if the river pouring out at Ripon Falls was the only outlet. He would then do the same for Lake Tanganyika—he and Livingstone had investigated only the Ruzizi—and, finally, he would take up Livingstone's last objective, a survey of the Lualaba to find where it led. He would follow the river downstream in a boat to its mouth, wherever that might be.

He set off for East Africa in August and by November he was at Bagamoyo. He had eight tons of baggage and a small army of porters. Such a great caravan offered a tempting prize to marauders, and by the time they reached Mwanza on the southern shore of Lake Victoria, at the end of February 1875, Stanley had lost a quarter of his men in the defense of his supplies.

Stanley's equipment included a portable barge, the *Lady Alice,* and he immediately had it assembled and launched. Leaving most of the expedition behind, he traveled up the eastern shore to Ripon Falls. Near there he encountered Mutesa, the same monarch who had fascinated and appalled Speke and Grant. Fourteen years had altered his style, if not his substance. He had apparently given up the lion stride, and there was no longer evidence of the murders and other atrocities that had been so prominent a feature of life at his court. Stanley found him charming and began a program of Bible readings to convert him to Christianity. Mutesa listened willingly and did not mention to

Stanley that he had marked the arrival of the last white man at his court by slaughtering 30 human beings in his honor. After nearly two weeks with Mutesa, which Stanley enjoyed thoroughly, the explorer continued his voyage around the lake. By the time he returned to Mwanza he had proven what Speke had only guessed: Lake Victoria was a single lake with one major outlet, Ripon Falls.

The next order of business was Lake Tanganyika, and Stanley reached Ujiji and launched the *Lady Alice* in June 1876. It took him only two months to sail around the entire lake and determine that there was no outlet that could possibly be described as the source of the Nile. The Burton–Speke controversy was at last resolved, with full honors to Speke.

Only the Lualaba river, on which Livingstone had placed such hope, remained. Stanley marched to the river, and the *Lady Alice* was reassembled yet again. It was a terrible journey, with every possible disaster. Smallpox and fever dogged the expedition; they nearly starved; they were attacked by riverside tribes; crucial supplies were lost; most of the accompanying canoes foundered, and men drowned; and the river went on and on and on. At last, 999 days after leaving Zanzibar, 115 survivors of the original 356-member expedition crawled out of the jungle at the Atlantic coast. As Livingstone had half suspected, the Lualaba led west to the Congo, not north to the Nile.

By the time Stanley returned to Zanzibar in 1877 by sea, three years after his departure, the mystery of the Nile existed no longer. There were details to tidy up, but the main questions were definitely answered. The floods across the Nile Valley, which brought life to the desert, were the result of rains that fell on the mountain streams feeding Lake Victoria and Lake Tana. Ptolemy's ancient map turned out to be surprisingly accurate, and the snowcapped equatorial Ruwenzori mountains east of Lake Edward, their slopes covered with bizarre gigantic plants, could be considered his Mountains of the Moon.

The Nile itself is now harnessed. Ripon Falls, where Speke saw the river emerging from Lake Victoria, has disappeared under the waters of Owen Falls Dam. Further downstream the massive Aswan High Dam has submerged Nubia under the waters of Lake Nasser in an effort to balance the flood periods so that the famines of a "low Nile" will be a thing of the past. The Nile is no longer considered a mysterious gift from the gods or a lure into an unknown hinterland but simply flows on, strong and steady, a ribbon of green in a sea of sand.

Stanley Ends the Mystery

Left: illustration of village life in East Africa from a book by Richard Burton, published in 1860. It was titled "The Ivory Porter, the Cloth Porter, and Woman in Usagara."

Chapter 6 The Mystery of the "Gilded Man"

Somewhere, according to legend, deep in the jungles of South America, is a city built of gold. It is ruled by El Dorado—"the gilded one" in Spanish—who is anointed daily with gold dust. The myth drew hundreds of adventurers into the impenetrable jungles of the Amazon basin, and most of them never returned. The few fortunate ones stumbled out of the forest years later, tattered, emaciated, and scarred from their ordeal. But the compelling lure of gold continued to draw hopeful fortune hunters who tortured the Indians they met until the Indians told them what they wanted to hear. What lies in the largely unknown Brazilian interior? Is there really an El Dorado?

It was in 1529 that reports of El Dorado—"the gilded one" in Spanish—first reached the conquistadors, who were then establishing tiny settlements on the Caribbean coast of South America. It was said that a mountain city existed where the people possessed so much gold that they covered the body of their king with the glittering dust. The story was irresistible to the gold-hungry Spanish, who felt they were on the threshold of a world filled with incredible riches. In 1521 Hernando Cortes had conquered the Aztec empire in what is now Mexico; in 1526 Francisco Pizarro had at last discovered indisputable proof of the wealth of the Incas in Peru, and in 1529 he was in Spain obtaining King Charles V's authority for an expedition of conquest. Anything seemed possible—gold and glory were there for the taking.

As the years passed the story acquired more details. In his high mountain kingdom each year the chief would ceremoniously strip naked and be covered with a sticky resin. His attendants then blew clouds of gold dust over his bare body until he glittered with the dazzling magnificence of a living golden statue. Gilded and gleaming, the king then led his people in procession to the shores of a lake, and he was rowed out in a canoe to the center. The king and his nobles threw gifts of emeralds and golden ornaments into the waters, and then, in a shimmering climax, the king himself plunged, shining, into the lake. When he emerged, the gold dust washed away, there was a festival of singing, dancing, and revelry.

Opposite: warrior's mask in gold, from the Museum of Gold in Bogotá. Colombia at the time of the Spanish conquest was inhabited by a number of small independent tribes. They kept their gold mainly for ceremonial and burial purposes, so consequently much of it remained hidden in graves, safe from the Europeans. Colombian Indian goldsmiths achieved amazing technical results with extremely primitive means. They knew about the lost-wax process of casting, soldering, rolling, wire-drawing, filigree-work, intaglio, embossing, and other sophisticated skills.

The Quest Begins

The obvious question was where this splendid place was to be found. That it lay somewhere in the unexplored interior was not doubted from the moment the story was told. The image of a people so rich they could coat their king with gold and then carelessly wash it away was a magnet for soldiers of fortune, so there was no shortage of men eager to find the golden city and claim its treasure. One by one, year after year, they set off into the unknown jungle, with a marvellous golden vision dancing before their eyes.

The first man to try to find El Dorado was a red-bearded German, Ambrosius Ehinger. He had been a merchant, and it was as a representative of a bank that he came to America. The wealthy banking house of the Welsers had supported Charles V of Spain in his claim to the imperial title of Holy Roman Emperor, so when Charles V became emperor he repaid the Welsers in 1527 with the territory of present-day Venezuela, naming them as the proprietary lords in perpetuity. Ehinger, accompanied by one other German and a party of hired Spaniards, arrived early in 1529 to take possession of the Welser property at the newly founded town of Coro, about a hundred miles east of the Gulf of Venezuela. Almost immediately after his arrival Ehinger heard the first hazy version of the story and he promptly, that very summer, set off to locate the king and his treasure.

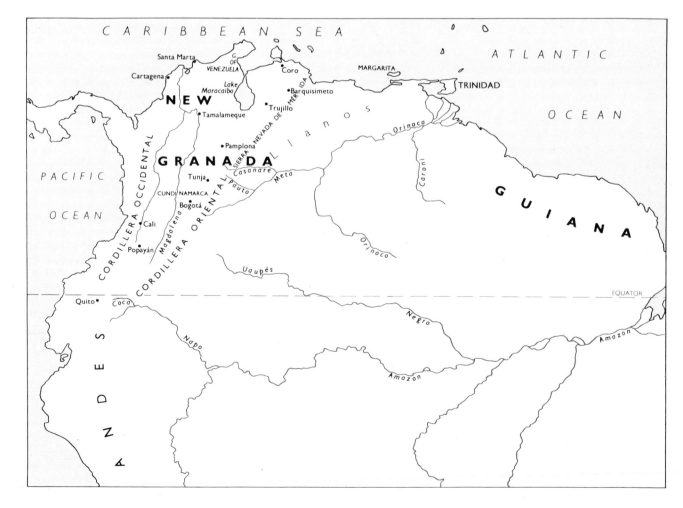

His quest was made considerably more difficult by the lack of knowledge of South American geography. Indeed, Ehinger believed that Venezuela was an island bounded on the south by the Pacific Ocean. Searching at random, he began by going west and setting up a garrison at the place where the Gulf of Venezuela meets Lake Maracaibo. From there he continued west, but after a year in which he found nothing he returned to Coro. He discovered that in the meantime he had been given up for dead, and a successor had been appointed as governor. However, as the successor had just died, there was no obstacle to Ehinger resuming his position.

Ehinger only remained in Coro for a year before he set out again in 1531. He retraced his earlier route, this time with several hundred Spaniards and a small army of Indian slave bearers, as far as Maracaibo and then turned southwest to the mountains. Although the terrain was difficult, Ehinger's advance was ruthless: he kept his Indian slaves together by means of a long iron collar that connected the chain of bearers in a single line, and if one bearer was unable to keep up because of illness or fatigue he was simply decapitated so as not to slow down the others. Ehinger met the attacks of hostile Indian tribes with the same methodical brutality, virtually depopulating whole villages as an example to others.

At Tamalameque, on the Río Magdalena, Ehinger claimed a rich store of jewels and gold, which he wrested from terrified Indians who had sought refuge on islands in the flooded river. But the treasure did Ehinger little good. He sent the loot back to Coro with a small party of only 35 men, who blazed a new route rather than retrace their steps and face the vengeance of the Indians they had devastated. Almost immediately they lost their

Above: conquistadors on their way to the port of Seville, in southern Spain, before setting out on a gold-seeking expedition in Venezuela. This watercolor was painted by a member of the expedition.

Opposite above: Charles V, Holy Roman Emperor, perhaps the last emperor to attempt a unified empire embracing the entire Christian world. He assigned to the Welsers, an important worldwide banking family, all rights to the territory of present-day Venezuela.

Opposite below: northern South America, across which first the Germans and then the Spanish roamed seeking gold.

Above: the galleon *Sancta Trinitas*, one of the ships carrying the Hohemut expedition to Venezuela, in a watercolor by Hieronymous Köler. Köler accompanied the expedition as an impressionable young lieutenant from Nuremberg and, though he was not a particularly good artist, his colors are vivid and believable and the record he provided is unique.

way and staggered through endless lagoons, swamps, and insect-infested rivers. The Indian porters escaped or collapsed and the Spaniards had to carry the heavy gold themselves. At last they could manage it no further and buried the treasure under a huge tree, hoping the tree would serve as a landmark. None of them ever reached Coro: reportedly one man survived, who was captured by the Indians and eventually adopted native ways. The treasure was never recovered, although many searchers came after it later.

Ehinger waited at Tamalameque for the party to return with reinforcements from Coro but, finally concluding that he had been betrayed, he decided to press on regardless. He went south, where advance scouts had reported cool, heavily populated, mountainous country. It was the eastern Cordillera (mountain chain), one of the three that make up Colombia's Andean mountains. The change in altitude combined with the icy temperatures killed off most of the native porters and many of the Spaniards. Ehinger survived, as did a few dozen of his men. By this time they were starving as well as freezing and were plagued by hostile Indians. Near present-day Pamplona Ehinger finally realized that it was futile to continue. He died on the return march, and only a handful of men stumbled into Coro in late 1533, gaunt and haggard. They had no gold to show for their ordeal.

Nikolaus Federmann, a young German agent for the Welsers

who arrived during Ehinger's first expedition from Coro, was to fare rather better. In September 1530, while Ehinger was making the final preparations for his second attempt, Federmann (then only 25 years old) went south from Coro into the rugged foothills of the Sierra Nevada de Mérida, reaching the area around what is now Trujillo before Indian attacks made it impractical to continue. He returned in six months with some gold he had seized from the Indians and a tantalizing story—soon to become bitterly familiar to the conquistadors—about the tremendous riches of a people who lived further west.

Ehinger's successor as governor was Georg Hohemut, from the German commercial town of Speyer. The Spaniards found his name totally unpronounceable (they had barely managed Ehinger, usually altering it to Alfinger or Dalfinger), and he is known in the Spanish chronicles simply as Jorge de Speyer (or Espira). Hohemut was as fascinated with the prospect of El Dorado as his predecessor had been. In May 1535, apparently relying on Indian reports of gold near the sources of the Río Meta, Hohemut set out with 400 men of whom a quarter were on horseback. Near what is now Barquisimeto (where Federmann had acquired his gold from the natives five years before) the expedition was decimated by fever in the hot, humid lowlands. Hohemut continued with less than 200 survivors, encouraged no

The Hohemut Expedition

Below: the Hohemut expedition landing on the northeastern coast of Venezuela. At the top of the hill are the Indians with pots of gold. This picture was painted by Köler.

A Golden City!

doubt by the success of others—by this time Pizarro had conquered Peru with all its gold. Just beyond the Río Casanare he found some friendly Indians who told him that over the mountains to the west was a grassy plateau that was populated by a gold-rich people who kept sheep. They pointed in the direction of what is now Bogotá, where they said was a city with a temple full of precious objects. They offered to guide the Spaniards to a pass through the mountains but turned out to be less familiar with the territory than expected, and after a prolonged and futile search the attempt was abandoned when a group of hostile Indians made a savage attack on the party. Hohemut continued south, probing for any way across the forbidding mountains.

They encountered the Uaupés Indians, who possessed some gold and silver and also confirmed the stories of a fabulously wealthy golden kingdom across the mountains—but still no pass could be found by which to reach it. Hohemut doggedly marched on until he was within one degree of the equator, and by then he had only 50 men fit for service—the rest were pathetic invalids. Carrying the treasure he had managed to find, Hohemut headed back to Coro which he reached in 1538, three long years after he had departed. In the end Hohemut himself paid dearly for his gold: exhausted, he died within a year of his return.

By that time, however, the quest for El Dorado was in full swing, and in 1538 three expeditions were underway, each recklessly spending lives in an obsessive search for the golden man. Three single-minded men, each with his own armed force, were steadily moving toward a preposterous confrontation. All three had set out in the spring of 1536. The largest party to start was that of Gonzalo Jiménez de Quesada, an adventurous young lawyer from Granada who had arrived in Santa Marta, one of the oldest Spanish settlements on the northern coast, in 1535. The next April Quesada set out with 620 men on foot and 85 horsemen, despatched by his governor on an urgent search for gold to meet the town's debts. From the beginning they were harassed by Indians, and after a short march through the desert to the mouth of the Magdalena they found themselves in trackless jungle. The Spaniards had to hack their way through the vines with machetes, malarial mosquitoes buzzed around their sweating bodies, and inevitably racking fever tormented them. They reached Tamalameque where they were attacked by Indians who were embittered by their earlier experiences with Europeans. After a halt there—during which they received some additional supplies from Santa Marta, brought by brigantines up the Magdalena—Quesada went on, following the river south.

Fever, jaguars, alligators, and the ubiquitous Indians with poison-tipped arrows all took an appalling toll. After four months only 209 men were still alive. There were no towns to raid for food; game was scarce, and when an animal was killed it had to be eaten immediately, otherwise it turned putrid in the oppressive damp heat. A dismal air of futility came over the Spaniards as the months wore on. The jungle seemed to continue forever, and the exhausted men were probably incapable of carrying on much further or of surviving the return march to Santa Marta. It was not until January 1537, nearly 10 long months after they had begun, that the Spaniards moved out onto

Above: Gonzalo Jiménez de Quesada (c.1495–1579), Spanish conquistador who led the expeditions that won New Granada for Spain. This is an anonymous 18th-century oil painting which is believed to be a good likeness.

Above: another of Köler's watercolors, showing Hohemut's men battling with Indians.

the high mountain plateau of Cundinamarca astride the Cordillera Oriental. The cultivated fields seemed like a miracle to the half-starved conquistadors. They had reached the mountain kingdom of the Chibchas.

Over a million Chibchas lived in their almost unapproachable highland plateau. Agriculturally self-supporting, their main foodstuff was the potato, and it was they who first introduced the Spanish to that useful tuber. They were expert in weaving and pottery, had developed an alloy of gold and copper which combined the greater strength of copper with the sheen of gold, and lived in substantial villages with large communal buildings. Realizing the high level of this civilization, the Spanish immediately looked for gold. The terrified Chibchas fled at their approach, first burying their gold. The soldiers pursued the Indians from settlement to settlement, capturing just enough gold to whet their appetite for more. At last they came to Tunja, which they approached so stealthily that the Spaniards were in the city before the inhabitants were able to hide their possessions.

It was truly a golden city: thin plates of gold tinkled musically outside the houses; the people were ornamented with golden pendants, earrings, and diadems of feathers embedded in gold. There were golden statues, gold-inlaid weapons, gold beads—and emeralds as well. Emeralds as big as walnuts were common. The soldiers ran wildly through the town, indiscriminately grabbing treasure. One man rushed up to Quesada, who was sitting quietly with the captured ruler of the city, and shouted in ecstasy, "Peru, Sir General, Peru! This is another Peru!"

Although they did not know it, they had found El Dorado. Just before coming into Tunja the conquistadors had passed beside Lake Guatavita—the very lake into which the gilded

The Lake of the "Gilded One"

Right: Lake Guatavita, cupped between the Cordilleras, northernmost of the Andes Mountains. It was here that the ceremony of the "Gilded Man" took place.

Above: priceless golden model, 7.25 inches long, thought to be a representation of the raft on which the "Gilded Man" and his attendants sailed out into Lake Guatavita. The ceremony involved coating El Dorado with a sticky resin and then covering him with gold dust, after which he jumped into the lake to rinse it off. Other golden gifts were also tossed into the lake as offerings to the Indians' god.

Right: gold miniature jar in the shape of a crouching person, made by the Tairona Indians of the northern coast of Colombia. The Tairona had reached a high level of development before the Spaniards arrived, both in engineering and in architecture.

Left: elaborately designed gold breastplate from the Calima region of Colombia, made with characteristically high-grade metal and excellent workmanship. The Chibcha of Cundinamarca were wiped out and became a mere memory after the Spanish looted their village, but many other Colombian tribes were at least as culturally advanced and often superior goldsmiths.

monarch had ceremoniously dived. But the real land of El Dorado had one major deficiency: it had no gold mines. The gold that so richly ornamented Tunja was all acquired by trade. Cundinamarca possessed salt mines, and the surrounding Indians readily traded gold for salt. Thus, after the Spanish had emptied the Chibcha cities of the gold that had been accumulated over generations, there was no more to be had. They learned this only gradually, and with that realization came the firm conviction that Cundinamarca could not be El Dorado after all. The legendary city of gold must lie elsewhere.

Quesada and his men paused to decide what to do next. The Indians had told him of a temple, the House of the Sun, which held far more gold than all of Tunja. It lay to the west, and that seemed the most likely prospect. But as he was assembling his force disconcerting news reached him. Another party of Spaniards was approaching.

The other party turned out to be commanded by Sebastián de Belalcázar, who had been one of Francisco Pizarro's lieutenants in Peru. Belalcázar had been sent north by Pizarro after the overthrow of the Incas, and in 1534 on his own authority he had conquered Quito in what is now Ecuador. In Quito he heard rumors of the dazzling Colombian El Dorado, and in 1536, just as Quesada was leaving Santa Marta, Belalcázar had set out from Quito. He came by way of Popayán and Cali, leaving men to hold both outposts as he continued north. After leaving Cali he marched his 200 infantry and 100 horsemen through progressively more difficult country, hampered by the vast herd of swine which he had brought to provide food for his men. The little army, moving at a pig's pace, was harried by Indians who made lightning attacks armed with the poisoned arrows that brought inevitable and agonizing death. They came through both icy mountains and jungle heat, and at last, in January 1539, they reached the high plateau of Cundinamarca. There they found Quesada's men, who had already conquered the Chibchas.

Incredibly, there was still more to come. Back in that same spring of 1536 a third force had set out for the golden city. Nikolaus Federmann, the young German based at Coro, had not waited for his governor, Georg Hohemut, to return from his expedition to the south before setting out himself with 400 men. He also went south, but he kept somewhat to the east of Hohemut's route. This took him through the grassy plains, or Llanos, of the Orinoco basin, territory later gold-hunters would come to know well. There are virtually no landmarks in the grassy marshes. In the dry season the heat is unremitting and almost unendurable; in the rainy months the rivers flood and the entire area becomes an appalling quagmire. Federmann and his men beat off attacks by Indians, their clothes rotted away on their backs, and their horses lost their shoes and stumbled on unshod.

Federmann wandered for nearly three years between the Llanos and the Cordillera, seeking a pass to the west. At last he came to the Indian village of Pasacote and discovered what he and Hohemut had both so profoundly hoped for—a pass into the high plateau. Only then did Federmann, in his turn, discover the galling reality—El Dorado was full of rival Spaniards. Then the final irony became apparent. Each of the three armies had

Above: portrait of Sebastián de Belalcázar, taken from the title page of Book VI of Antonio de Herrera's *History* of 1730. It also depicts several incidents that occurred between the various conquistadors.

exactly 166 survivors. Three precisely equal forces faced each other on the remote, mountain-encircled plateau.

In the end, although the rival armies muttered among·themselves, the three generals met the unprecedented situation with grace. (The discovery that there were no gold mines in Cundinamarca probably helped to soothe relations.) Besides, all three were in a somewhat irregular position. Belalcázar had far exceeded his authority from Pizarro in continuing beyond Quito; Quesada had sent none of the gold he had seized back to Santa Marta, where the governor was desperately in need of it; Federmann had left Coro while Hohemut was away and had made definite efforts to avoid his returning soldiers, when Hohemut might have reasonably anticipated some help. Therefore Belalcázar shared his pigs, Quesada shared some of his gold, and all three agreed to sail to Spain together where the king could distribute the governorships of the newly discovered lands. Prudently, they followed the Magdalena to Cartagena and sailed from there to Cuba—none of the three attempted to revisit the bases from which they had set out.

In Spain Belalcázar was given the governorship of Popayán. Federmann discovered he was out of favor with the Welsers, who felt aggrieved that he had abandoned his duties to wander in the Llanos for three years—without even reaching El Dorado in first place. Disappointed, Federmann never returned to South America. Quesada, indisputably the first to reach Cundinamarca and conqueror of the Chibchas, arrived at court to find that his claim to the governorship of New Granada (as he had named the plateau) was challenged by the son of the governor of Santa Marta. The governor had died in 1536, just after Quesada left, and his son (who had stolen Santa Marta's gold and escaped to Spain the year before) claimed not only the governorship of Santa Marta by right of inheritance but that of New Granada as well, saying it was as a representative of his father that Quesada had acted. The son had married well and had rich relatives to support him, and in 1540 the king gave both Santa Marta and New Granada to him. Quesada left Spain in disgust, and it was 10 years before he returned to South America.

When the three generals set off for Spain Quesada's brother Hernán was left in command of New Granada, and he also attempted some further gold hunting. By this time Lake Guatavita had been identified as the lake of El Dorado, and in 1540 Hernán attempted to drain the lake to recover the golden objects that had been thrown into it. When tremendous efforts produced only a large quantity of thick mud and very little gold, Hernán concluded that it simply could not be the true lake of gold. El Dorado must lie elsewhere. As the Quesada expedition had explored west and north of the plateau and found nothing, and as Belalcázar had come from the south and not discovered the land of gold, Hernán decided that it must then lie to the east. (He ignored the awkward fact that Federmann had approached from that direction.) For a full year Hernán and nearly 300 Spaniards, with 5000 Indians, hunted through the Llanos and found nothing but Indian arrows and appalling heat. Half his men died; all the horses perished, and the expedition returned on foot, gaunt and haggard. They had discovered no gold.

Confrontation at El Dorado

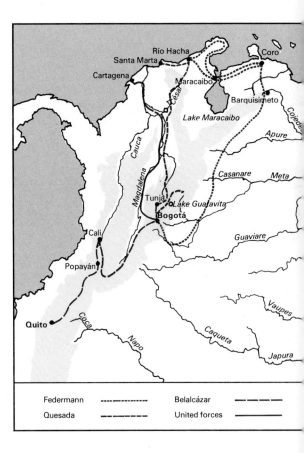

Above: map showing the routes of march of each of the three conquistadors who eventually converged on Cundinamarca and that of their combined forces to Cartagena where they embarked for Spain.

Disappointments and Disasters

Above: Pedro de Urzúa, in a portrait from Book III of Andreis Gonzalez de Barcia's history of the West Indies, published in 1749.

Another younger brother who searched in the same general area was Gonzalo Pizarro, whose elder brother was the conqueror of Peru. Gonzalo left Quito in 1541 to follow the golden legend. By this time the tale had become so embroidered that the king was said to wear powdered gold as his ordinary attire, and the ceremony of the lake was disregarded. Seeking El Dorado, Pizarro and his men started out by crossing the eastern Cordillera, a ghastly experience in the course of which more than a hundred Indians froze to death. Once on the other side, Gonzalo became frustrated when the local Indians were unable to tell him where El Dorado lay, so he had them tortured on makeshift racks. When they still had no information to give, he had a few devoured by his dogs.

When word of his methods had spread from tribe to tribe he found no lack of extravagant reports of wealth, always possessed by a people who lived some distance to the east. Excited by the prospect of at last finding the golden city, the Spanish floundered further and further east through swamps and an endless maze of deep, fast-running creeks. Men and horses drowned, food was scarce, and even the ferocious hunting dogs were consumed as meat. So many of their Indian bearers died or deserted that the Spaniards were reduced to carrying their heavy equipment themselves. By this time they were following the wide Coca River, and Pizarro decided to build a boat to carry the surplus baggage and sick men downstream. A brigantine was built, and for a few weeks it moved slowly down the river beside the men, who marched wearily along the banks. Hunger was becoming a major problem, so just after Christmas 1541 the brigantine sailed ahead out of sight to search for settlements further on, where they could obtain food for the starving men upstream. But the brigantine, captained by Francisco de Orellana, never returned. Whether Orellana deliberately deserted Pizarro (as one of the men on the brigantine claimed), or whether he was unable to return upstream because of the fast-moving current (which he himself maintained), he went on to gain fame as the first to navigate the Amazon River. Pizarro, despairing at last and concluding that he had been betrayed, gave up the golden vision and struggled back in August 1542. Less than a third of the proud men who had set out returned to Quito, and those who did were in rags, wan and wasted beyond recognition.

While Pizarro was living out his nightmare east of Quito, another expedition was hunting for the same golden goal to the north. Philipp von Hutten, another young German, had been sent out by the Welsers from Coro to seek the golden "temple of the sun," which was now believed to exist east of the Colombian Cordilleras. Hutten was no more successful than any of his predecessors, but he did hear from friendly Indians that a wealthy tribe called the Omagua lived along the northern shore of the Amazon. He even managed to get a glimpse of their city from a distance, and viewed from a hilltop the city did indeed seem to glitter like gold. But by that time he had only a few men left, and they were beaten back by the ferocious Omaguas. They straggled back to Coro in 1545 where they discovered a usurper in command, who had Hutten beheaded. It was the end of Welser rule in Venezuela: the Spanish authorities stepped in, and the usurper

himself was seized and executed. But no more Germans came to search fruitlessly for El Dorado.

The next episode was particularly grisly and bizarre. The governor of Peru in the mid-16th century came to the sensible conclusion that the search for El Dorado was an excellent enterprise on which to send the unruly ruffians who had nothing to do but cause trouble once the conquest was complete. In 1559, therefore, an expedition set out headed for the upper Amazon, where El Dorado was then assumed to be located. The young nobleman given command, Pedro de Urzúa, had the misfortune to recruit among his disorderly rabble a homicidal maniac called Lope de Aguirre, and Urzúa himself was very soon hacked to death in a mutiny. His beautiful mistress (whom he had unwisely chosen to bring with him) and his successor Guzmán met a similar fate, and the madman took command himself. All thought of finding El Dorado was abandoned as the bloodthirsty pirate band groped north toward the coast of Venezuela. Aguirre garroted or stabbed anyone he suspected of disloyalty—and he was a suspicious man. When they reached the coast they crossed

Above: Spaniards throwing Indians to be eaten by their dogs, in a colored engraving from Theodor de Bry's *Grands Voyages*, published in 13 volumes between 1590 and 1634. Word of the Spanish methods of extracting information passed quickly, and eventually the Indians would say anything, as long as it meant their torturers went elsewhere.

Above: Spanish treatment of their Indian porters, who were forced to carry tons of baggage through unfamiliar jungle to help satisfy the European lust for gold. This is another engraving from de Bry's *Grands Voyages*.

to the Spanish settlement on Margarita, an island just offshore. There they attacked, looted, and murdered their fellow countrymen. Aguirre sent off a long, rambling letter of defiance to the king of Spain, declaring one of his own followers (whom he nevertheless executed in time) "Lord and Prince of Peru." The angry Spanish authorities at last acted, and Aguirre found himself encircled. In his final desperation, just before he was captured and killed on the spot, Aguirre stabbed his own daughter to death.

The horrifying behavior of Aguirre and his gory progress did not slow down other seekers of El Dorado—but each of them in the end met the same dismal fate. The jungles of the upper Amazon swallowed them up and the expeditions foundered, exhausted by heat, enfeebled by starvation and disease, and continually harassed by hostile Indians and their terrible poisoned arrows. Illusions were dissipated: Hutten's "golden city" proved to be just another Indian town. Monotonously the skeletal survivors crept back to their home bases empty-handed, El Dorado ever elusive.

One of the most forlorn returns was that of Quesada, the conqueror of Cundinamarca, who had been dispossessed of his rightful title to New Granada at the court of Spain. In 1550 he had returned to Bogotá, the city he had founded, as a poor but highly respected man. Over the years he gradually acquired property, but he was as obsessed with the idea of the golden city as ever, and in 1568 he mortgaged all he possessed to launch out once more in search of El Dorado. He was still convinced that the city lay in the Llanos, in spite of the fact that the area had been crossed and recrossed by many expeditions. He was nearly 70 when he set out from Bogotá with a proud flourish, and four years later the pitiful fragments of his glittering procession crept back to the city. At their head was Quesada, still straight in his saddle, on a half-starved horse. He had staked everything on this final bid for glory, and he had lost it all. At least he was alive: of the 400 men who accompanied him from Bogotá only 25 returned.

Although Quesada himself never again led a search for El Dorado, his conviction that it existed never wavered. In his will —he died in 1579, at the age of nearly 80—he made two bequests. One was for a well to be built on a hill in Peru, where the climate was hot and no water was available for wayfarers; Quesada had known his share of thirst. The other was the governorship of the unconquered land he had explored in his search for El Dorado, between the Orinoco and Amazon rivers. That he bequeathed to the husband of his niece, his only living relative, with the proviso that he continue the search for El Dorado.

Thus Don Antonio de Berrio, a professional soldier who was then about 60 years old, was catapulted into the quest for El Dorado by the indomitable determination of his wife's uncle. In 1580 he arrived in New Granada with his family and set about his inherited task. By this time the search for El Dorado had been going on for half a century, and Berrio, with the clearer vision of the outsider, considered that both the Andean plateaus and the Llanos to the east had been combed so thoroughly that there was no point in further investigation there. Berrio decided instead to

Berrio Sets Out

try east of the Llanos, where there might be mountains. He had not forgotten—as many had—that the original reports of El Dorado had always mentioned a lake surrounded by mountains. In 1584 he set out to see. He crossed the eastern Cordillera from Tunja with only about 80 men and pushed briskly across the Llanos. Either he was more efficient than his predecessors or he had learned from their errors, because it took him only a few months to cross the maze of rivers and swamps that had so often defeated others. There before him were the mountains, east of the Orinoco River in what is now southern Venezuela. Although he reached the foothills, he was caught by the rainy season, and too many of his men fell ill with swamp fevers to try to go on. Berrio sensibly decided to retreat. He returned to New Granada 17 months after leaving, having lost only eight men.

He did not stay there long. In the summer of 1585 he was again on his way, crossing the Cordillera and the Llanos with his usual brisk despatch and, reaching the foothills again, marched along them for nearly 600 miles without finding a pass through the mountains. After two years of this his men rebelled, and most of them followed a mutinous captain back to New Granada. Thus reduced in manpower to below what he considered a safe level, Berrio abandoned further attempts at exploration and returned home himself. He was by now nearly 70 years old.

But in 1590 he was off again. By this time he knew exactly where he was going, and he traveled mainly by river. He went down the Pauto southeast to the Meta, and from there into the mighty Orinoco. His ranks thinned from day to day: some men

Left: the tropical jungle terrain through which the conquistadors marched in their search for El Dorado. The sheer physical difficulty of navigating through the interior meant that many never returned.

The Incredible Juan Martinez

died in the swift-running current, and others deserted. The horses had to be turned into rations for those who remained. But Berrio's leadership prevailed (the Englishman Sir Walter Raleigh, his opponent in days to come, wrote that he was "a gentleman well descended . . . of great assuredness, and of a great heart"). He had heard that behind that implacable mountain range was a lake where, said the Orinoco Indians, lived a tribe of great power and splendor; he was determined to reach it. What was more, he was told that these Indians had only arrived recently and had gained their power through military skill and payments in gold. For years it had been whispered that some of the Incas had escaped Pizarro and his terrible victory by fleeing eastward: Berrio must have imagined his quarry as Incas and El Dorado rolled into one.

He was told that the mountains came to an end near the mouth of the Caroni, a tributary of the Orinoco which joins the river just above the vast Orinoco estuary. But progress directly up the Caroni was impossible because a mighty waterfall blocked the way only a short distance upstream. Berrio therefore camped just beyond it. His manpower situation was again critical: only 50 of his men had survived, and of these scarcely a dozen were in good health. Although the Indians assured him that the riches of El Dorado lay within four days' march, Berrio was unable to advance. The gold was as unattainable as ever. Berrio sent letters via Indian guides to the governor of the island of Margarita (which Aguirre had brutalized 30 years before) asking for supplies and reinforcements, but there was no answer and no help. He watched his men grow more feeble and their provisions diminish daily, and eventually he had to abandon this attempt, too.

But this time instead of returning to New Granada, Berrio continued down the Orinoco to the sea and sailed to Margarita. There the old man, greatly tired by his monumental journey across the continent, discovered that Juan Sarmiento, the governor of Margarita, saw him as an obstacle in the governor's own path to the riches of El Dorado. It was Berrio, after all, who had the legal right to search the Orinoco area. He was of necessity Sarmiento's guest, but although he was aware of the threat of treachery beneath the cordial façade he was helpless to do anything except write letters seeking aid from the authorities.

In the midst of this unhappy situation occurred an extraordinary event which electrified the population of Margarita. It was rumored that a man who called himself Juan Martínez had suddenly appeared, dressed as an Indian and speaking Spanish haltingly as if it were unfamiliar to him. He reportedly claimed that he had gone into the Llanos on a Spanish expedition over a decade before. Every man except himself had died, but he had been captured by Indians and lived among them for 10 years before he escaped. During this time he had actually been taken, blindfolded, to the great city of the Gilded Man and had seen with his own eyes the golden skin of the king and his courtiers. For seven months he had lived amid unimaginable wealth in a city he called Manoa. Then he was blindfolded again and allowed to leave, loaded with treasure. Unfortunately he had lost all of it to robbers on his way to Margarita.

The man was never actually seen by anyone in authority, and all the accounts agree that he died very shortly after his appearance. Still, it was an absorbing tale, almost too incredible for disbelief. To Berrio, this was confirmation of all he had hoped for; the possibility that Juan Martínez was lying or had lost his wits during his years in the jungle—or, indeed, that his story was a complete fabrication—seems never to have occurred to him.

Berrio had left the Orinoco late in 1592, and by the spring of 1595 he still had not managed to return. Every attempt to seek assistance had come to nothing, seemingly producing only more rivals. "The devil himself is the patron of this enterprise," Berrio declared in bitter frustration, according to Sir Walter Raleigh.

Raleigh himself was to become Berrio's most formidable rival. The English had made their presence felt first in 1594, when a party arrived at Trinidad, sent by Raleigh on a reconnaissance voyage to check out the possibilities of an English attempt on El Dorado. Berrio, who by then had managed to establish a garrison and was living at Trinidad, away from Sarmiento's malignant hospitality, received them peaceably enough; but later an ambush (whether engineered by Berrio or not is unclear) resulted in

Above: the Orinoco river at Puerto Ordaz. The Orinoco estuary acted as a great natural barrier to Berrio and the later seekers after El Dorado.

The Englishman Joins the Search

eight men having their throats cut. Sir Robert Dudley, another Englishman, arrived in February 1595 but was understandably wary. Again Berrio was friendly, but Dudley chose to stay on the opposite side of the island and used it as a base for a brief and abortive attempt on the Orinoco estuary, where his men collected a few golden trinkets. In April, unsuspected by Berrio, Raleigh himself landed on Trinidad. He defeated the few soldiers sent out to investigate and swept into Berrio's stronghold with the advantage of surprise. The garrison was burned, 20 Spaniards were killed, and Berrio found himself a prisoner on Raleigh's ship.

Sir Walter Raleigh was a fascinating man. Courtier, philosopher, poet, soldier, and liar, he had been a favorite of Queen Elizabeth I until he provoked her wrath by secretly marrying one of her maids of honor. He and his new wife were promptly imprisoned in the Tower of London, and even after his release the queen looked upon him with cold dislike. Raleigh's attempt on El Dorado was his bid to regain her favor and win back her preference by heaping her with gold from the New World. Raleigh also, in common with most Britons of his era, deeply distrusted and despised the Spanish. He felt that it was imperative for the English to weaken Spain by drawing off some of her South American treasure, which might otherwise finance Spanish aggression in Europe.

While Berrio was his prisoner Raleigh developed a cautious respect for the old Spaniard, and verbally the two men fenced politely. Berrio was willing enough to talk of El Dorado, but he emphasized the hardships and exaggerated the distances. Berrio told Raleigh of the reports of Juan Martínez and his gold, but he also told him of the sandbars and swift currents of the Orinoco estuary. Raleigh concluded that Berrio was simply trying to discourage and mislead him.

But in the event he found the difficulties real enough, beginning with the fact that the waters of the estuary were too shallow for his boats. Using makeshift craft, he wandered vaguely through the complicated system of waterways. When the water was low, progress was slow because of the mud flats; when the water was high, the current pushed them back. In spite of it all, Raleigh pushed stubbornly on until he reached the mouth of the Caroni. Here the Indians told encouraging tales of the riches of Manoa, beside the lake on the other side of the mountains. Raleigh started up the Caroni but the falls stopped further progress. His men fanned out to gather ore samples that seemed to glitter like gold and stones that looked like sapphires. But the winter rains were beginning, and Raleigh decided it was time to return. The journey back to the coast was easier, as this time they traveled with the current.

In England he was given an unenthusiastic welcome. He had no gold, and many of the ore samples were worthless. The queen was even less favorably disposed toward him than before, and Raleigh was given no opportunity to return to South America. In 1596, the year after his return, he did manage to send back his lieutenant, Laurence Keymis, to maintain contact with Raleigh's Indian allies. Keymis discovered that Berrio had reached the mouth of the Caroni and had established a fortification there,

Opposite: Sir Walter Raleigh with his son, painted in 1602. In a doomed attempt to regain favor at court he set out to find the fabulous city of gold in the jungles of Venezuela.

Above: Raleigh (spear in hand) in 1595 at the burning and sacking of San José de Oruña, founded by Antonio de Berrio on Trinidad in 1592. Berrio and his companions (walking with manacles) were taken prisoner. This drawing is by de Bry.

which blocked access to the area in which Raleigh had found small amounts of gold ore. Later expeditions backed by Raleigh were no more successful.

Raleigh himself did not return to South America for nearly 20 years. In the meantime Berrio, after a series of disappointments, had died in his jungle fortress at the mouth of the Caroni, unable to penetrate further. In England Raleigh fared little better. After Queen Elizabeth died in 1603 her successor, James I, had him imprisoned in the Tower again at the instigation of his enemies. For 13 years he remained there, dreaming of the day he would be free to set out again for El Dorado.

When he did, in 1616, it was under almost impossible conditions. James was then following a pro-Spanish policy, and he released Raleigh for the expedition only with the proviso that he search for the gold of El Dorado without setting foot on Spanish territory or inflicting injury on any Spanish vessel. In addition, Raleigh still had a death sentence hanging over him, and he was not to be pardoned unless he returned successful.

Not surprisingly, he failed. Bad luck dogged him throughout: the voyage across the Atlantic was terrible, and at the end of it Raleigh—then well over 60—was too ill to lead the expedition ashore himself. His faithful lieutenant Keymis went on with Raleigh's 24-year-old son Walter. For all his loyalty, Keymis brought both Raleigh and the expedition to the verge of disaster by blundering into a battle with the Spanish at the mouth of the Caroni. The English took the fort, but young Walter was killed and the terms of the commission had clearly been violated. To add to the debacle, there was no gold to be found. After wandering around aimlessly in bitter misery, Keymis at last brought his force back to the waiting Raleigh, who received his report of failure heaped upon failure with cold anger. In despair Keymis retired to his cabin, where he killed himself. Raleigh sailed back to England with a disappointed and mutinous crew. He was immediately imprisoned and, on October 29, 1618, he was beheaded.

Raleigh was to be the last of the heroic seekers after El Dorado. The Spanish abandoned the quest after the failure of Berrio; the Dutch, British, and French were more concerned with the tangible profits of trade and slaves in the Caribbean than with the illusory riches of El Dorado. Neither Raleigh nor any other man ever found El Dorado in the territory of Guiana. The golden myth had become a fatal will-o'-the-wisp leading men deeper and deeper into the jungle to their destruction. To the extent that the golden man—El Dorado—had ever existed, he existed in Cundinamarca on the high Andean plateau. But no reality could ever live up to the golden legend, and so—although the fabled lake was found early in the search—the quest went on and on, moving further eastward as each supposed site was found to be barren. There were no gold mines in Cundinamarca; there was no gold along the Amazon; and finally, when the mountains of Guiana were breached, it was discovered that there was no city of Manoa. The lake of which the Indians had told was simply formed when winter rains flooded the shallow banks of the rivers.

The interior of South America is only slightly less forbidding now than it was in the days of Quesada, Berrio, and Raleigh. The more remote Indian tribes are little more affected by civilization. Even today some people wonder if somewhere in the deep jungle El Dorado might await discovery. The will to believe is still as curiously persistent as it ever was.

Was There Ever a "Gilded Man"?

Left: European version (by de Bry) of the myth of El Dorado. The "Gilded One" of the Chibchas is here anointed with resin while another attendant blows gold dust over him. In the background are Indians drinking a liquid made from corn out of golden goblets. The actual attire of the Chibchas was a long, heavy cotton poncho rather than the feathered wear pictured here.

Chapter 7 Unconquered Fortress of the Inca

When the Inca empire was destroyed in the 16th century by the Spanish conquistadors under Francisco Pizarro, a fiercely stubborn remnant of the Incas retreated to a mountaintop city where the Europeans never found them. The jungle relentlessly encroached on the terraced palaces, temples, and fountains over 8000 feet up in the Andes, concealing the great plazas and magnificent stonework. But what was it like to live in Machu Picchu before it was finally abandoned? How did the last Incas, emperors of the Inca kingdom, manage to protect the fortress-city for so long? Are there perhaps other Inca cities, now masked by undergrowth, awaiting discovery?

It was cold. The mountain mist hung heavily over the stone terraces, and the woman on the stairway shivered slightly and drew her white woolen shawl closer around herself. In the early morning the entire stone city seemed gray. Not until the dawn lightened further would the green of the garden terraces soften the severity of stone against stone.

Above the city rose the precipitous cliffs of the two mountain peaks, one to the north, the other to the south. Between them lay the city itself, clinging to the ridge which dropped off sharply on either side. It was a natural fortress, well guarded against any unauthorized intrusion. All around were spectacular mountain vistas and breathtaking views of the splendor of the Andes in which the city perched preposterously.

The woman looked at none of this. She had lived among these mountains since childhood, and if the austere magnificence had ever compelled her attention it did so no longer. The mountains were simply there, as the cold morning mist and the unyielding stone beneath her sandals were there. She reached the top of the stone staircase, turned into an open doorway, and vanished into the dark interior. She was a Mama Cuna, a Chosen Woman who supervised and taught her younger companions, and she had neither the leisure nor the inclination to admire the scenery. A new day was beginning, and there was work to do. The new emperor—the Inca—was in the city, somehow dispossessed of his traditional capital, Cuzco, where the "bearded ones" were

Opposite: Machu Picchu, named after the mountain peak that towers above it since its Inca name is unknown. Its role in Inca life is also unknown, although archaeologists think this was probably religious. The only certainty is that Machu Picchu was never found by the Spanish, which insured its survival more or less intact.

Hiram Bingham Finds the City

suddenly in command. Everything was strange; all the rules that had seemed fixed and sure for generations were now upset. In the midst of the confusion the daily pattern of life stubbornly continued, as if people believed that if they repeated what was known and familiar the nightmare would pass: sanity and stability would return. Thus the Mama Cuna made her way through the city in the early dawn, following her accustomed path as if none of the murder or madness in the valleys below had ever happened.

Nevertheless the days of the city were numbered. At some date not long after, though it was never conquered, the city was to be abandoned. The Spanish never knew of its existence, hidden as it was within its mountain barriers. But for some reason—which we may never know—orders must have been given to leave the city. The gold and silver, the beautiful fine woolens woven by the Chosen Women, the pottery, and the sacred mummies of dead Incas were all taken out of the fortress city. Whether any of the Chosen Women remained behind is not known.

The city remained wrapped in mountain mists and silence, and slowly the jungle crept in through the fortifications and gradually covered the stone steps. The thatched roofs decayed and collapsed. From time to time descendants of the Inca people, by then reduced to scraping out a miserable existence under Spanish colonial rule, probably climbed the mountains to search the burial sites for treasure. But nothing remained of much value: broken pottery was a poor reward for an exhausting climb. Over the centuries the city was forgotten, and now no one even knows its name. It is simply called after the mountain peak which towers over it—Machu Picchu.

Not until this century was it rediscovered. The Spanish had tightened their grip on the land of the Incas, and the once proud land became a colony of the Spanish throne. But all the gold of Peru was not sufficient to sustain an overextended empire, and in time Spain's power waned and the Republic of Peru was established. In 1911 an American historian and explorer, Hiram Bingham, heard stories of interesting ruins in the Urubamba valley north of Cuzco. The way up from the valley was long and hard (the Inca road leading to the city gate had long ago been destroyed by rockfalls and covered over by jungle), but scattered Inca ruins offered tantalizing promise of what might lie ahead.

After nearly a month of steady climbing, through increasing heat and humidity, Bingham mounted a last ridge and saw before him a great flight of beautifully constructed stone terraces. Past the terraces were houses made of the finest Inca stonework. There was what might have been a royal mausoleum, and, at the top of a ledge, a graceful semicircular building followed the natural curvature of the surrounding rock. Everywhere he looked were walls of white granite ashlars fitting perfectly together without mortar, in the traditional Inca style. Even covered as they were with mosses and vines, bamboo thickets and trees, the ruins were spectacular. For Bingham—and for everyone else since his time who has come upon the magnificence of the ruined city—the questions well up instantly: what was this city? How was it so successfully hidden? What sort of people were capable of building such incredibly fine buildings on the shoulder of the Andes?

Above: Manco Capac, the first Inca ruler, as depicted with a cocoa pouch on his right arm and a parasol in his left hand by Felipe Poma de Ayala. An obscure Inca artist, Poma de Ayala spent nearly 40 years collecting information about his people's history and traditions and illustrated it with his own pen-and-ink drawings. In 1908 the book was rediscovered in the Copenhagen Royal Library.

The answers remain wrapped in mystery. In 1527 Francisco Pizarro first set foot on the shore of what is now Peru at Tumbes, then the northernmost coastal city under the control of the Incas. Over the centuries since then soldiers, priests, historians, and archaeologists have recorded what they saw and remembered about the Inca empire, but their information suffers from two essential difficulties. The first is that no outsider ever saw the empire at its most powerful; when the Spanish arrived it was in the midst of an unprecedented political crisis. But the second difficulty is even more crucial—the Incas, like other South American Indians, had no written language. Inca history is

Above: the baths built by the Incas at Tambo Machay, near Cuzco. They are constructed of granite blocks of various sizes fitted together without cement. They are placed so exactly that it is impossible to insert the point of a knife between them.

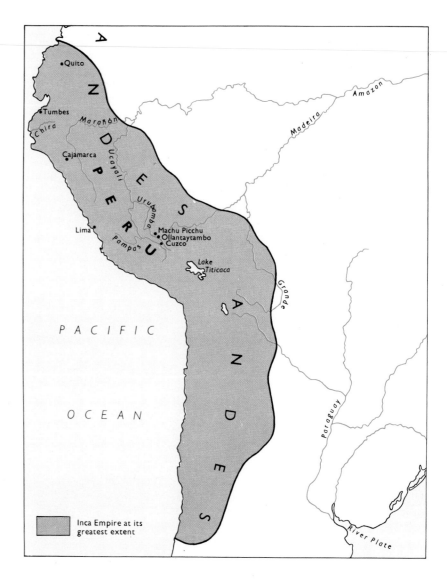

Right: map of western South America
showing the territory of the Inca empire as
it was when conquered by the Spanish.

Below: design painted on a pottery drinking
vessel or *kero*, made around 1532 for
drinking *chicha*, the ritual beer of the Incas.
It shows a warrior carrying an ornate club
and featherwork shield and surrounded by
patterns and stylized rainbows.

Inca Empire at its
greatest extent

entirely a matter of remembering tales passed by word of mouth.
By the time the brutal Spanish conquest was complete, few official "rememberers" were left.

But even in the days of their glory the Incas were very careful
about what they chose to have remembered. The central premise
of Inca history was that the children of the sun, Manco Capac
and his sister-wife Mama Occlo, were created on the Isle of the
Sun in Lake Titicaca and set out from there to teach the arts of
civilization to a barbarous world. This idea, that the Incas were
the pioneers of advanced culture in previously primitive surroundings, we now know to be untrue. The Incas actually built
their remarkable civilization on well-established cultural foundations. The fact is that the Incas (or rather the people who called
their kings Incas—we do not know what they called themselves)
were almost certainly one of a number of small tribes living near
Lake Titicaca who fought their way northward to a fertile valley
where they established what became their imperial capital of
Cuzco. Archaeological evidence suggests that initially the Inca
people were no different from their neighbors. Like them they
cultivated potatoes and maize; like them they used only stone

tools; and like them they relied on the llama, which had been domesticated for centuries. What appears to have been uniquely their own was a genius for organization.

The Incas distinguished themselves by the society they established, in which the individual was a disciplined cog in a massive governmental machine. Each person had his or her place and duty, and people who were unable to provide for themselves were supplied with necessities. Conquered tribes were firmly and benevolently incorporated within the Inca framework; their individual histories were suppressed and forgotten as they became identified with Inca power. Inca warriors were valiant and for the most part victorious, but the Inca arts of peace are what still compel our attention.

The basis of political organization was the *ayllu*, or tribal division. The ayllu was small and tightly knit so that the accomplishments or shame of any member reflected directly upon the entire ayllu. The ayllu held land, crops, and animals in common, and under normal circumstances most individuals were born, lived out their lives, and died within the confines of their ayllu. Only marriage altered membership in that one could not take a husband or wife from within the same ayllu, and upon marriage a woman left her father's ayllu to join that of her husband. Marriage was only partially a personal affair, because if a man had not selected a wife by the time he was 20 years of age a marriage would be arranged for him by an official during a periodic visit.

For women, however, marriage into another ayllu was not the only possibility. Young girls were carefully watched and, by the time they were eight or ten years old, those who possessed unusual beauty or grace or showed particular talent in weaving were called to the attention of the visiting officials, who sent them to become Chosen Women or *aclla cuna* (Virgins of the Sun). The young Chosen Women were closely supervised, and they were taught exquisite spinning and weaving and the rituals of the sun

"Chosen Women" of the Incas

Below: modern farmer near Cajamarca in Peru, still using the irrigation methods developed by the Incas.

The Key to the Inca System

Below: two aspects of the Incas' elaborate and sophisticated bureaucratic system of governing their vast empire—a royal courier (top) and the supreme council (bottom).

(the god and father of the Incas). Chosen Women dressed in fine white woolens and were rigidly segregated from the rest of society. Some were of noble birth, but within the order there were no gradations in status.

Chosen Women fulfilled several functions. Some remained virgin priestesses all their lives; a very few were selected for the infrequent human sacrifices to the sun; and the most beautiful became concubines of the Inca, earthly representative of the sun. Others were given by the Inca as wives to favored generals or conquered chiefs. A Chosen Woman who remained in a convent, unmarried, became a Mama Cuna with the duty of passing on her skills to the younger girls. As many as 15,000 Chosen Women lived in sacred enclosures around the empire. The pattern of their lives behind the high stone walls remains a mystery: the bleak rows of cells of the Inca ruins suggest that it was austere. Certainly the fate of a Chosen Woman who was discovered in a sexual liaison was harsh—she was buried alive, her lover was strangled, and his ayllu was razed to the ground; the site was then sown with stones. There could be no mercy for a woman who dared to be unfaithful to the sun god, or for a man who infringed the rights of the Inca.

The ruling authorities were those the Spanish called "Big Ears," who were all born into the original Inca tribes. Their caste was indicated by their earrings, because the children of the nobility had their ears pierced, and the holes were gradually enlarged until an egg could pass through them. Adults wore the characteristic Inca earrings—rounded bejeweled golden disks. The privileged men of this class were allowed several wives and concubines, elaborate clothing, and extensive estates. But the aristocracy worked hard as the administrators of the state. Idleness in all ranks was punishable by death.

Below these aristocrats born to their station were those who were Incas by privilege. They were not born into the royal ayllus but had in some cases risen through ability. At its peak the Inca empire was expanding too rapidly to be governed solely by the small ruling caste, and inevitably outsiders became necessary. Other Incas by privilege, who were called *curacas*, were sons of conquered chieftains. Once vanquished, tribal chiefs were often reestablished as rulers while their sons were sent to Cuzco to be impressed by Inca grandeur and trained in Inca ways. They dressed as Incas, had their ears pierced for Inca earrings, and often selected their wives from among the Chosen Women. When they returned to their native territories they were part of Inca power and carried important responsibilities. Most significant, they were bound to the Inca empire—their one-time enemy— with bonds of loyalty for favors received. Their old positions were enlarged and magnified by the glory of the Inca empire.

The key to the Inca system was the realization that military victory was only the beginning of conquest, that only with a contented and productive population could the empire continue to expand. If a community near the frontier was found to be restive, the population was simply moved in its entirety to an area closer to Cuzco, where the people could be awed by Inca splendor and government officials could keep a close eye on them. The ayllu which had occupied that territory exchanged it for the frontier

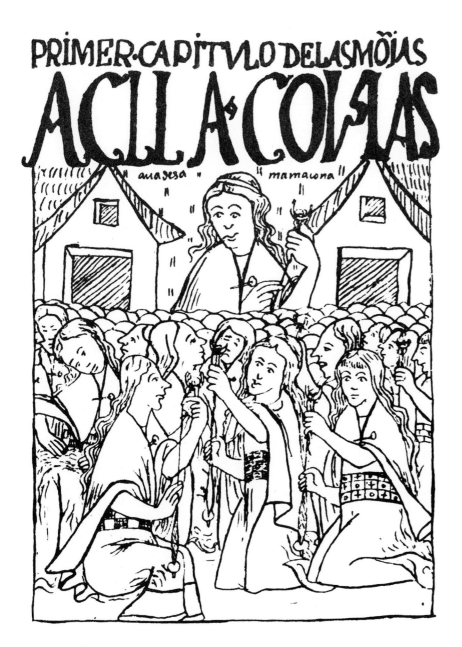

PRIMER·CAPITVLO DELASMÕIAS
ACLLACOILAS

anaxeza   mamauona

Left: the Virgins of the Sun spinning thread.
The production of beautiful textile fabrics
made of alpaca or llama wool, highly
specialized work, was one of the tasks of
the Chosen Women.

area thus vacated. Simultaneously potential troublemakers were
thus brought under close watch and a loyal outpost was established. Like many Inca policies, this was sensible, efficient, and
totally unconcerned with individual preference.

To record the affairs of this far-reaching government an ingenious system was developed. Lacking any written alphabet,
administrative officials employed the *quipu*, a linked group of
knotted cords of many colors. The color denoted the subject
while the knots indicated numbers in a decimal system. Although
the Incas had no writing and never developed the wheel, it is
interesting that they were among the few peoples in the history
of civilization to understand the concept of zero. The quipu itself
was a simple and ingenious device meant to aid the memory of
skilled interpreters, whose job it was to translate the knots into
information. The connotations of the quipu were standardized
and were taught to Inca aristocrats as well as to professional

Above: the grand treasurer (top), a high Inca official, reading a quipu. As the keeper of accounts, this nobleman would have to be able to count accurately in hundreds of thousands everything that went on in the kingdom—feasts, holy days, months, years, and every Indian town and village. The inspector of bridges (bottom) was another of the host of government officials who traveled up and down the empire making sure essential work was carried out.

Right: a quipu, a cord from which many smaller knotted strings, sometimes of different colors, were hung.

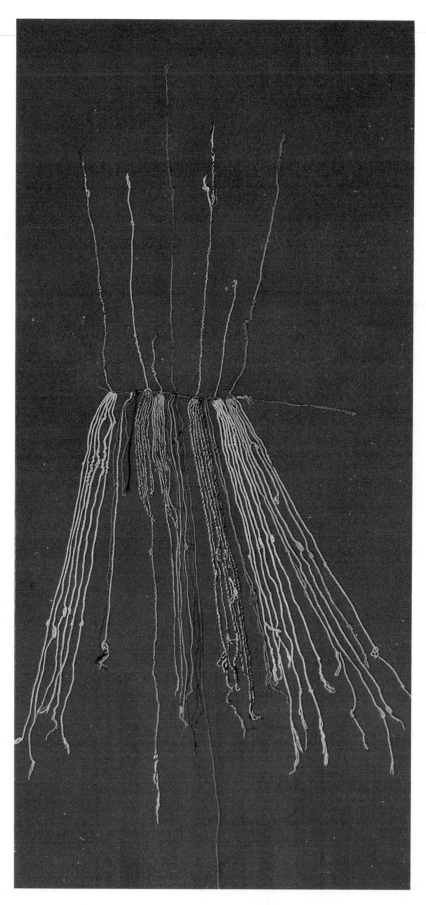

interpreters. A noble may not have had to use a quipu himself, but ideally he should always be able to check the calculations of his accountants. Not only did the colors of the wool threads have meaning, but the methods of tying the knots or twisting the threads and the distances between the knots were also significant. Initially skeptical, the Spanish were gradually impressed by the skills of the quipu readers, but unfortunately their conquest marked the end of them. Zealous Catholic priests, believing them to be books of the devil, destroyed the archives of knotted cords which recorded the history of the Inca empire, and as the quipu interpreters gradually died off their knowledge was no longer handed down. Now the quipus are mute and lifeless, random pieces of string in museum cases, and their meaning is forever shrouded in oblivion.

Without historical evidence, therefore, any dates in Inca history—with the momentous exception of 1527, the year Francisco Pizarro landed—remain educated guesses. It seems likely that the Inca people first emerged as distinct from the surrounding Andean tribes around the 12th century, so in traditional Inca terms this would be the date for the semilegendary Manco Capac. For the next two to three centuries the Incas established themselves in the Cuzco valley. By the 14th century the Incas had begun to expand outward, first south and north and then in all directions. The great Inca Pachacutec had conquered all of what is now Peru by approximately 1466; his successors extended the frontiers to include Chile (in 1492—the same year that Columbus arrived in the Caribbean islands) and parts of Colombia (in 1498—coinciding with Columbus' discovery of the South American mainland).

By 1500 the Inca conquest was complete, and the empire was at its largest. In Cuzco the Inca presided over a magnificent court. He ate off plates of gold and silver, held by his Chosen Women; his clothes were of finest soft vicuña wool, and he wore each garment only once, after which it was destroyed. His nobles were self-assured and competent. Government control was pervasive, leaving no one needy, hungry, or without shelter. Money did not exist—the Incas valued gold purely for its glittering beauty—and taxes were paid by days of labor, from which the aristocracy was excused. But the nobles had their own administrative responsibilities, and death was the penalty for assignments uncompleted.

Inca roads ran the length and breadth of the empire, and bridges of fiber cables spanned the gorges and rivers. The roads were not meant for ordinary coming and going—people could not leave the land of their ayllu without specific permission—but for the traveling officials and, most importantly, for armies on their way to war. As there was no wheeled traffic, the roads were built in steps when the grade was too steep for comfort and safety. Considerable speed was possible for the trained couriers: fish fresh from the ocean reached the Inca's table in Cuzco, 130 miles away, the same day it was caught.

Gold mined from swift-running mountain streams was carried along the Inca roads to skilled goldsmiths who crafted the gleaming metal into exquisite objects. For the Incas gold was "the sweat of the sun," and all gold and silver belonged to the Inca himself;

Inca Couriers and the Quipu

Below: the bridge of San Luis Rey, most famous and perhaps the finest of all the Inca bridges. It spanned the precipitous gorge of the Apurimac river. The cables, made of braided and twisted rope as thick as a man's body, were 148 feet long with a further 40 feet embedded in the rock on each side. More cables formed the floor of the bridge, which was then covered with wooden planks. First built in 1350, it was used until 1890. There was no way to steady the bridge in the wind, and the first Spaniards to arrive in Peru crossed it in abject terror.

Above: a gold funerary mask, decorated with emeralds, from northern Peru. It was not made by the Incas but by another gold-working Indian tribe. Very little remains of true Inca craftsmanship because the Spanish melted so much of it down to send back to Spain.

as the sun's representative he was entrusted with its safekeeping. It was shaped into magnificent ceremonial objects or jewelry and was used to decorate buildings. One great golden sheet covered the end wall of a building which illustrated the sun and moon among the stars and an outline of the history of creation. Like all the other beautiful objects the Spanish seized, it was melted down for easier shipment to Spain, but its glory was remembered in Indian tradition.

Of all their accomplishments, it was in building that the Incas most excelled. Proof of their mastery still stands centuries after the builders completed their work. Massive polygonal blocks lie so close together that it is impossible to insert the point of a knife between them. Using only stone and bronze tools, they constructed buildings so sound that they have survived despite all the quakes and tremors that have beset this earthquake-prone region. Spanish colonial buildings have collapsed, but their Inca foundations have outlasted them.

But the seeds of destruction were sprouting both within the empire and beyond its boundaries. In 1513 Vasco Nuñez de Balboa saw the Pacific, and the Incas began to hear the first vague rumors of "bearded ones." Nearly 10 years later the Spanish in Central America first heard of the Land of Gold to the south, and they began their inexorable approach, drawn by the golden lure. In 1527 Pizarro arrived at Tumbes with 13 men on a preliminary reconnaissance, and he took some Indians away with him to be trained as interpreters in anticipation of his return. Reports of these remarkable happenings were immediately forwarded to Cuzco, but the administrators there had other pressing concerns. A terrifying epidemic raged (which may have been acquired from the Europeans in the north), and Huayna Capac, the eleventh Inca, was dying in Quito, which he had established as a base during his campaigns in what is now Ecuador.

With the Inca's death the problem of the succession became acute. Under normal circumstances the procedure was quite straightforward: the reigning Inca selected the most competent of his sons by his *coya*, his empress and principal wife, who was also according to tradition his sister. However, Huayna had spent many years in the north and wished to leave part of his empire to Atahualpa, his son by a princess of Quito of whom he was particularly fond. The major part of the empire—all of it, in fact, except for the new additions he himself had made by his northern conquests—he left to his legitimate heir Huáscar, who lived in Cuzco.

The division was unprecedented and calamitous. Civil war inevitably broke out between the half-brothers, and battlegrounds were heaped with bloody carcasses before Atahualpa (an experienced general who had fought with his father) eventually triumphed. Huáscar and all his offspring were massacred by his brother's victorious forces. Even his unborn children were ripped from the wombs of their dying mothers. The empire reeked with blood and vengeance as Atahualpa made his way toward Cuzco, a once proud city which had finally been forced to yield to an outsider.

It was at this point, on May 13, 1532, that Pizarro returned to Peru with 106 foot soldiers and 62 men on horseback. Atahualpa was resting before his entrance into Cuzco at Cajamarca, a sulfur spa high in the Andes, where he was recovering from a leg wound received during the war. Pizarro set out from Tumbes, where he left a garrison, for the natural harbor at the mouth of the Chira river, where he founded the settlement of San Miguel. Here he was told about the five-year-long civil war. It was obvious even to an outsider that the deep divisions it had caused had not yet begun to heal, and Pizarro, who had come to conquer, was elated to discover a crack of vulnerability in the massive empire he was about to challenge.

Atahualpa, for his part, was interested but unconcerned by the progress of these curious strangers. He knew that they were few while his own forces were tremendous. Pizarro, once he knew where the Inca was to be found, began the 350-mile journey to Cajamarca. The Spanish soldiers sweated across the coastal desert in their heavy armor and gasped for oxygen as they climbed the precipitous heights. They walked along narrow roadways overhung by massive fortresses, and yet they suffered only random attacks. The Spanish crept across suspension bridges that drooped ominously in the middle and swung disconcertingly in the wind, and yet no one took advantage of their exposed position. Atahualpa, secure in his invincibility, ordered no move against them but simply had them watched. As they neared Cajamarca he sent out one of his nobles to invite the white men to enter the city as his guests.

As the Spanish clattered through the streets of Cajamarca on November 15, 1532, they found the town strangely quiet: there was no one to greet them. At last Pizarro sent his brother Her-

Coming of the "Bearded Ones"

Below: portrait of Francisco Pizarro (1478?–1541), conqueror of Peru. Pizarro was over 50 years old when he set out with a handful of fortune hunters to topple the largest empire in the New World, stretching more than 2500 miles down the west side of the South American continent. He was known among his men for obsessive single-mindedness and an utter disregard for his own personal comfort.

The Deceiving of Atahualpa

Below: the Inca emperor Atahualpa, painted by an unknown artist of the Cuzco school. He fought a five-year civil war with his half-brother Huáscar over control of their father's empire, only to lose it to the conquistador Francisco Pizarro.

nando, with Hernando de Soto, to seek out the Inca while Francisco waited to make a dignified approach. The Spaniards found the Inca seated on a golden stool surrounded by his nobles. They were impressed by his regal calm, and Hernando Pizarro invited him to come and dine with his brother. At first Atahualpa made no reply, but when the request was repeated in more courteous terms he spoke. He was fasting that day, he said, but he would come the following day. As they were leaving Hernando de Soto tried a flourish of Spanish horsemanship. Mounted, he wheeled and galloped toward the sitting monarch before drawing up so sharply (according to the Indian chronicles) that Atahualpa could feel the horse's breath on his face. The surrounding nobles involuntarily flinched, but Atahualpa, who had never even seen a horse before, sat impassive and dignified.

The next day the Inca and his nobles came to meet the Spanish. As guests, unarmed, they walked into a carefully planned ambush. A friar came out to meet the Inca and demanded that Atahualpa declare his allegiance to the Catholic church. Annoyed at the impudence of this insignificant man, Atahualpa tossed the Bible he offered to the ground and pointed to the sun, saying, "My god still lives." At this Pizarro gave a prearranged signal, and the Spanish soldiers and cavalry charged the unarmed Indians. After only 30 minutes the proud force of retainers was dead, and Atahualpa was Pizarro's prisoner. As one of those who took part in the battle later commented, "As the Indians were unarmed they were defeated without danger to any Christian."

With the Inca held captive, the clockwork efficiency of the Inca empire was stopped short. It was run by a totally centralized administration, and now that center was powerless. The shock waves reverberated across the vast communication network of Inca roads as officials waited for someone to tell them what to do, as they had always been told before. But there was no one to give the orders. Atahualpa tried to exploit the inexplicable Spanish passion for gold in a bid for freedom. He promised to fill the room in which he was kept in Cajamarca with gold to a point as high as he could reach. The room was 22 feet long by 17 feet wide, and the mark of the Inca's reach about 7 feet high. Runners traveled all over the empire collecting precious objects of the finest craftsmanship to meet the ransom. The room was filled as agreed, but the Spanish dared not free Atahualpa, since they were still so very few against so many. Pizarro, over the protests of Hernando de Soto and his own brother Hernando, finally decided on judicial murder. Atahualpa was accused of treason (trying to raise a force to overthrow the Spaniards), incest (because of his legal marriage to his sister), and of usurpation of the Inca throne rightfully belonging to his dead half-brother Huáscar. Predictably enough, he was sentenced to death and executed. The gold ransom was melted down into ingots and shipped to Spain.

With the Inca dead Pizarro marched on Cuzco. The city—already savaged by Atahualpa's men after the fall of Huáscar—was systematically looted and its inhabitants tortured, raped, and murdered. The Inca people had been trained for generations in unquestioning obedience: now this obedience was interpreted as cowardice by the Spanish, who had no mercy. The complex machinery of government that had controlled irrigation, organ-

ized agriculture, and maintained the roads and services was allowed to collapse in disarray. Those Indians who survived the first brutal attacks waited dumbly for whatever the unfeeling heavens might unleash upon them next.

After the execution of Atahualpa Pizarro cast about for a successor and found a young son of Huayna Capac. His name was Manco Capac, and he had escaped the occupation of Cuzco by Atahualpa's men by retreating over the Andes to the east. Pizarro declared that Manco Capac would be the new Inca. He was installed with an impoverished attempt at the traditional ceremony, but crowned or not, Manco Inca and all in Cuzco knew that he was solely a puppet of the Spanish.

Beneath the façade of obedience to his Spanish masters, how-

Above: the trial and death of Atahualpa. After fulfilling his promise to Pizarro and amassing a fortune in gold objects for his Spanish kidnappers, Atahualpa was tried on trumped up charges, sentenced to death, and murdered (he was strangled) by the Spaniards.

Above: the Spanish fight the Incas for the city of Cuzco. At first the Indians under Manco Inca, experienced in mountain warfare, laid ambushes for their enemies with relative impunity. But eventually they allowed themselves to be drawn into open battle on the plains near Lima, and there the Spanish defeated them.

ever, Manco Inca was plotting and organizing. In the spring of 1536 his opportunity came. Playing on the Spanish greed for gold, he had requested that he be allowed to celebrate the April harvest in his traditional lands north of the capital, where at the same time he could hunt for some of his father's fabulous gold treasure which had disappeared from the city and which the Spanish coveted. Using those lines of communication permitted by the Spanish for the puppet government, supporters of Manco Inca had meanwhile organized an army. With the Inca safely out of the city, the secret army attacked Cuzco during Easter week. Spanish communications were severed between Cuzco and the coast, and Spanish settlers in the countryside were seized and beheaded.

For over a year the Inca's forces kept the city under seige. The Spanish counterattacked furiously, relying upon allies among the Inca's subject peoples, who grasped this opportunity to re-

Retreat to the Mountain City

venge themselves upon their former masters. At last, in 1537, the Inca forces met the Spanish in battle on the plains near Lima, the new capital established by Pizarro. As guerrillas attacking from mountain fortresses the Incas were unconquerable, but on the open plain the Spanish were in their element. The forces of Manco Inca were vanquished, and the Inca himself, along with the remnants of his army of supporters, retreated deep into the Urubamba valley northwest of Cuzco. Hernando Pizarro made one determined attempt to seize his fortress, Ollantaytambo, but his forces retreated in disarray from the Indian defense, a deluge of stones shot from slingshots and even gunfire from captured muskets. Never again did the Spanish attempt to storm the Incas in their mountain strongholds. Manco Inca and his men melted back into the Andes, and the Spanish were left in command of the fertile plains and coastal cities. But it had been a near thing—the Incas had come close to reclaiming their land.

It was probably then that Manco Inca retreated to the fortress of Machu Picchu and the stone city became, for a time, the royal residence. The most spectacular buildings there must have already been standing: the depleted resources at Manco Inca's command would not have permitted much ambitious construction. The stones are silent as to what role the city played before it became the fugitive Inca's refuge. Skeletons found in the burial caves near the city are almost entirely those of women, so perhaps the magnificent ruins were once a vast temple to the sun, populated mainly by the Chosen Women who devoted their lives to the rituals of worship. No one can now say if the Inca emperors before Pizarro made pilgrimages to the citadel in the mountains. But the presence of buildings much less carefully constructed than the superb central structures suggests that the city was hastily enlarged to accommodate the loyal remnant of the Inca's followers who came with him to the city we now call Machu Picchu.

Meanwhile in the valleys below there was another Inca. The Spanish, still seeking a veil of legitimacy for their rape of the empire, elevated another surviving son of Huayna Capac. His name was Paullu Capac, and for 12 years, from 1537 to 1549, he cooperated with the Spanish in Cuzco. Paullu reasoned that the only possibility of Inca survival lay in some measure of collaboration with the Spanish, and he even fought with them against Manco Inca's forces in their desperate uprising. In 1543 he was baptized a Christian and became Don Cristóbal Paullu Topa Inca. He was granted a Spanish coat of arms and founded the first chapel in Cuzco.

Manco Inca remained in the mountains. During these years the Spanish had other concerns which prevented them from stamping out the last pockets of Inca resistance. With the conquest virtually over the conquistadors fell upon one another, and for 11 long years, beginning in 1537 after the defeat of Manco Inca, the people of Peru watched helplessly as their new masters clawed and tore at each other, and the land sank deeper into anarchy. The chief rival to the power of the Pizarros, Diego de Almagro, was defeated and executed by Hernando Pizarro in 1538; three years later his vengeful supporters murdered Francisco Pizarro himself in his palace at Lima. Manco Inca was not

Above: Diego de Almagro (1475?–1538), one-time close friend of Francisco Pizarro. The conquistadors fell out over the division of the spoils of the Inca conquest, and their personal quarrel resulted in a civil war between the invaders that last for 11 years.

Below: the murder of Francisco Pizarro at his palace in Lima. Although the conquistador was actually killed by Diego de Almagro's followers three years after their leader's death, the Indian artist Poma de Ayala has depicted Almagro himself thrusting a sword through Pizarro's heart.

untouched by the wrangling. In 1542, after the death of Pizarro, a handful of refugee Almagrists reached the outlying settlements of the Inca's truncated territory and, swearing loyalty to Manco Inca, were permitted to remain.

What followed was either stupid folly or deliberate treachery. The accounts vary, but most of them agree that the renegade Spaniards taught the Inca to play various European games— bowls, quoits, and even chess and checkers. Reportedly, Manco Inca had a bowling green made at the settlement where the Spanish refugees lived (there is no indication that the Spanish ever saw the city of Machu Picchu or knew that it existed). It was during one of these games that one of the refugees lost his temper in the heat of competition and insulted the Inca. Manco Inca struck the hot-tempered Spaniard and warned him to consider with whom he talked—and the furious Spaniard killed him, either with a dagger or with his bare hands. Titu Cusi, one of Manco's sons, claimed that the Spaniards deliberately set upon the Inca during a game of quoits and stabbed him to death—to win favor, it has been suggested, with the new Spanish viceroy of Peru.

Whatever the circumstances, Manco Inca was assassinated in 1545. His eldest son, Sayri Inca, succeeded him and ruled his mountain retreat in peace for 10 years. In 1555 he was coaxed out by the viceroy, who offered him a more comfortable residence nearer Cuzco. Sayri Inca seems to have been pleased with this opportunity to see more of the world that up to then he had only heard about, and he accepted the Spanish offer. But he lived only two years among the Spanish; although he was apparently well and respectfully cared for, he died of what the viceroy said was disease. His nobles claimed he had been poisoned.

His half-brother Titu Cusi remained in the mountains, safe-guarding a younger brother, Tupac Amaru, by placing him "into the House of the Sun with the Chosen Virgins and their Matrons" —almost certainly in the city of Machu Picchu. Titu Cusi survived until 1571, meeting Spanish emissaries in his jungle city of Vilcabamba and listening to missionaries, always—the missionaries thought—on the verge of conversion, but never yielding in the end. He died of natural causes, still supreme in his mountain stronghold.

The forehead fringe—the mark of Inca sovereignty—then passed to Tupac Amaru, but he proved no match for the Spanish. A new viceroy, Francisco de Toledo, had arrived in Peru in 1569, determined to regularize the administration of the colony by ending the power of the Incas for all time. He sent out an ambassador, and, unwisely, Tupac Amaru's men murdered him. The Spanish then dispatched a full-fledged expeditionary force to capture the Inca and take revenge.

By then the Inca warriors had been reduced to a forlorn handful who had forgotten the tactics that had gained them an empire. They tried to hide their Inca in the jungle valley of the Pampas river, but it was not remote enough. The Spanish followed, and the last Inca was captured trying to protect his pregnant wife. Back in Cuzco she was mangled before his eyes. Tupac Amaru himself was baptized and beheaded, only 39 years after Atahualpa had been murdered by Pizarro.

Toledo gained little by his barbarism. When he returned to Spain the king refused to see him, saying he had been sent to serve kings, not to kill them. But the colonial system which Toledo established lasted for the next 200 years.

For how many of those years did the fortress city of Machu Picchu live? The city was stripped of all its furnishings, so it seems that at some time someone gave the order to abandon it. Was it Tupac Amaru? Were any of the Chosen Women left behind to continue their rituals and petitions to the sun god, who seemed to have forgotten his people? Did a last surviving priestess watch the sun rise and set as she waited patiently for death in the silent stone city?

No one knows. The years passed, and the jungle crept in over the stones. The terraces were overgrown and forgotten. The city remained, awaiting the visit of the scholar and archaeologist, the swarm of tourists, and rush of the 20th century. It stands as it has stood for centuries, an irrefutable monument to the grandeur of the Incas. They themselves may have perished, but their sun still shines upon their temple, and the stone city endures.

What Happened to Machu Picchu?

Below: Inca construction carved from solid rock at Cuzco. The stone was beaten into shape and polished by stone balls repeatedly dropped on it. It was important for the joints between stones to fit accurately and for the balance of weights to be precise so that when the frequent earthquakes jolted the cities the stones would jump up and then fall back into place without any danger of collapse.

Chapter 8
The Maya Enigma

While Europe lay gripped by the depression and stultifying monotony of the Dark Ages, across the Atlantic Ocean in the New World a brilliant civilization was in full flower—that of the mysterious and enigmatic Maya. Their daily life revolved around religion, and the cities they carved out of the jungle, over 100 of them, were living temples. During the 8th century their way of life reached a peak—then, suddenly and inexplicably, it disintegrated. For 1000 years the cities remained buried under dark, tangled rain forest, until the Spaniards stumbled across them in the 18th century. Whatever happened to the Maya? How could such a thriving, highly evolved civilization suddenly abandon its cities to the jungle?

If it were not for chewing gum, we would know even less than we do about the mysterious Maya of Central America. Their incredibly sophisticated civilization rose to its greatest height in the six centuries after 300 A.D. and then inexplicably collapsed, completely and entirely. What had once been a thickly populated territory returned to virtually uninhabited virgin forest. The Maya cities are now nearly submerged in smothering vegetation. The tips of the tallest pyramids, green with creeping vines, may rise above the treetops, but most of the buildings are completely hidden, their locations suggested only by gentle swellings in the surface of the all-enveloping overgrowth. The only people who now walk the warm and humid forest paths are native chicleros, who collect the sap from the sapodilla trees which provides chicle, the base for chewing gum. The ancient Maya also gathered the sap centuries ago, but they used it as an adhesive.

Only the chicleros now know the forest paths, and they were the ones who guided the archaeologists to the half-forgotten Maya ruins. The once-bustling ceremonial courts, the patchwork of cultivated fields surrounding the cities, the multitude of scattered huts that housed artisans, craftsmen, builders, and farmers —all were abandoned abruptly to the forest, leaving only their enigmatic hieroglyphic carvings behind. What happened? Where did the people go? The forest is silent now, except for the chattering of birds and monkeys.

Archaeologists can offer only suppositions and theories for the

Opposite: the central acropolis and Temple IV at Tikal, Guatemala. Probably built around 750 A.D. during the late classic period, this example of Mayan architecture is from one of the best-excavated sites in the Central American jungle.

A Legacy of Hieroglyphs

many gaps in the history of the Maya. They were the only people of the New World to develop a true writing system for which they used hieroglyphs, but, maddeningly, most of what has been deciphered is simply numerical and calendrical calculations. The great preoccupation of the Maya seems to have been the passage of time. They learned to calculate millions of years into the past, and much of their writing records these computations. The rest is a mystery awaiting the gifted scholar who can finally crack the script, as a codebreaker cracks a code.

But without the clues to be found in their own writing about themselves, the Maya remain elusive. Using only stone tools they managed to build great cities in areas of jungle and forest where the victory over relentlessly encroaching undergrowth was not a single achievement but a daily battle. Though they never grasped the principle of the wheel, yet they charted the heavens accurately. They never learned to weigh a sack of corn, but their mathematicians contemplated eternity and performed elaborate calculations. They never made the short step from the corbeled to the true arch, but the magnificence of their architecture is visible still, even clothed in jungle vegetation.

Their accomplishments have fascinated those who stumbled on the ruins of their greatness since the time of the Franciscan Diego de Landa, who in the 16th century burned all the Maya books he could seize because they "contained nothing but superstitions and falsehoods of the Devil." But after his return to Spain, where he was summoned to explain his excesses, he wrote a history of the Yucatán area in which he recorded the customs, religious beliefs, and history of the Maya calendar, illustrated with drawings of the glyphs. Thanks to his account we know something of these mysterious people, and from the three books (*codices*) which survived and are now in European museums we can piece out a bit more. But still we can only glimpse the Maya dimly, through the shifting perspectives of the past: even Landa, the earliest European, arrived seven centuries too late.

The Maya built their civilization in the central lowlands of the Yucatán peninsula. They did not call it Yucatán—we do not

Below: a page from the Dresden codex, the earliest of the three surviving Maya codices to escape the zealous book burning of the Spanish friars. It shows a series of elaborate astronomical calculations recording the rhythm of the planet Venus.

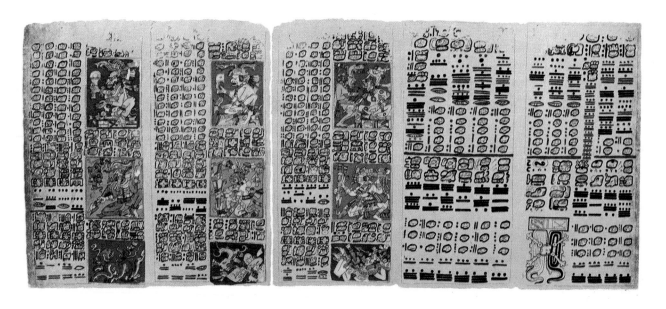

Above: Central America, site of the Maya and Toltec empires.

know what they called it or what they called themselves. When the Spaniards first skirted the coastline and saw the well-constructed buildings, they asked (in Spanish) who had built them. The Indians answered, "Ci-u-than," which meant "We don't understand you." The Spanish took that to mean the land was called Yucatán.

Whatever it is called, the Yucatán peninsula, which now is divided between Mexico and Guatemala, is not a hospitable part of the world. The Maya people inhabited, as they still do, the entire peninsula as well as the adjoining mountainous spine of Central America. The land ranges from arid limestone in the Mexican states of Yucatán and Campeche and the territory of Quintana Roo to the volcanic ranges of highland Guatemala and neighboring El Salvador. Between lies the central lowland area, which includes what is now the Petén district of Guatemala and the adjacent parts of Mexico and Belize. The territory is mainly low-lying limestone with only a thin layer of soil. It has been described as singularly lacking in natural resources—except, perhaps, for the limestone itself, which is an excellent building material.

Normally there is abundant rainfall during the rainy season, which begins in May and lasts until December or January, but water runs through the limestone quickly, and the supply of water was an abiding Maya concern. In January the dry season begins. Archaeologists have long limited their site work to the dry months; during the rainy season the swamps become an impassable morass. Even in the dry season the humidity is oppressive: one archaeologist working at Tikal, one of the best-excavated Maya cities, had continuous problems with his ear which were only resolved when a doctor removed several tiny mushrooms which had taken root in his auditory canal.

No matter how unpromising the territory, it is an indisputable fact that at one time a substantial population lived in the now-abandoned central area. Their method of agriculture is one of the many controversial aspects of Maya life. The theories—and guesses—are based on the method of farming practiced by

A Wasteful Agriculture

Above: stone head and torso of the young corn god, from Copán, Honduras. It is 28 inches high and dates from the late classic period. The corn god was one of the most important Maya deities.

Maya farmers today, who live on the fringes of the central area. It is the system known as slash-and-burn agriculture or, in the Central American region, the *milpa*.

In the milpa cycle the farmer cuts vegetation in either virgin forest or an abandoned field during the dry season. At the end of the dry season, but before the rains start, the dried debris is burned to produce ash that fertilizes the soil. Then the farmer pokes holes in the cleared land with a digging stick and drops in grains of corn. With luck and under normal circumstances, the rains then come and water the fields, and the grain flourishes. But so poor is the soil—and so great the competition from stubborn clumps of grass that relentlessly return to the cleared land—that after a second year of cultivation the crop is no longer worth the effort expended, and the farmer abandons that plot to the forest and clears new ground. The abandoned field is left fallow for years, never less than three and most commonly between six and eight. By the time the field is again farmed, natural processes have built up its fertility again.

Such a system is obviously wasteful of land, since for every plot farmed in a given year there are three or four fallow. Among modern milpa farmers in lowland Central America, population density ranges from 25 to 100 persons per square mile in a highly decentralized pattern. Milpa farmers cannot live together in towns: the walk to the field cannot be so long that the farmer has no energy left for farming when he reaches it. One of the main problems for archaeologists trying to reconstruct the pattern of Maya life has thus been to explain the existence of Maya cities. It is true that they were not cities in the sense that New York or Amsterdam or Tokyo are cities, but they none the less represented concentrations of population. Almost all of the buildings in the excavated Maya cities appear to have been temples and ceremonial structures. The people lived outside the cities near their fields.

Even so, the concentration of homesteads around the ceremonial centers is far higher than the milpa system of farming apparently could support. Tikal is probably the largest of the central Maya centers and is one of the most thoroughly excavated. In the six square miles surrounding the site there are enough house mounds to have accommodated 11,000 residents. That works out at a density of about 1600 persons per square mile—16 times the maximum density now living within a milpa system.

If the climate of the lowland area was similar to what it is now, and the bulk of the evidence seems to indicate that it has not changed, then it seems impossible that the Maya should have been able to gather thousands of workers to live near the ceremonial centers. But the centers are there, and for six centuries the people were, too.

Furthermore, theirs was not a bare subsistence economy. Millions of man-hours went into the construction of Maya cities, which were built of stones joined together with pulverized limestone cement. These were then polished and glazed. A surplus of food would have been required to feed the builders. There were craftsmen and artisans—potters whose skills matched or surpassed those of ancient Greece, sculptors who carved images of

Above: farming today near Oaxaca, Mexico. The milpa or slash and burn system is still used in many parts of Central America, and this has made it easier for archaeologists to theorize about Maya customs.

astonishing vigor and beauty, and painters who produced vivid murals. There must also have been many priests. All these people had to be supported by a food production system which could supply more than the needs of the farmer and his family alone.

Many suggestions have been formulated to explain how Maya food production worked. Although corn, or maize, was the center of Maya life, and the youthful corn god was a particularly revered member of the pantheon of deities, they might well have grown other crops as well—root crops such as yams, sweet potatoes, and cassava; and nuts from the ramon or breadnut tree, an excellent source of vegetable protein. The soil might conceivably have been more fertile until overfarmed, although in that case one would expect that over the centuries it would have reverted to its natural state. Or the fallow period in ancient times might have been much shorter than it is now. Which, if any, of these hypotheses are correct we do not know. With no direct evidence scholars can only theorize. Modern techniques, including the sophisticated analysis of ancient pollen, are no help here. Root crops leave no pollen and ramon trees exist abundantly in the natural vegetation, so the presence of their pollen

Above: Olmec terra cotta figurine of a baby, found in Mexico. This dates from between 500 and 100 B.C.

would not be conclusive. The problem is simply one of many that presently remain unsolved.

Perhaps the most elementary of Maya mysteries, however, is where the tribes came from in the first place. There has been no dearth of suggestions. When they were first discovered, Europeans were convinced that the civilizations of the New World must have been transplanted from somewhere else. The sophisticated Maya artefacts were variously attributed to remnants of the Lost Tribes of Israel (by Bishop Landa himself), survivors of the "lost continent" of Atlantis, and Phoenician settlers who crossed the Atlantic from the Mediterranean. In the 18th century it was suggested that American Indians in general were descended from Noah, and according to this school of thought the Ark was built in America. Another idea was that America had been colonized by survivors of one of Alexander the Great's fleets, recorded to have been lost in the 4th century B.C.; or perhaps crews from Kublai Khan's ships had been driven across the Pacific by a great storm in the 14th century; or the American peoples might have descended from Trojans, Etruscans, Chinese Buddhists, Norsemen, African Mandingos, Tartars, Irish, or Huns.

Amidst this plethora of proposed origins, most archaeologists today choose the less spectacular theory that the Maya were simply themselves, descendants of several scattered migrations from Asia to America over the then-existing land bridge which is now Bering Strait. The consensus of opinion holds that those migrations took place 10 to 20 thousand years ago. According to this interpretation, by 2000 B.C. the people who were to become the Maya were probably established in the southern part of what is now Maya territory, and over the next two millennia they developed in the same ways as their neighbors. Early researchers, dazzled by the magnificence of the Maya ruins, believed that Maya culture inexplicably blossomed on its own. But further excavation and study have indicated that the Maya and their neighbors to the north in what is now Mexico—the Zapotec of Oaxaca and the Olmec, centered at La Venta in the state of Tabasco—were developing at nearly the same time. The Olmec, in fact, almost certainly predated them, and many archaeologists now give them credit for beginning the development of what became the Maya calendar, and even for inventing writing.

Other archaeologists speculate that the Olmec in fact spoke Maya (one site in Belize in what was once British Honduras, thought to be pre-Olmec, shows Maya building characteristics), and the problem of which group came first becomes yet more convoluted. In any case, focusing on the Olmec simply moves the mystery back in time: Olmec development is as enigmatic as that of the Maya, and their society collapsed just as suddenly around the beginning of the Christian era. In any case, the entire fragile structure of theoretical sequences and influences may change drastically at any time, since in the mile upon mile of uninvestigated jungle and forest the find of a single new site could conceivably alter much of the picture.

By about 250 A.D. the lowland Maya had evolved a "civilized" culture. This was once believed to have been a sudden jump in

Where Did the Maya Come From?

development, which lent strength to the theories that Maya brilliance was an import from somewhere else. More recent study, however, has uncovered clues showing that Maya traits were being developed during the formative period which began around 500 B.C. During that period the Maya were building pyramids, proper study of which is unfortunately greatly hindered by the Maya custom of building later pyramids on top of existing ones. Their burials show that differences in social rank were emerging. The burials also share typical features with later Maya culture — the presence of stingray tail spines, for instance, which were imported for use in ceremonial blood-letting. In a child's burial the finger bone of an adult was found; this is interesting because throughout the Maya period and up to the Spanish conquest it was customary for a mother to bury one of her own terminal finger bones with her dead child. Clearly the tradition is very old.

The Maya were probably, then as now, a fairly homogeneous people. Their descendants speak about 15 Maya languages or major dialects, similar in their relationships with each other to those within the Romance group of European languages. Some dialects are mutually intelligible while others are only somewhat alike, as is the case with French and Italian. Generally speaking,

Above left: Olmec bas-relief of a serpent and priest. This artifact, found near the Gulf of Mexico, was made by a tribe who almost certainly predated the Maya and may have begun the development of the Maya calendar.

The Riddle of the "Palaces"

the Maya are stocky with broad faces, straight or slightly wavy black hair, and almond-shaped eyes. Many Maya have large, hooked noses and a slightly drooping lower lip, traits which were considered very beautiful by the ancient Maya and are faithfully recorded in their art. A broad, sloping forehead was considered so desirable that Maya infants were strapped between boards during their first few days of life in order to set their soft skulls in the required deformation. Slightly crossed eyes were also admired, so a ball would be suspended a short distance above the baby's nose for it to focus on.

However food production may have been organized, inevitably most laborers would have been involved in farming. They lived with their families in small, rounded huts built on low, stone-walled platforms, and it is the existence of these platforms which makes it possible to estimate the population during the peak of Maya development. Maya descendants to this day are exceptionally clean and place a high value on orderliness, and the archaeological evidence shows that this is no recent characteristic. The huts were built in small, neat clusters, often with carefully paved plazas in between. The riches of Maya civilization seem to have reached the most humble social levels: in remote peasant households archaeologists have found hand-painted, multicolored pottery like that used in the ceremonial centers, as well as imported stone implements for grinding corn.

Wealthier people and priests probably lived closer to the main centers or in smaller centers which boasted their own temple pyramids and one or more "palace" structures. What exactly these palaces were used for has not been satisfactorily determined. It seems unlikely that they were residential buildings, since many of the walls are massively thick and the rooms are small, ill-lit, and airless. Nor has any domestic debris from the classic period been uncovered within them. Some archaeologists have suggested that they might have been used for solemn religious ceremonies not held in public; others have theorized that they were used by the administrative and bureaucratic workers

Above: Mayan bas-relief of a man with the characteristic hooked nose and thick, drooping lip of the Maya Indians.

Right: terra cotta figurine of a woman weaving, probably an evocation of Mayan daily life. This piece comes from Jaina, Mexico.

who must have gathered in the local centers and cities. Lacking any direct contemporary evidence, however, the suggestions remain only educated guesses.

The cities themselves were magnificent, clearly the jewel and pride of the Maya people. They were almost entirely devoted to religious worship, which seems to have been the center of Maya life in general. Their all-powerful gods were worshiped, placated, and sacrificed to; a knowledge of their good or bad intentions was considered essential for the success of any enterprise. It seems clear that at the top of the social pyramid stood the priests, whose power and authority with the gods was supposed to guarantee the greatest possible benefits for the people. The conquering Spanish thought the Maya gods innumerable; certainly

Above: "Arraignment of the Prisoners," a scene from the wall murals of Bonampak, an ancient Maya ruin. Painted around 800 A.D. in the late classic period, the actual fresco was crumbling when Bonampak was discovered in 1946, and this painting by Antonio Tejeda was made as a permanent record. On the upper tier of the picture stand richly attired priests and nobles. Below them, awaiting sentence, sprawl prisoners of war. Various minor officials and attendants are ranged on the lower terrace. The Maya's use of bright colors without perspective creates a rich, decorative effect.

Above: the pyramid and Temple of the Inscriptions at Palenque in southern Mexico, dating from about 700 A.D. (the late classic period). Palenque represents the peak of Mayan architectural achievement and was only rediscovered by the Spanish in 1773. In 1950 a burial crypt was discovered under the pyramid, joined to the upper levels by an internal stairway. This was the first and so far the only case of a tomb being found beneath a pyramid in Mexico.

there were a great many. The Maya year was a rich tapestry of festivals, dances, and music devoted to the seasons of the gods. There were processions, ceremonies, and sacrifices. During the festivals the great cities must have been thronged with people drawn in from the neighboring countryside. The great pyramids, with their steep narrow steps ascending precipitously to temple platforms at the top, must have been awe-inspiring when immaculately clean, shining in the sun. The great plazas and ball courts had stepped accommodation for spectators and must have been crowded with men, women, and children. To this day prayers and offerings remain an important feature of Maya religious life, now a curious amalgamation of Catholicism with aspects of the traditional pagan faith.

Sacrifices played a key part in the religious ritual, and the remains of offerings abound in Maya ruins. Human sacrifice was practiced during the classic period between 350 and 900 A.D.,

Sacrifice in Maya Religion

Left: detail of the architecture of the so-called "Nunnery Quadrangle" at Uxmal in southwestern Yucatán. This site has been broadly dated as 9th or 10th century A.D. The Nunnery is actually a palace group made up of four separate rectangular buildings arranged around an interior court. The masonry façades include representations of the thatched roof huts of ordinary farmers as well as latticed, crisscross designs.

Below: lintel 24 from house G in the Maya ceremonial center at Menche, Yaxchilán, Guatemala. It shows a richly robed woman penitent kneeling before the ruler and mutilating her own tongue (and drawing blood) by passing a rope of thorns through it. The inscription shows the Round Calendar date 5 Eb 15 Mac, which probably occurred during 709 A.D.

though not to the same extent as in the decadent period which followed the Maya collapse; the surviving Maya were heavily influenced by the Mexican peoples' emphasis upon the need of the gods for human hearts. Self-sacrifice by blood-letting seems to have been immensely important throughout Maya history, however, and blood was apparently shed freely from the tongue, ears, elbows, and penis during preparation for and in the course of important festivals.

The Maya were obsessed by time to a degree not equaled by any other great pre-modern civilization, and a prominent feature of all Maya cities are the *stelae*. These are limestone shafts carved or painted with stylized portraits of gods and hieroglyphic texts which report the inexorable passage of time. It is as if New York were to have a sequence of monuments down Fifth Avenue, each recording the date it was erected and the positions of the moon and the planets at the time, with information on ruling gods.

Wizardry in Mathematics

Right: Mayan calendar on a lintel from house D at Yaxchilán, a major Maya center strung out along a terrace on the banks of the Usumacinta river. Yaxchilán is famous for its many stone lintels, carved in relief with scenes of conquest and ceremonial life. The Jaguar dynasty ruled the site in the 8th century, and the lintels begin with the exploits of Shield Jaguar, who was succeeded by his son Bird Jaguar in 752 A.D.

For the Maya, each day was not merely influenced by a god: each day *was* a god, or rather a number of gods. They visualized the divisions of time as burdens carried by relays of gods through eternity. For instance, imagine May 10, 1979 carried by six bearers: the god of the number 10 carries May on his back; the god of number 1 carries the millennium; the god of number 9 carries the centuries; the god of 7 the decades; and the god of 9 carries the years. At the end of the day the May load is transferred to the god of the number 11, and after this momentary halt the procession moves off again. These burdens came to be equated with the expected good or ill fortune of the year: the day with which a new year started was its bearer, and the aspect of that god governed the year. If the year began with the god Kan it meant a good harvest, since Kan was an aspect of the maize god. On the other hand, a year beginning with Ix was likely to be disastrous because the god Ix was malevolent. To predict these matters and mollify the evil aspects of gods were clearly major concerns, and these seem to have been the basis for the elaborate Maya systems of calendrical and astronomical cal-

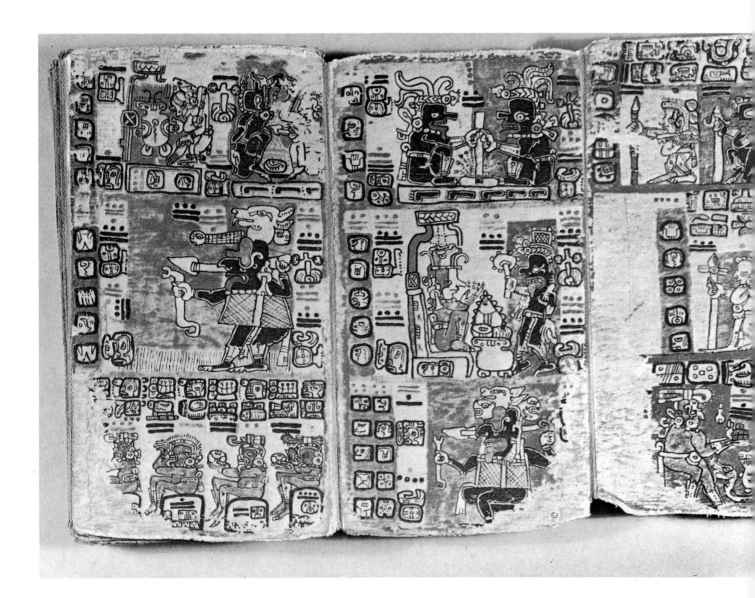

Above: Mayan gods and dignitaries from the Codex Troano Cortesianus, a later codex dating from the 15th century. The Maya had a bewilderingly large number of gods—in one 18th-century manuscript 166 deities are mentioned by name—resulting from the fact that each god had many aspects. The Maya clergy's duties included "computation of the years, months, and days, the festivals and ceremonies, the administration of the sacraments, the fateful days and seasons, their methods of divination and their prophecies, events and the cures for diseases, and their antiquities and how to read and write with the letters and characters."

culations. They believed that history was cyclical and that what had happened at a given point in the past would be repeated when that point was duplicated in a later cycle. Given the same influences, history would repeat itself.

These cycles were themselves greatly complicated. A Sacred Round was a cycle of 20 repeating days, each of which was a god, and 13 repeating numbers, which interlocked to form a total of 260 days. The secular year was divided into 18 months of 20 days each, ending with a period of five days which was considered almost outside the year and was desperately unlucky. While it lasted one tried to do as little as possible lest misfortune fall on one's enterprises; one devoted the time to fasting, continence, and prayer. These two calendars, of the Sacred Round and the secular year, intermeshed so that each date was expressed in terms of both: 1 Imix, 19 Pop—rather as if we used our ordinary calendar and a liturgical (Hebrew or Muslim) calendar simultaneously.

The two Maya calendars only repeated the same coincidence of dates every 52 years, which was known as the Calendar Round.

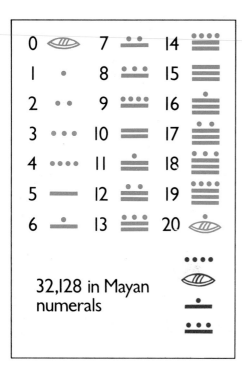

32,128 in Mayan numerals

This poses a problem in deciphering Maya inscriptions in that they are sometimes dated according to the Calendar Round alone, rather like our habit of abbreviating dates—as in May 15, '78—so that its position is located within a century, but exactly which century is not indicated. As the Maya wanted to count time in long periods, they also had the Long Count method, which may have been invented by the Olmec. This system (which in its turn interlocked with the Calendar Round) included the *tun*, an approximate year of 360 days; a cycle of *katuns*, periods of 20 tuns or 7200 days; and *baktuns*, periods of 20 katuns or 144,000 days. Larger measurements of time existed but were less commonly used.

The entire complicated system has been likened to a series of engaged cogwheels, with the reservation, of course, that the Maya themselves never visualized the process as mechanical but rather as a series of complicated interactions between the relevant gods who took turns ruling the world. To record these intricate calendrical calculations the Maya developed a positional system of representing written numbers, like our own. In our system the numbers 2001 and 1002 use the same digits, but their different positions give them different values. We use a decimal system;

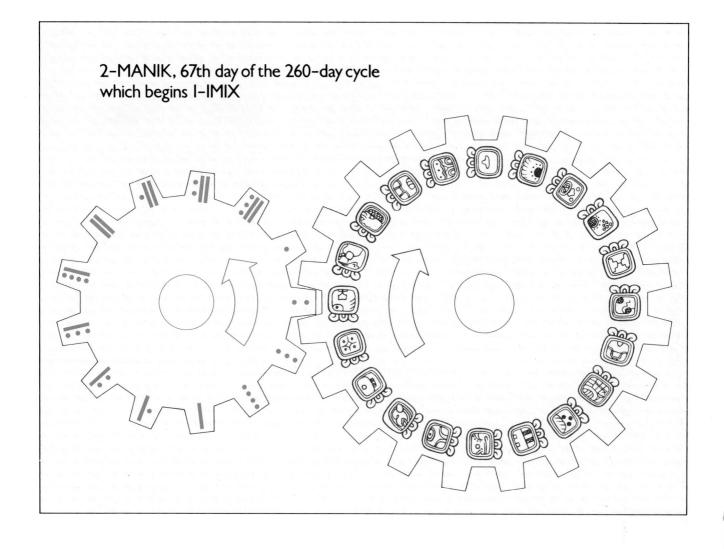

2-MANIK, 67th day of the 260-day cycle which begins 1-IMIX

the Maya used 20 rather than 10 as their base and used bars and dots for notation. A bar was 5 and the dot was 1. Numbers could be written both vertically and horizontally. It was a much more flexible and subtle system than the contemporary Roman numeral system then in use in Europe, which had no concept of zero. The Maya mark for zero was usually a stylized figure of a shell.

Maya expertise in astronomy was as great as their skill with numbers and dates, and it is particularly impressive in view of the environment, in which it rains for nearly nine months of the year making consistent observation difficult. The Maya were mainly concerned with the movements of the moon and the planet Venus. As they had no concept of a round earth, the movements of heavenly bodies were seen simply as repeating events in the same way that time itself was repetitive. The astronomical patterns were another aspect of the Maya enthusiasm for working out parallel calculations and then intermeshing them. The surviving Maya works—the three codices and the multitude of carved glyphs on stelae and other sculptures—are filled with calendrical and astronomical information.

The last three centuries of the Maya classic period, from 600 A.D. to roughly 900, were years of rapidly expanding population growth and a significant increase in monumental architecture. Pyramids and temples as well as palace groups rose like mushrooms all over the lowlands. These buildings showed an interesting change in emphasis: whereas the earlier builders had apparently concentrated on temples, the later Maya increasingly replaced temples with secular palaces. There seems also to have been a rise in military activity. Although the presentation of prisoners had been a dominant theme in Maya art from the beginning, in the late classic period there are more scenes of actual fighting.

Who the opponents were is not clear. The individual Maya cities seem to have been self-ruling and independent and have often been compared to the ancient Greek city-states, but the evidence is not definite. There are indications of friendly relations between the cities, and they certainly shared the same language and culture, but until more of the Maya writing is deciphered we are unable to say what their political relationship was; warfare might, then, have occurred between the cities. During the late classic period none of their once-powerful non-Maya neighbors was strong enough to pose much of a threat.

Lacking details, therefore, we are left with the image of a society in full and flamboyant flower. The vast lowland area, once forest, must have been studded with countless ceremonial centers—from simple, thatched hut-temples to the vast grandeur of the massed pyramids, temples, and palaces of the great cities. The land would have been a busy patchwork of cleared fields and clusters of huts grouped together. The people were building, always building, erecting more stelae to mark the passage of time, more temples to honor the gods, and more palaces to reflect the power of the rulers. Sculpture expressed sensitivity; the pottery was the result of skilled experimentation with new techniques of shaping and decoration; buildings were spacious. The civilization was reaching its climax.

Two Maya Calendars

Opposite above: Maya base-20 numeration. Number signs increased in value from bottom to top in vertical columns, so that symbols in the first and lowest place were valued in units of one, the combination of symbols in the next place would be multiplied by 20, the next by 400, etc.

Above: Maya pottery vessel with the figure of a dignitary and date glyphs painted on it.

Opposite below: schematic representation of the Maya's two simplest and most fundamental time cycles. The Calendar Round of 52 years consisted of two permutating cycles, one of which was the 260-day count. This Sacred Round represented the intermeshing of a repeating sequence of the numbers 1 to 13 (left) with another cycle of 20 days (right), each of which was named after a god. The Sacred Round was then read along with the tun of 360 days (with 5 unlucky days added at the end). The result was the 52-year Calendar Round, during which period no date would be repeated. Other intermeshing cycles, covering periods ranging from centuries to millions of years, added further layers of complexity to their time scheme.

Above: the Temple of the Magician (named by the Spanish friars) at Uxmal. The site is dominated by two mighty temple-pyramids, this one and that of the Dwarf.

Opposite above: terra cotta figurine of an important official in full regalia, from Jaina.

Opposite below: Ball Court in the ancient temple-city of Copán in northwestern Honduras. A rough game was played with a rubber ball in the narrow courtyard between the sloping benches.

Then it collapsed, quite abruptly, over the course of less than a century. In 790, at the end of one 20-year katun, 19 cities erected stelae (as was usual, although this was the largest number ever to do so). In 810 12 cities erected stelae; in 830 only three did so. The last stelae with full inscriptions from the Long Count dating system were carved in 889. Building stopped; house mounds in the countryside surrounding the cities were abandoned. The palace structures in the city of Tikal, though inhabited, were in a state far from their former glory. Roofs collapsed from lack of maintenance, and the debris was pushed to one side so that the impoverished inhabitants could continue to live in the rubble.

Garbage piled up on stairways, in courtyards, and in abandoned rooms—all of which had once been swept clean. The survivors clung on for a while, but estimates suggest that a century later only 10 percent of the previous population remained.

Where did they go? What could have happened? So far no single explanation seems conclusive. The increasing importance of military power might point to a series of suicidal civil wars, but there is no evidence that the cities were overthrown by force, and in fact there is no sign of anything but natural decay following abandonment. The peasants might have risen in revolt against increasingly powerful priests and nobles. There might have been invasion from abroad (of which there is no evidence). There might have been epidemics (but the endemic diseases of which we know—malaria, yellow fever, and hookworm—are almost certainly post-Columbian importations). Did the Maya simply overpopulate and overfarm their limited rain-forest environment? Of all the possibilities, overpopulation is generally accepted as at least one of the factors leading to the disaster.

For disaster it certainly was. Some of the people of the lowlands may have migrated to the surrounding areas, but there is no archaeological evidence to prove that they did, and in any case nowhere nearby could the total Maya population have possibly been accommodated. One authority does point out that we are not talking about jungles piled high with rotting corpses: the collapse, swift as it was, did extend over four or five generations, and it is an inescapable fact that each generation dies out in any population. The decline may have taken the form of a marked drop in fertility or disproportionately high death rates (perhaps due to malnutrition) among young women and children.

Monumental Architecture

The Mysterious Itza Invaders

Only in the Maya lowlands was the light snuffed out entirely. In Yucatán—or, more precisely, in the northern Maya area comprising the modern Mexican states of Yucatán, Campeche, and Quintana Roo—the civilization actively continued, although it was altered and increasingly influenced by ideas from Mexico. While most of the Maya cities in Yucatán and Campeche were apparently abandoned about the same time as the lowland sites, some were revived later during the so-called Mexican period from about 975 to 1200. The Itzá, described as foreigners who spoke broken Maya, in 987 seized the famous Chichén Itzá site, which had been a Maya city of some importance during the classic period.

Who the Itzá were is another topic of vigorous scholarly debate. Most likely they were Toltecs, whose culture developed in Tula, about 50 miles north of modern Mexico City. Even if not actually Toltecs, they were clearly influenced by Toltec culture, for Chichén Itzá has Toltec ornaments and additions built on top of Maya structures. The name Chichén Itzá itself means *cenote* of the Itzá (meaning a natural limestone reservoir). Human sacrifices of young virgins were thrown into the depths of the Sacred Cenote, according to stories which circulated from the time of the conquest. Determined archaeologists dredged it, and, although they found human remains, of the 42 identifiable skeletons recovered half were of children, 13 were of men, and

Above: Toltec figures at Tula in Mexico, where the Toltecs settled soon after 900 A.D. Tula was finally destroyed by violent internal dissensions in the middle of the 12th century, but many Toltecs under their king Topíltzin were forced to leave and fled south at an earlier stage, probably in 987 A.D. The Toltec style is dominated by the image of the warrior.

the remaining 8 were women, all but one apparently past the normal age of marriage.

Toltec domination of Chichén Itzá lasted for more than two centuries, but we do not know whether any other cities were taken over or how much of the surrounding countryside was under their control. They were succeeded by the rulers of Mayapán, a more recently established city not far from present-day Mérida. For the next 250 years Mayapán governed Yucatán, keeping tight control over subject cities by requiring that their rulers live in Mayapán itself. Mayapán was an ordinary city in the sense that most of its buildings were residential. The ruins are extensive and are surrounded by a massive stone wall, now collapsing, which is over 5 miles long. Obviously a defensive device, the wall suggests that conditions were more dangerous.

The ruins of Chichén Itzá show a decline both in the quality of art and the craftsmanship of building, and in Mayapán both continued to degenerate. The Maya fires were burning low; revolts against Mayapán in the 15th century meant only that the independent chieftainships, which had succeeded its centralized rule, warred bitterly against each other. The intertribal rivalry was ended in 1525 with the coming of the Spanish. The conquest of Yucatán was complete 16 years later. Although the last Maya settlement, at Tayasal, a small island in Lake Petén Itzá in what is now northern Guatemala, was not conquered until 1697, the

Left: Chichén Itzá, a Mayan site which was revived by Itzá invaders and ruled by them from the 10th to the 12th century A.D. Under the rule of these people, probably Toltecs forced to leave Tula, Chichén Itzá became the supreme metropolis of a united kingdom. The fortress-city is most renowned for its Sacred Cenote or Well of Sacrifice, reached by a 900-foot-long causeway leading north from the Great Plaza. However, the peak of the sacrificial cult was reached after the decline of the Toltec influence, and it continued into colonial times. The Toltecs seem to have abandoned their mighty capital by the early 13th century.

glory of the Maya was long past. But the strength of Maya traditions remained: imported Mexican gods were eventually forgotten, while the Maya rain gods were remembered in primitive ceremonies.

Today Maya ruins still lie in the rain forest, a tantalizing reminder of a greatness we cannot grasp. The evidence remaining is incomplete and elusive, and it involves trying to reconstitute a culture from a handful of calendars and three books—it is as if we were to use an almanac, *Pilgrim's Progress*, and a manual on astrology to try to visualize our own culture. The magnificence

Magnificence of the Maya

Left: east façade of the Nunnery at Chichén Itzá as it was first discovered, in a drawing by the Victorian architect and historian Frederick Catherwood. The building is elaborately ornamented with hieroglyphs and figures of the sky serpent, and it is typical of Maya architecture of the end of the late classical period. Other structures in Chichén Itzá are representative of the amalgamation of Toltec and Maya culture dating from the early postclassic period.

of the Maya accomplishment is indisputable, but what did it mean? What was it like to be a Maya? How did they see their world?

If we are ever able to read their inscriptions we may come closer to an answer. For the present the Maya remain one of history's enigmas. They took one of the world's most unpromising environments—the evergreen tropical rain forest—and built within it some of the world's most remarkable structures. But the forest has since swallowed nearly all traces of them, and only their memory, incomplete as it is, remains.

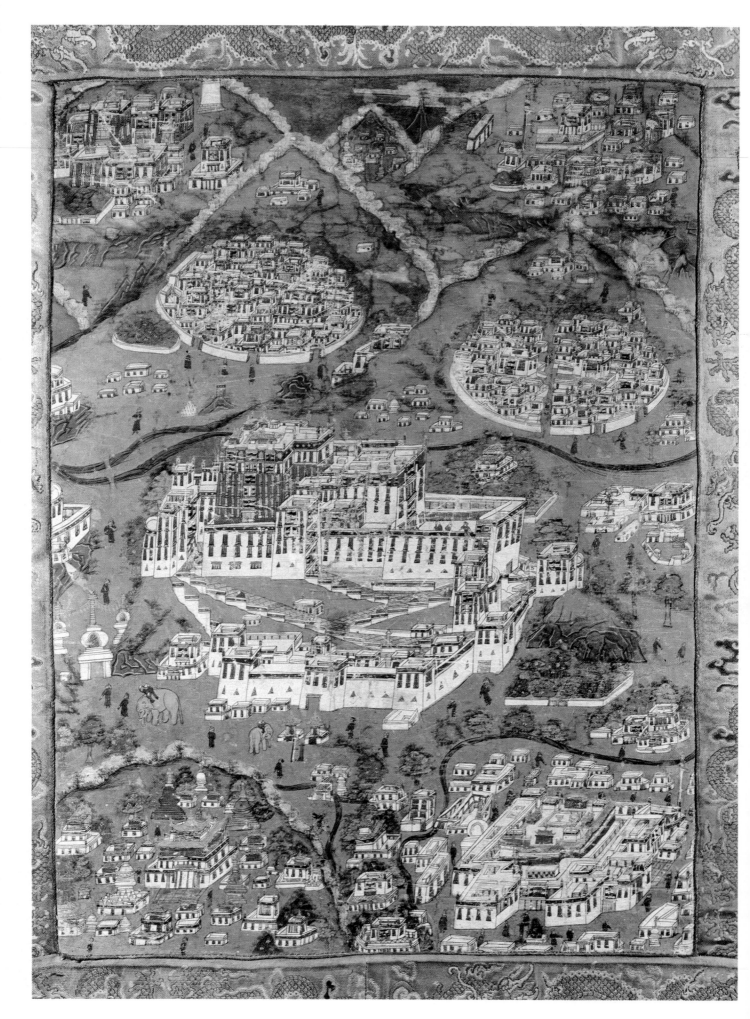

Chapter 9
The Inaccessible Land

The first the Western world heard of Tibet was a rumor of a strange people whose priests wore black robes, never married, and performed rites similar to Christian baptism, confession, and communion. Could it be a lost Christian colony? In the 17th century Jesuit missionaries working in northern India became the first Europeans to penetrate the dangerous mountain passes which guarded Tibet. Later they were followed by adventurers, merchants, and soldiers. All were received without enthusiasm—some were immediately sent away. A few were never heard of again. What is Tibet really like? How do its people manage to live in the lap of the Himalayas? What is life there like now, behind the Chinese "bamboo curtain"?

The Dalai Lama was dead. Monks searching for his new incarnation fanned out over the countryside and discreetly consulted with local oracles both within and beyond the political boundaries of Tibet itself. In accordance with tradition a regent was assigned to rule until the new Dalai Lama (priest-king) had reached his majority. The regent went to the mystical lake of Lhamo Latso, two or three days' journey southeast of the capital city of Lhasa. The first Dalai Lama was said to have had a vision in which he was told that his patron goddess, the guardian of this sacred lake, would always watch over his successors. So now this particular regent traveled through the mountains to the lake far above the tree line, where the barren ground slopes down to the water's edge and only an occasional boulder breaks through the delicate dusting of snow. On reaching the lake the regent sat and quietly stared into its clear depths, waiting. Deep beneath the surface was a kind of shimmering. It cleared, and on the surface of the water a reflection appeared. It was not a reflection of the mountain peaks surrounding Lhamo Latso—instead it was a typical landscape of eastern Tibet near the Chinese border. The waters shimmered again and, when they cleared, a picture formed of a typical peasant homestead with a stone wall around it. The wall was broken by a gate which led into an inner courtyard, and in the courtyard was a mottled brown and white dog.

On his return to Lhasa the regent was unsurprised to hear that one of the search parties, headed by a revered abbot, had found

Opposite: the Potala, residence of the Dalai Lama in the Tibetan capital of Lhasa. This painting, done in the 13th century, shows the original Potala. In the mid-17th century the fifth Dalai Lama had it razed to the ground and built a new and grander edifice in its place. The new building was the one that was seen and admired by the missionaries and explorers of the 1700s and 1800s. The later Potala served the same functions as its predecessor—palace, monastery, and well-defended fortress.

A Mountain Stronghold

Opposite above: caravan of traders in Ladakh making their way through the mountains. The difficult terrain such caravans had to negotiate can be seen here. Even in summer the mountains are covered with snow, and huge glaciers continually grind down into the valleys.

Below: Tibet surrounded by its neighbors, China and India.

the reincarnated Dalai Lama in eastern Tibet, at a homestead surrounded by a stone wall and guarded by a brown and white dog. The little boy was only four years old but had instantly recognized the abbot, who was disguised as a servant. The boy had surprised everyone—not least his family—by proving himself knowledgeable in the official court language, which nobody in his remote village had ever heard before. The child was shown two sets of prayer beads, one of which had belonged to the previous Dalai Lama. He immediately snatched at that set, claiming that it was his and asking how the abbot had acquired it.

The signs and omens all seemed favorable; the child seemed quick and bright. But other candidates had also been produced by other teams of searchers, and in a matter of such importance no chances could be taken. A lottery, consecrated by a special ceremony, was held in which a number of names were carefully entered on fluttering pieces of paper. When one was drawn it bore the name of the four-year-old child from Tsinghai province, China.

This was in 1939. He was enthroned in 1940, but 20 years later Bstan-'dzin-rgya-mtsho took off his splendid robes, left his gold-encrusted private apartments, and, disguised as a simple monk, escaped from Lhasa and the ruling Chinese Communist forces across the border into India. There he has remained ever since with a group of followers, waiting to return to his people and his mysterious land.

Tibet has always been a mysterious and hidden land—perhaps never more so than today, when it is firmly included within Chinese territorial boundaries, and the mountain passes are efficiently guarded by Chinese military units who permit no traffic except with China itself. Tibet's first line of defense against

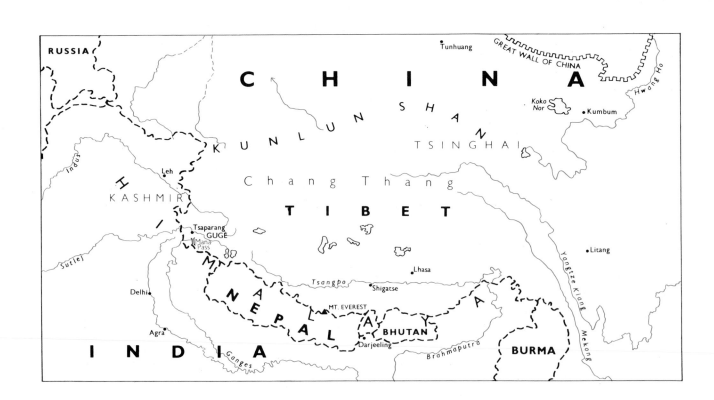

a predatory world has always been geographic. The narrow river valleys which shelter nearly all its people lie within a formidable circle of mountains. The Himalaya range curves around to the south (Mount Everest itself is on the Tibetan–Nepalese border), and the Kunlun range guards the north. Just south of the Kunlun mountains is a high, rocky plain called Chang Thang, which accounts for nearly half the area of Tibet. But Chang Thang is barren, with virtually no rain or snow, and it is inhabited only by scattered nomadic herdsmen who move their flocks of sheep from one sparse grazing area to another. Between Chang Thang and the long lowland valleys of southern Tibet lie still more mountains. The first Tibetans settled in the protected valleys that slope down to the Tsangpo river. They were probably nomadic people from central Asia who over the centuries made their way through the high mountain passes.

In about the 5th century A.D. the small local groups were united by a single dynamic chief, Songtsen Gampo, who is generally considered the first Tibetan king. A man of varied and unexpected talents, Songtsen Gampo managed to extend Tibetan influence northeast toward China. Alarmed, the Chinese sent him an ambassador, of whom Songtsen Gampo demanded a Chinese princess as a wife. When the Chinese refused he led his armies to the very frontiers of what was then China, past the

Below: the present Dalai Lama (sixth from the left) with his Khamba warrior guard in exile in India. Their weapons vary from flintlocks with fixed bayonets to modern submachine guns.

Above: lamas wearing aprons made of human bones. The Tibetans' traditional attitude toward the physical remains of their dead was one aspect of Tibetan culture that many outsiders found hard to accept. The lamas, grouped into monasteries, owned much of the arable land, which was farmed by peasant tenants.

brackish lake Koko Nor and toward the Great Wall itself. The Chinese emperor capitulated and a princess, Wen Cheng, was dispatched to Tibet.

Wen Cheng brought more than prestige to the Tibetan court. She was a Buddhist, and she brought with her to Lhasa her priests and teachers and an enormous statue of the Buddha made of a mysterious alloy of gold, silver, and bronze which was said to have been miraculously created. (It is still in Tibet, in the temple built to honor the princess' arrival.) Buddhism had already reached Tibet from India, but strengthened by Wen Cheng and another Buddhist royal wife, a Nepalese princess, it began to have a noticeable impact on the traditional Tibetan shamanistic faith known as Bon. Over the centuries imported Buddhism and

Land of Monks and Monasteries

Above left: a lamasery of Likir in Ladakh. Endowed with a splendid view of the valley spread out below and the snowcapped mountains in the distance, it still looks as it did centuries ago.

indigenous Bon formed a singular amalgam to produce the distinctive Tibetan Buddhism sometimes called Lamaism.

In Tibet Buddhism was securely rooted in royal patronage; in Europe Christianity was similarly propagated and firmly established by emperors who were converted to the faith. Between the 10th and the 15th centuries social and cultural developments in Tibet and Europe were broadly similar: in both, the hierarchy of the church played a pervasive role in secular affairs, and religion shaped the everyday life of ordinary people. But in Europe the 15th century saw the beginnings of the Renaissance and the regeneration of knowledge in practically every sphere of human activity. There was no Renaissance in Tibet. The best way to minimize the intrusion of Tibet's more powerful neighbors was to remain aloof; the best way to remain distinctively Tibetan was to remain a backwater. Locked behind formidable mountains Tibet chose to go its own way.

Life centered around the monasteries. Much of the arable land was owned by the communities of monks (although it was actually farmed by their tenants), and roughly a fifth of the population were attached to monasteries. A huge gulf separated the nobility, which provided the civil service, and the peasants. Every lay official had a monastic counterpart. The most powerful monasteries—those with great houses, vast lands, and traditional prerogatives—wielded enormous influence. Most were ruled by abbots who were often believed to be incarnate lamas descended from the original founders of the monasteries.

This concept was based on the Buddhist belief that for a monk the highest ideal is to achieve the possibility of permanent release from life's sufferings (roughly the state called Nirvana) and then to renounce it in order to return to life for the benefit of others. Sometimes this return becomes a regular and recognizable series of rebirths in human form, as for the Dalai Lama. The abbot of an ordinary monastery, however, is considered to be a lesser level of incarnation. The Dalai Lama is believed to be a living incarnation of Buddha in his aspect of Changchub Sempa, the patron deity of Tibet. The present Dalai Lama is the fourteenth: the first Dalai Lama to be recognized as such was Bsod-nams-rgya-mtsho, the third hierarch of the Yellow Hat sect, who lived in the 16th century. His two predecessors were then also retrospectively declared to have been the Dalai Lama.

A Lost Colony of Christians?

Above: contemporary portrait of Antonio de Andrade (1580?–1634), a Portuguese priest living in northern India, who was convinced that hidden in the valleys of the Himalayas were pockets of forgotten Christians. He became one of the first Europeans to reach Tibet.

By the time of the third Dalai Lama the balance of power in Tibet had shifted decisively from the monarchy toward the great monastic establishments. Political events had aided this development: the Tibetans had escaped the terrible ravages of the hordes of Genghis Khan during his westward march by meeting his representatives at their border and there accepting Mongol overlordship. In return, the Buddhist Mongols accepted Tibetan lamas as their religious teachers, evolving a patron/priest relationship which strengthened the power of the lamas at home as well.

It was about the time of the third Dalai Lama that stories of a strange land locked behind the mountains began to drift down to the Portuguese Jesuit missionaries then busy establishing the first Christian outposts in India and China. For centuries a series of rumors had gone around Europe of a Christian king—Prester John—who was supposed to rule a fabulously wealthy Christian kingdom somewhere in the East. In fact, when the first reports of the Mongol advance across Asia reached Christendom, some hoped that the Mongols might in fact be the forces of Prester John, waging a holy war against Islam. When it became painfully clear that the Mongols did not intend to spare the eastern Christian lands any more than they had the lands of the unbelievers, such optimism was regretfully abandoned, but the idea of a hidden Christian kingdom persisted. Therefore, when the Jesuits in India heard of this place called Tibet, where priests wore black robes, never married, and performed rites which sounded very similar to baptism, confession, and communion, the Europeans were tantalized by the idea that behind those mountains might be the lost Christian colony.

The most determined was Antonio de Andrade, a Portuguese priest who was working in northern India in the early 1620s. When he encountered a Hindu pilgrim caravan in Delhi about to depart for a holy shrine near the Tibetan border, Andrade disguised himself as a Hindu and, with a similarly disguised lay brother, Manuel Marques, joined the pilgrims. It was an arduous journey, and the difficulties increased as they moved higher into the mountains. The caravan crept up a narrow path which sometimes became a mere ledge only inches wide, when they were forced to cling to the edge of a cliff hundreds of feet above a roaring river.

When they reached the Hindu shrine the two Jesuits paused only long enough to observe the sacred hot springs. While the rest of the pilgrim caravan worshiped, the Jesuits pressed on to the Tibetan border. Traveling without the protection of a caravan, tormented by snow-blindness and cold so bitter that Andrade lost part of one finger and only discovered it when he noticed the stump bleeding profusely, they finally crossed the Mana Pass into Tibet. They were the first Europeans to reach the hidden land.

They found themselves in the small Tibetan state of Guge, in the town of Tsaparang, far to the west of Lhasa. Although Andrade was disappointed in his hopes of discovering fellow Christians—he described the local lamas as "souls bred in laziness"—he found the local ruler surprisingly receptive to his message. Although the Jesuits had to return to India almost immediately before the pass was closed by autumn snows,

Andrade promised to return the next year. A local war delayed him, though, and it was not until 1624 that Andrade was able to reach Tsaparang again, where he opened a mission. The ruler himself paid for a permanent church a year later, which was built next to his palace for "the lamas of the West."

The mission thrived for several years, but shortly after Andrade left in 1630, to become Jesuit superior at Goa, the local lamas overthrew the impressionable ruler, sacked the church, virtually imprisoned the Jesuits in residence, and sold their converts into slavery. When Andrade heard of the catastrophe he dispatched another priest to Tsaparang, but, although he was successful in winning the release of the Christian slaves, the local people were too frightened of the lamas to respond to the re-

Above: detail from a 17th-century painting showing the Portuguese colony of Goa off the west coast of India. The vignette at the top shows St. Francis Xavier arriving at the colony, which became the headquarters of Jesuit missionary work in this part of Asia. Andrade left Tibet to become an abbot at a monastery in Goa.

maining missionaries. The Tsaparang mission was abandoned altogether in 1635.

It was nearly 30 years before other Europeans reached Tibet, and when they did they came from China. By the 1650s Dutch merchants had broken the previous Portuguese monopoly on trade with Asia, and the sea routes to China had become increasingly hazardous for Portuguese ships. Faced with the problem of maintaining contact with their headquarters in Rome, in 1661 the Jesuit mission in Peking sent two young priests to discover an overland route to Europe. Although both John Grueber, an Austrian, and Albert d'Orville, a Belgian, were trained geographers, like all Europeans they knew very little about central Asia. It seemed that a route through Tibet to India might shorten a journey known to be long and dangerous, and so after leaving China by way of Hsi-ning, a frontier city on the Great Wall, they turned southwest toward Tibet. Beyond the Wall was the desert; beyond that, mountains and high barren plains; and beyond that, towering mountain ranges guarded Tibet itself. It took them three months of continuous travel— long days of riding, long nights of fitful sleep, during which they were always watching for the bandits who might sweep down upon a caravan—to reach Lhasa.

Their most striking initial impression was of the improbable Potala hill, which rises abruptly at the edge of Lhasa and is crowned by an enormous palace, the residence of the Dalai Lama. The palace was newly built when Grueber and d'Orville reached Lhasa. It was the work of a remarkable individual, the fifth Dalai Lama, who is still known to his people as the Great Fifth. In secular matters he was a skilled military leader and politician who completed the final unification of all the small states of Tibet under a single government and then managed to thread his way through both Mongol and Chinese political maneuvers to emerge successfully as the sole secular ruler of an independent Tibet. As a religious leader he was no less over-

Right: letter given by Simon da Cunha, resident in Japan, to John Grueber and Bernard Diestel, charging them with finding a land route from Peking to Europe. The Jesuits used these letters as licenses or passports. In the lower lefthand corner d'Orville's name was substituted for Diestel's when the latter died before the mission began. In the lower righthand corner Henri Roth's name is substituted for d'Orville's after his death in Agra in 1662.

Two Europeans Reach Lhasa

Left: engraving of the Potala in Lhasa, made in 1667 from sketches drawn by Grueber when he was there.

whelming. He reorganized monastic life so that his own reform Yellow Hat sect was clearly in the ascendant, although the traditionalist Red Hats continued to follow their beliefs unmolested, and he centralized the control of both religious and secular life under his own leadership. Wishing to honor his tutor, the fifth Dalai Lama declared him an incarnate lama as well and ordained him Panchen Lama. His seat was at Shigatse, and his position was second only to that of the Dalai Lama himself. From that time onward when the Panchen Lama died a search was instigated to find his new incarnation in the same way as for the successor to the Dalai Lama. One of the two hierarchs would always perform the initiation for the other.

When Grueber and d'Orville reached Lhasa Tibet was basking in power, security, and new-found internal unity. The Jesuits were fascinated, if often appalled, by Tibetan life. They found the obeisance shown to the Dalai Lama particularly shocking: such reverence, they felt, was due only to the Catholic pope. Like other visitors through the centuries, they remarked on the brilliance of the courtiers and the lack of personal cleanliness of ordinary Tibetans, a characteristic which has been explained as an adaptation to the high altitude, where ultraviolet rays attack skin not protected by a rich layer of natural oils and accompanying grime. Whatever the reason, both the grubbiness and the pervasive aroma of yak butter have often been noted.

Grueber and d'Orville were, however, greatly impressed by the richness of the Potala. Like their Jesuit predecessors, they were struck by the similarities between Christianity and Tibetan Buddhism, but unlike Andrade they did not linger to establish a mission. Their duty was to find an overland route to Europe, and after a short rest stay they continued south to Nepal. In 1662 at Agra, in India, d'Orville died, exhausted by his travels. Grueber pressed on, and he finally did reach Rome.

The "Merry One"

Above: wooden figure of the chief lama of Bhutan, a member of the traditional Red Hat sect. While Desideri was in Lhasa the Yellow Hat reformists, a Mongol prince called Latsang, and the Red Hats became locked in a power struggle which led to the intervention of the Dzungar Mongols.

Their route was clearly too difficult to be used regularly, though, and no other missionaries followed in their footsteps through Lhasa. But the Jesuits in Goa still cherished the dream of a permanent mission there, and in 1715, over 50 years after Grueber and d'Orville's visit, another pair of missionaries set out northward from Delhi to the mountain ramparts of Tibet.

Their names were Emanuel Freyre and Ippolito Desideri, and they were an ill-matched pair. Freyre, a Portuguese Jesuit in his late 50s, was crotchety, sour, and less than enthusiastic about leaving his work of 20 years in the Indian plains. His companion was a young Italian priest, 30 years of age, who volunteered for the mission while still in Europe. Although Freyre was the elder and nominal leader, Desideri was clearly the driving force.

Desideri had come out to India specifically for his Tibetan mission, and he joined Freyre in Delhi. Rather than follow Andrade's grueling route, they decided to enter Tibet by way of Kashmir, a longer but somewhat easier approach. Even so, Desideri compared their climb through the mountains to a march up "staircases piled one on top of another," made of ice "resembling marble in hardness." Freyre seems to have been timid by nature, and he viewed most of their hardships as personal affronts. No sooner had they reached Leh in Ladakh (now a district of Kashmir but then considered part of Tibet itself), where Desideri had intended to set up the first mission, than Freyre insisted that he would return to India even if he had to go alone. Rather than return the way they had come, Freyre proposed to find an alternative route through eastern Tibet. Unwilling to let his elderly companion struggle back on his own, Desideri reluctantly left Leh with him.

The two made their way with considerable difficulty to the edge of the barren Chang Thang plain. There they were able to join a caravan bound for Lhasa—the captain of which was a charming Mongol princess. She was the first aspect of Tibet that old Freyre approved of, and his report of the journey is full of her kindness. She even saved his life. Freyre, apparently traveling at the back of the caravan, discovered that his horse was dying from the altitude and looked·up to find himself alone in the bitterly cold darkness. The princess (alerted by Desideri, who had belatedly realized his companion had fallen behind) sent riders back to search for him. They found him huddled for warmth next to the belly of his dead horse, weak from exposure but vigorously indignant. The old priest was bundled up and brought to the camp where the solicitous princess nursed his weary body and soothed his aggrieved spirit. Shortly afterward the caravan entered Lhasa, and within a few days Freyre, after a dour look around, left for Nepal on his way back to India. Desideri cannot have regretted seeing him go.

Desideri himself was fascinated with Lhasa. After Freyre left he was the only European in the city—a Capuchin mission had been established in 1708, but the friars had been withdrawn four years later. He found the political situation in Tibet very complicated. The Great Fifth Dalai Lama had died, but his grand vizier (suspected to be his bastard son) had managed to hide the fact of his death for several years. The search for the sixth Dalai Lama therefore did not begin until nine years after his presumed birth, and the boy was not finally identified until he was at least 12 years old. Whether because of his late entry into monastic discipline or because he was simply unsuitable, the sixth Dalai Lama did not work out as expected, and he was never ordained a monk. A poet of considerable gifts, his most notable and spectacular characteristic was his love of women. Before the coming of the Chinese in 1951 some brothels in Lhasa were still painted yellow in proud memory of the time when the sixth Dalai Lama had visited them himself.

In spite of his unorthodox behavior he was loved by his people—he is still spoken of as the "Merry One"—but the long gap between the death of the Great Fifth and the sixth's assumption of power had permitted a Mongol prince, Latsang, to install himself as king and assume secular supremacy with the backing of the Chinese Manchu emperor. The Yellow Hats resented the king's power, and in this situation the king found the popularity of the "Merry Sixth" a thorn in his side.

What happened next, like so much in Tibet, is ambiguous and subject to several interpretations. Latsang apparently sent the Merry Sixth on a journey to China and arranged that an assassination would be attempted at Litang, just short of the Chinese border. On the other hand, some Tibetans believe the sixth Dalai Lama simply chose to disappear at Litang and spent the rest of his life as a holy beggar. In any case, Latsang declared him dead and—without following any of the traditional rules for finding a new incarnation—boldly produced a 25-year-old monk as the new Dalai Lama, a "true sixth" to replace the dissolute pretender. The enraged Tibetans (particularly the Yellow Hat lamas) adamantly refused to accept his candidate and, using their usual methods, discovered a new incarnation, a seventh Dalai Lama, near Litang itself. Latsang countered this move by having the Chinese kidnap the child and take him into China.

It was at this point that Desideri arrived in Lhasa. Obviously more used to kings than Dalai Lamas, Desideri was impressed by Latsang, who listened to his message sympathetically and granted him permission to establish a mission. The priest had high hopes that Latsang himself would accept Christianity, and he learned Tibetan so that he could produce a long treatise which he hoped would convert the king. The king read it and then made a proposition: Desideri would take part in a public debate with leading lamas in which Christianity and Buddhism could be publicly compared. To prepare for this, he suggested, Desideri should enter a Tibetan monastery and learn the dogma and traditions of his opponents. Desideri eagerly accepted.

The proposition was made primarily for diplomatic purposes. Latsang had other, more pressing problems, and whereas he felt it unwise to offend a foreigner of unknown influence, he was not particularly concerned about religious debate. His Yellow Hat opponents had sought outside aid from the Dzungar Mongols, who lived in the northern part of what is now Sinkiang province in China. While Desideri watched, fascinated but helpless, from his monastery, the Mongols, supported by many Tibetan monks, stormed through the mountain ramparts at Lhasa, where they seized the Potala and killed Latsang before he could escape from the city.

Above: a modern young incarnate lama of the Yellow Hat sect. He is the seventeenth in a line of lama heads of the Kye monastery in Spiti, on the border between Tibet and Ladakh in Kashmir. Tibetans believe that when any great lama dies his soul is immediately reborn in another body, and a search is undertaken for the reborn leader.

When the Yellow Hats and their Mongol allies had triumphed an unpleasant interval followed, during which the Mongols looted Lhasa and the Yellow Hats fell upon their Red Hat rivals. Desideri, associated with the former king, was in considerable danger and fled to a monastery several days' journey from the capital. Meanwhile the Chinese, disinclined to accept calmly an extension of Mongol power which might contribute to a unification of the Mongols—and thus a direct threat to China itself—took a hand. Before his death Latsang had appealed to the Chinese emperor for aid, who dispatched an army. But bad logistical planning and the rigors of the desert crossing broke the strength of the Chineses forces, and the survivors were encircled and massacred by the Mongols. The emperor promptly sent a much larger force to avenge the first, and in the vanguard was the young seventh Dalai Lama, included in order to convince the Tibetan people that the Chinese wanted to restore the old order and drive out the alien Mongols.

As the Chinese advanced orders were given under the name of the Dalai Lama that all Tibetan men over the age of 12 should join the invading force (even Desideri in his monastery was drafted, but he was exempted at the last moment). After four days of battle with the ferocious Mongols, who were unable to retreat but scorned surrender, the Chinese were triumphant. As promised the Dalai Lama was restored to his throne and the alien Mongols were evicted—but in their place were installed two Chinese *ambans*, or political residents, who were to remain in Lhasa, backed by a permanent Chinese military garrison, to protect the emperor's interests.

Desideri himself was unable to stay in Tibet. In Rome the Tibetan mission was assigned to the Capuchin order, which claimed priority on the basis of its previous mission. In 1721 Desideri reluctantly left for India, and the Capuchins reestab-

Below: outsiders were unwelcome in Tibet under the Chinese ambans. This sketch was made by one of two Europeans who, disguised as Indian fakirs, attempted to infiltrate the mysterious Himalayan kingdom.

lished their mission. It was tolerated for 20 years by the suspicious lamas (and even more wary Chinese) for the medical work they performed, but increasing hostility forced the dwindling mission to close in 1745. For Europeans, the door to mysterious Tibet swung firmly shut.

Before Manchu authority had been established in Lhasa, Tibet's mysteries had been protected by her inaccessibility: if an enterprising foreigner succeeded in conquering her guardian mountains—as did Andrade and the others—he was greeted with courtesy and polite interest. Now Tibet's isolation became a matter of policy. Below on the plains of India first the Portuguese and then the British were making their influence strongly felt. The Chinese, wary of any encroachment on their territory, saw the Himalayan mountains of Tibet as the outermost ring of their own defense, which they were unlikely to open to any interloper. Under normal circumstances the Chinese ambans did not intervene in Tibetan affairs, but implicit in their presence was the threat of Manchu power, and any dealings with foreigners immediately attracted their suspicious attention.

This the British discovered when, in 1774, the East India Company sent a young Scot named George Bogle to Tibet to investigate the possibility of opening trade. By the time of Bogle's visit the seventh Dalai Lama had died, and since his successor chose to lead a contemplative life, all administrative power was left to his regent (under the watchful eyes of the ambans). Most of Bogle's dealings, therefore, were with the sixth Panchen Lama, who was a vigorous person with sufficient autonomy to deal directly with Bogle up to a point. The Panchen Lama himself apparently favored trade, or at least some contact with the British, but his freedom of action was circumscribed by the Chinese in Lhasa. He clearly liked Bogle, who seems to have been a personable young man, and during the six months that Bogle remained in Tibet a warm friendship grew up between the two. But the authorities in Lhasa never relented, and in the end Bogle left Tibet and his friend the Panchen Lama without a trade agreement.

One result of his stay there, however, was a lively set of progress reports which he sent to his superiors in India. Bogle's descriptions of Tibet show him to have been a keen observer with a willingness to comprehend the Tibetan motives for customs which appeared extremely bizarre. Earlier visitors had reported their macabre method of disposing of the dead: bodies were taken to a nearby mountain where they were cut into small pieces to be devoured by birds and wild beasts. Bogle commented that, because there was little wood in the country, cremation (practiced in other Buddhist areas) was impractical. He was even prepared to explain the Tibetan aversion to washing, on the grounds that getting wet was "uncomfortable in this cold climate." He remarked on the Tibetan custom of polyandry, in which several brothers married the same woman, but he apparently did not recognize it as a way of keeping property together. All the brothers and their wife lived on the land they inherited from their parents, and if one brother chose to leave and take a wife of his own he lost his rights to any of his father's land. Bogle called the system "women's revenge."

The First Briton Explores Tibet

Above: George Bogle (1746–1781), chosen by Warren Hastings of the East India Company to be the first British envoy to Tibet in 1774. He became a close friend of the Panchen Lama, but could not form a British-Tibetan trade agreement because of the unwillingness of the Chinese in Lhasa.

The Great Survey

Despite Bogle's charm and intelligence, however, the Chinese remained implacably opposed to any Tibetan association with the British. Other envoys continued to try in successive years, but the response continued to be negative.

In 1845 two French missionaries, Evarist Huc and Joseph Gabet, reached Tibet from China disguised as lamas. They arrived at Kumbum, a Buddhist sanctuary in northeastern Tibet, where they abandoned their disguise, and from there they proceeded to Lhasa. There they were viewed with suspicion but were taken to the regent (the Dalai Lama at the time was a young child), who was quite taken with the foreigners and their modern marvels. The regent was particularly fascinated by a microscope, which made a louse plucked from the silk robes of a lama appear as big as a rat. Nevertheless the Chinese were as disapproving as ever, and rather than provoke a crisis between the regent and the ambans the two missionaries took their leave.

But Tibet was too important strategically to be left alone. Manchu power was on the wane in central Asia, and both Russia and Great Britain were eager to fill the vacuum; each suspected the ambitions of the other. The British, at work on their Great Trigonometrical Survey of India during the entire 19th century, managed to infiltrate Tibet with specially trained native surveyors known as *pundits*. They were taught to walk in exactly measured paces and to use various surveying instruments, which were ingeniously disguised and hidden in their belongings. The pundits were given code names and were sent out to survey the forbidden territory. In a narrow sense their activities were not political: the only mysteries they set out to expose were geographical. The Tibetans, however, viewed their work as acts of

Below: drawing by a British Survey officer, J. B. Bellasis, of himself conducting a survey from a camp in India. The British East India Company had begun the process in the mid-18th century, when it began extending its control over the entire subcontinent of India.

Left: map of 1876 taken from a report of the Great Trigonometrical Survey, showing the scale of the undertaking.

Below: Kishen Singh, the pundit code-named Krishna. He marched from Kashmir to the Chinese frontier at Sachu, arriving at the Survey office in Darjeeling, in north-eastern India, almost five years later. He had accurately charted 2800 miles of incredibly difficult mountain terrain.

straightforward espionage, and the fate of a captured pundit was not a pleasant one. Those who succeeded did so brilliantly.

One of the most notable was code-named Krishna, or A.K., who performed the magnificent feat of marching from Kashmir, through Lhasa and across Chang Thang, to the Chinese frontier at Tunharang. He finally appeared at the Survey office in Darjeeling five years later. Neither his pace-counting, for which he used the Survey's specially adapted prayer beads, nor his calculations of position ever faltered in all that time, so that after walking 2800 miles across the highest mountain terrain in the world, he was only 9.5 miles south and 2.5 miles west of his own estimated position.

While the British were mapping Tibet with the information brought back by the pundits, the Russians were probing her northern frontiers. The noted geographer Nikolai Przhevalski made four attempts to reach Lhasa between 1871 and 1885 but each time was turned back by the wary Tibetans. Russia's most successful attempt to influence Tibet was made by a Buriat-Mongol from southeastern Siberia named Arguan Dorjiev, who had worked for the czar before going to Tibet. In 1885 Dorjiev, who had been trained as a Buddhist monk, became the tutor and companion of the young thirteenth Dalai Lama, and he managed to persuade his student that the czar was actually a Buddhist at heart. He further convinced the young man that only Russia was in a position to defend Tibet from the pressures of Britain on the one hand and China on the other. By 1902 the Dalai Lama was thinking of visiting St. Petersburg, and plans were being drawn up to link Tibet to Russia with a branch of the Trans-Siberian Railroad.

Above: Younghusband's 1904 expedition with part of his mule train. He had left India with 7000 mules and 5000 bullocks.

This was more than the British would tolerate. In 1903 Lord Curzon, the aggressive viceroy of British India, sent a military mission to Lhasa to force the Dalai Lama to renounce his Russian affiliations. The expedition was to be a last thrust of British imperial power. Francis Younghusband, the young British officer who was chosen to head the mission, was both direct and unyielding, and when the Tibetans refused to negotiate with him at Lhasa his army mowed down their soldiers with rifles. The British marched into Lhasa on August 2, 1904. The Dalai Lama fled into Mongolia with his tutor, so it was his resentful regent, disillusioned that the Russians had not come to his aid, who capitulated to the British.

Ironically, Younghusband and Curzon had gained more than the British wanted. There was no practical way to maintain communication links to India for a permanent garrison in Tibet, and in any case such British dominion over Tibet would upset the delicate central Asian balance of power. Therefore Britain agreed with Russia that China would have full sovereignty over the kingdom, since its collapsing Manchu dynasty presented no threat to anyone. By 1907 the treaty had been signed by Russia and Britain, and the great powers turned their attention elsewhere.

The embittered Tibetans, handed around like a bag of laundry, held their peace. In 1910 the Dalai Lama returned to Lhasa; in 1912, a year after the Republican Revolution swept the Manchu dynasty out of power, Tibet declared its independence. The thirteenth Dalai Lama ruled until his death in 1933; in 1939 his successor, the fourteenth, was proclaimed; and in 1951 the

Right: the last meeting. The Tibetans came to Younghusband's tent in a cavalcade for a final 'palaver," at which time they reiterated their request that he retreat to Yatung where they would negotiate. The British insisted on being allowed into Lhasa, and this led to the clash on the Guru plain.

The Younghusband Expedition-1904

Left: photograph of the thirteenth Dalai Lama (1876–1933) at the age of 24. Four years later he was forced to flee to Mongolia with his tutor, the Russian agent Dorjiev, as Younghusband's British forces approached the Tibetan capital of Lhasa.

Chinese Communists came, and nothing was the same again.

What is Tibet like now? It is difficult to know. There is no shortage of reports—they range from searing tales of oppression from Tibetan refugees, most of whom had belonged to the monasteries or the nobility, to uplifting accounts of the emancipation of subjugated peasants from Chinese sympathizers who have been permitted to visit the new Tibet. The reality, as usual, probably lies between the two extremes. Even the original reason for the Chinese invasion (or, as the Communists claim, the Chinese reappearance) is debatable. Pro-Western commentators claim that China wished to secure her own southern border, as

Tibet-Pawn in the Power Game

Right: Lhasa today as the capital of the Autonomous Region of Tibet.

Below: a Chinese soldier and a Tibetan peasant working together in modern Tibet, whose mountain scenery remains essentially unchanged since before Andrade's time despite massive political and religious upheavals.

she had tried to do for centuries; pro-Chinese observers claim that Tibet had always been part of China, and that because American agitators were threatening to detach Tibet entirely, Mao Tse-tung resolved to liberate the area from the dangers of foreign influence.

Tibetan armies were then either defeated or "won over by the extraordinarily good behavior of the Red armies," depending upon the viewpoint. In 1959 an uprising was attempted, and the Dalai Lama, who until then had cooperated with the Chinese, had to flee to India. Since then Tibet has been deliberately and systematically incorporated into the Chinese nation. Buddhism, for so many centuries the central pattern of life, has been replaced by Communism and the thoughts of Chairman Mao. Some of the peasants, who for centuries were subject to the monasteries, undoubtedly feel that life has improved. Others may experience much of the same personal misery under their new masters, but bereft of the religion that once sustained them. A considerable number of Chinese now live in Tibet—it is im-

THE INACCESSIBLE LAND

Above: part of a network of highways, covering more than 7000 miles, that has been built in Tibet since it became part of China. According to the Chinese, this has altered the former inaccessibility of Tibet by linking the country more firmly to China. However, it is still difficult for non-Chinese to penetrate its mountain barriers. ·

possible to say exactly how many, as there are no statistics—and they are attempting to raise the Tibetan standard of living. Roads have been built; peasants are becoming factory workers; literacy rates are rising. It is claimed that the Chinese are teaching the young Tibetans to wash—not even the Red Guards can induce the older people to bathe.

From his exile in India the fourteenth Dalai Lama has declared a new constitution for Tibet which would correct some of the worst abuses of monastic power. Since, as his predecessors discovered in the past, the outside world shows little enthusiasm for coming to Tibet's aid except in order to promote outside interests, it seems unlikely that the Dalai Lama will ever be in a position to implement his reforms. A whole generation of Tibetans has now grown up under Communism; whether they would welcome a return to religious rule is certainly open to question. For centuries the secluded land of Tibet has been a puzzle to those outside its frontiers. Behind the "bamboo wall" it is now more of an enigma than ever.

Chapter 10
The Forbidden City

Surrounded by the emptiness of the Arabian desert, the holy city of Mecca has been a magnet for Western adventurers through the centuries. Since the time of Muhammad no non-Muslim has been permitted to enter the sacred city of Mecca—even today infidels may not pass the stone gateposts 15 miles away. A pilgrimage to its shrine, the Kaaba, is an important spiritual obligation for every follower of Islam. The lure of the forbidden has combined with the attraction of mystery and remoteness to draw travelers and adventurers, who risk death if detected. What is Mecca really like? What was reported by the disguised Europeans who ventured beyond its stone pillars? Is Mecca today still a forbidden city?

Mecca lies on the barren Arabian plateau, parts of which are composed of hard, gravelly clay while others are soft and treacherous. The sun is hot and terrible; when the humid air of the Red Sea coast meets the hot, dry central Arabian atmosphere electric storms are often generated, and lightning sometimes leaps from mountaintop to mountaintop in spectacular displays that last for hours. Only seldom do these storms bring any rain to the dry earth. Occasionally in winter a sudden cloudburst will pour rain down the arid gullies to wash away whatever lies in its path and then disappear quickly into the desert sands.

Normally, however, the Meccan plateau is parched and rainless, and the mere presence of water is a miracle. The town that is now Mecca began to form around a well, believed to be a particularly remarkable well even in a land where any well is notable. The tradition is that this well was a special gift from God, for here, after Abraham had cast her out with only a small supply of water, the handmaiden Hagar had searched unavailingly for water for their baby son. Eventually she hid him away so that she would not have to watch him die of thirst. Despairing, she cried out to God, who heard her. She "opened her eyes, and she saw a well of water; and she went, and filled the bottle with water, and gave the lad drink." The well still exists in Mecca, and the Arabs trace their descent from that boy in the desert, Abraham's son Ishmael.

Probably it was the well that first attracted worship, and soon

Opposite: Mecca today. Barred to non-Muslims since the time of Muhammad, Mecca has remained a more religiously oriented city than Jerusalem, for instance. Even as Saudi Arabia becomes more developed, its Muslim leaders remain steadfast in their adherence to ancient Islamic prohibitions against desecration by "infidels."

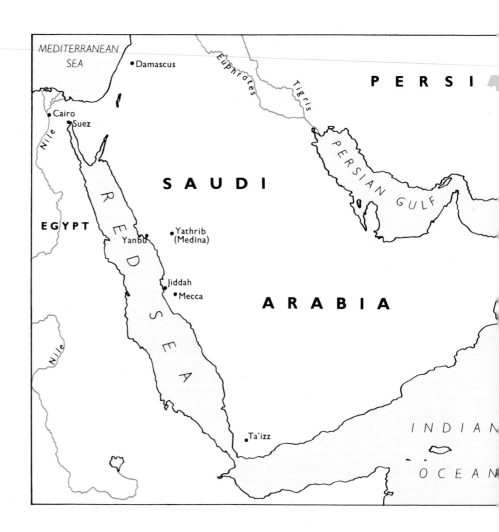

Above: the holy city of Mecca was founded near a well in the midst of the Arabian desert peninsula.

after came the Kaaba (meaning "cube"), which according to tradition was built by Abraham and Ishmael together as a replica of God's house in heaven. It exists today as an austere cube of undressed stone draped by a black cloth, the *kiswah*, which is ornamented with sacred quotations. A particularly holy black stone is set in the eastern corner of the Kaaba and is believed to have been given to Abraham by the angel Gabriel, who also delivered revelations to Muhammad. At one time there was a statue of Abraham in Mecca, along with many others. The Kaaba and Mecca became such popular places of pilgrimage that Greek writers commented on the city's temple, and, during one autumn month, fighting among the local Bedouin tribes was forbidden by mutual consent to enable pilgrims to make their journey in safety. To this day the Muslim lunar calendar still includes that month—the name of which means "forbidden"— as a reminder of the ancient holy truce. By the time Muhammad himself was born, in about 570 A.D., Mecca was already one of the chief cities of Arabia. Two thriving caravan routes passed through the town: one was the spice road from southern Arabia to Syria, and the other connected Persia with the Nile valley in Egypt.

We know practically nothing about Muhammad's early life except that he was well born: he came from the tribe of Quraysh, a leading group in Arabian politics, although his own family belonged to an impoverished branch. His father died before Muhammed was born, and the child was only six when his mother also died. From that time he was raised first by his grandfather, who had been the custodian of the pagan Kaaba, and later by his uncle.

By the time he was 25 years old he was a trader and had earned the nickname "the Reliable" for managing camel caravans for their owners. One of these owners, a wealthy widow named Khadija, was so impressed by the young man that she first made him her business manager and then married him. Although she was 15 years his senior, their marriage seems to have been a happy one, and they had two sons (neither of whom survived infancy) and four daughters. Although polygamy was common in their society, Muhammad did not take another wife until after Khadija's death.

Mecca at this time was a cosmopolitan community including large groups of Jews and Christians, but nonetheless it remained predominantly Arab. The prerogatives of powerful families had increased sufficiently by the 6th century for a structure based on

Mecca and the Rise of Islam

Above: 19th-century engraving of Hagar and Ishmael, illustrating the Old Testament story of Abraham's handmaiden and her desperate need for water for herself and her son.

Left: plan of the Kaaba enclosure in Mecca, painted on a Turkish tile in the 17th century. The Kaaba is the central point of the Muslim pilgrimage to Mecca.

The Life of Muhammad

classes of "haves" and "have-nots" to develop in the town. Muhammad himself probably experienced at least some of the injustices of the system due to the poverty of his family, though as part of an important tribe he was better off than many. As

he grew older, he increasingly often turned his back on the bickering and selfishness of Meccan society and went up into the dry, bleak hills near the town to meditate.

No one knows the precise date, but it is commonly accepted that it was during the month of Ramadan (now the month for ritual Muslim fasting), when Muhammad was about 40 years old, that he was spending the night in a cave and the archangel Gabriel appeared to him in a dream. The angel brought him his first revelation of a monotheistic god who was displeased with the pagan idols of Mecca. Muhammad's first reaction, according to tradition, was terror. He was fearful that he was being possessed, like the soothsayers of the time, by *jinn*, or wandering spirits.

He went home to his wife with the story of his eerie experience and also told her of his misgivings. Khadija reassured him. She herself had been told by a seer that her husband had been visited by the same angel who visited Moses and the Hebrew prophets, and she was immediately convinced of the truth of the message. Muhammad underwent an initial period of soul-searching and hesitation, but when the next revelation came, urging Muhammad to warn others of their iniquities, Muhammad was ready to accept his mission.

All this must have happened in about 610 A.D. The next years were not easy for Muhammad. He preached his message, but at first he could convince only a tiny circle of believers, most of whom were members of his family (his first convert was his wife). Both his insistence on the oneness of God and his attacks on idolatry soon earned him persecution from the trading magnates of Mecca, who derived much of their income from the pilgrim caravans which came to worship the many gods of the Kaaba. In addition, Muhammad's message included a strong emphasis on social reform: the revelations of Allah (the name Muhammad

Above: 16th-century miniature from a Turkish manuscript showing the Prophet Muhammad with some of his first followers —Abu-Bakr, Umar, Osman, and Ali.

Opposite: the birth of Muhammad, illustrated in a manuscript from Turkey painted in the 1500s.

Left: the Kaaba as seen from Mount Keyis, in a photograph taken in 1901.

The Five Pillars

applied to the One God, which had previously meant the supreme pagan god) consistently demanded the exercise of mercy and benevolence as a necessary complement to religious belief. None of these ideas made him popular with the local rulers.

Around 620 the situation deteriorated sharply. When pressure on his family to control their inconvenient relative proved unsuccessful the entire branch to which he belonged was ostracized for two years. Skeptics demanded that if Muhammad were God's prophet he should do miracles, but Muhammad continued to insist that he was only a man, and that miracles were not his mission. His only miracle was the Koran—the collection of his revelations presented in magnificently rhyming, rhythmic Arabic prose. Whether Muhammad was illiterate, as tradition claims, or not, he was certainly not a literary man, and the Koran is by any standards an outstanding literary achievement. But this was not miracle enough for the threatened Meccans.

In 622 Muhammad and his disciples slipped out of town to escape would-be assassins. They fled to Yathrib, a nearby city, whose people had invited the believers in the new Muslim beliefs to come. This migration, or *hegira*, is the most significant date in Islamic history, and the year 622 became the first year of the Muslim calendar. At Yathrib, which was then renamed Medina, or "The City," the new religion flourished. Muhammad became ruler as well as prophet, and the Medina section of the Koran, which records the revelations he received there, shows him to have been one of the world's great legislators. He was also a gifted military leader. Preliminary skirmishes with the forces of Mecca ended with a great force of 10,000 men, led by Muhammad himself, marching on the holy city.

The Quraysh rulers, recognizing inevitable defeat, met the prophet when he was still a day's journey away and offered to submit to the new faith. The Muslims thus entered the city in peace, and Muhammad himself destroyed 360 idols in the Kaaba, proclaiming, "God is great! Truth has come. Falsehood has vanished!" The people of Mecca were treated with unusual magnanimity and restraint, and only four men were executed. With astonished gratitude thousands of Meccans formally adopted Islam. It was the crowning achievement of Muhammad's life.

He then returned to Medina. His wife Khadija had died years before, and since then Muhammad had married 11 times, mainly in order to bind himself to many of the important tribes of Arabia. The wife he loved most, however, was a young girl, Ayesha, who was the daughter of one of his earliest converts. When she married him she was still so childlike that she had taken her dolls to her husband's house. But it was to her that Muhammad turned as he felt his strength failing, and he died in her arms in 632. Her father, Abu-Bakr, became the first caliph ("successor") and announced the death to the faithful assembled outside. "O Muslims! If any of you has been worshiping Muhammad, then let me tell you that Muhammad is dead. But if you really do worship God, then know ye that God is living and will never die!"

This point is a central issue in Islam. Muslims are not Muhammadans in the sense that believers in Christ are Christians:

Above: the mosque of Yesil Camii, at Iznik, Turkey. It was built between 1378 and 1391 A.D. and shows how far Islam had spread 750 years after Muhammad.

Above: the opening pages of a Near Eastern Koran, probably dating from the 15th century, showing an aspect of the style of Islamic calligraphy and manuscript illumination.

Muhammad explicitly denied that he was in any way divine. His role was to be the last of the prophets, bringing a message and laying down a pattern of life for all those who submit themselves to Allah.

The Muslim pattern of life is simple and is based on five clearly stated obligations called the Five Pillars. The first is the profession of faith: "There is no god but Allah, and Muhammad is his prophet." This is the first phrase spoken into the ear of a newborn baby and the last on the lips of the dying. It is uttered by the faithful no less than 20 times daily.

The second obligation is that the believer should offer a ritual prayer five times a day. A tradition says that when Muhammad first approached Allah about this matter, he was told that believers must pray 40 times a day. When he protested that such frequent prayer would be impossible, God accepted the point and lowered the requirement to 30. Again Muhammad protested, and again it was lowered, and so it went on until Allah and Muhammad arrived at the final compromise of five. Historically it seems that during the earliest stages of Islam only two prayers were required, at sunset and at dawn. Later a third prayer was added, apparently through the influence of the Jewish tradition of three prayers a day, and later still the last two prayers became part of the believer's obligation. They are now performed just before sunrise, immediately after midday, in the late afternoon, at sunset, and after dark. At each of these times believers are called to prayer by the voice of the muezzin chanting his ritual

Prayers and Pilgrimages

Right: the great prayer outside the town wall of Mecca at the end of an important festival. All the worshipers' backs bend in the direction of the sacred Kaaba.

Opposite above: the ihram, the costume worn by Islamic pilgrims to Mecca. The pilgrim must follow strict rules of ritual purification which include the discarding of his or her usual clothing.

Opposite below: the pilgrims arrive at Mount Arafat, the last holy place that must be visited in order to complete the hajj.

cry from the mosque. The worshipers face Mecca as they pray; pilgrims in Mecca itself pray in the direction of the Kaaba, which is thus encircled by kneeling forms and the only spot in the world where all Muslims do not face the same direction.

The third obligation is to pay a tax, which is used primarily for charity toward the poor, and the fourth is that the believer should fast throughout the daylight hours during Ramadan, the ninth month of the Muslim lunar calendar. It periodically falls when the days are at their longest, and in the long, hot days of summer the absolute prohibition against eating or drinking can be a severe physical and mental ordeal for fasters. As the month progresses their stamina inevitably decreases and tempers become shorter. At the same time, however, the fast is a cohesive force binding the entire community, linking them together in the solidarity of Islam.

After Muhammad's pilgrimage to Mecca in the eighth year of the Hegira he received the revelation, "Verily the idolators are unclean: let them not come near unto the Holy Temple after this year." From that time on Mecca has been a city forbidden to outsiders. In fact, no infidel is permitted to pass a set of stone pillars which mark the farthest point (about 15 miles away) from which the light of the sanctuary can be seen. For a believer, on the other hand, passing these stone pillars represents the beginning of the culmination of his religious experience, for the fifth

religious duty of every Muslim is to make a pilgrimage to the
sacred monuments of Mecca at least once during his life.

This applies to all those who are physically able and can afford
to make the journey, so that the pilgrimage becomes not only an
individual declaration of belief but the occasion of an immense
coming together of Muslims from all over the world. They meet
under conditions which level all social inequalities. No matter
what status the believer has at home, in Mecca he is simply
another pilgrim. Each person discards his usual clothing, neither
shaves nor cuts his hair, and before entering the sanctuary dons
two seamless cloths. One wraps around the waist and falls to
just above the knees, and the other is wrapped around the
shoulders. Leather soles are strapped to the feet instead of shoes,
and the head is left unprotected from the fierce desert sun.

The great pilgrimage, or *hajj*, may take place at any time after
the end of Ramadan, but the last month of the year (Dhu
al-Hijjah, or month of pilgrimage) is the traditional time, and
the climactic ceremonies occur on the ninth and tenth days of
that month. Each pilgrim must circle the Kaaba seven times,
ideally kissing the sacred Black Stone each time, though the
pressure of numbers usually means this is an exercise in persistence and determination. The pilgrimage also includes visits to
the holy well, to another sacred stone upon which Abraham is
said to have climbed when he was laying the upper courses of the
Kaaba, and to nearby Mount Safa. The pilgrim runs from there
to Mount Marwah and back seven times, thus commemorating
Hagar's desperate search for water before God provided her with
the well.

The culmination of the pilgrimage takes place at Mount
Arafat, outside Mecca, where the pilgrims gather for a sermon.
They then go on to Mina, where each person stones a pillar with
seven small pebbles in remembrance of the tradition that Abraham escaped from Satan, who tempted him there, by casting
seven stones at the devil. The ceremony ends with the sacrifice
of an animal, usually a sheep or goat. Part of it may be eaten by
the owners, but the rest is distributed among the poor of Mecca.

Above: African pilgrims to Mecca dressed in the traditional two lengths of cloth, facing the Kaaba. The shrouded, cube-shaped building contains the Black Stone, consecrated by Muhammad, that the archangel Gabriel is believed to have given to Abraham.

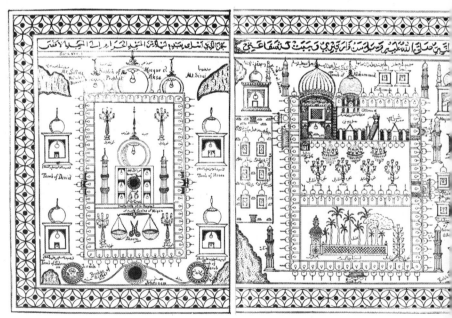

At the end of the sacrifice ritual the pilgrims have their heads shaved and their nails cut, and at this point they are considered partially desanctified. Only after a final circling of the Kaaba is the pilgrimage complete and the pilgrim returned to his secular condition. From that time on he is entitled to be called "Hajj."

This extraordinary religious activity captured the attention of the people of the outside world as soon as they heard of it—and it was not long after Muhammad's death that his message began to be carried far beyond Arabia. Muhammad died in 632 and by 710 Arab warriors, united by their faith, had spilled out of Arabia and reached much of the Mediterranean basin and southwest Asia. They reached the Atlantic at Morocco and the Indus river in what is now Pakistan, and they crossed the Strait of Gibraltar into Spain. Arab horsemen were soon raiding as far north as the Loire and Rhone valleys of France, and the Monts des Maures (Mountains of the Moors) in southeastern France are named in their memory. After the initial Islamic explosion the two communities, Islam and Western Christendom, became mutually suspicious and remained locked in confrontation for centuries.

The first Christian known to have penetrated Mecca was an Italian who wrote a book about his travels, which was published in 1510. His name was Ludovico di Varthema, and he had probably been a soldier before becoming a traveler. He reached Mecca by way of Damascus in Syria, where he apparently picked up a working knowledge of Arabic. He appears to have been practical rather than intellectually brilliant, and his account is factual and down-to-earth.

In choosing his disguise di Varthema took advantage of the existence of a special army of men called Mamelukes. From an original group captured as children, enslaved, and forcibly converted to Islam, they were to become the power which sustained the rule of Muslim caliphs in Egypt, Palestine, and Syria.

First Christian to Visit Mecca

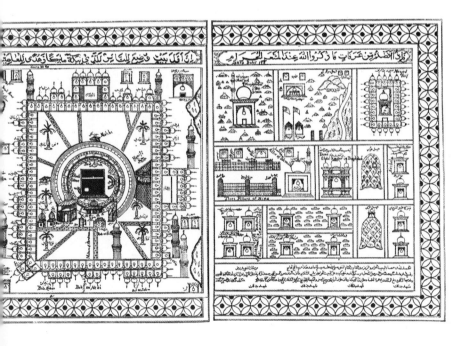

Left: a Mecca certificate, given to pilgrims who have visited the sacred city. It shows the various landmarks of the complete pilgrimage. As every Muslim is commanded to make at least one pilgrimage to Mecca during his lifetime, if at all possible, this certificate could almost be considered as, in part, a passport to heaven.

Mameluke guards did not marry: their ranks were renewed by yet more European and Circassian children captured for slaves. Therefore they did not look like Arabs, but—as Muslims—they were not only entitled but obliged to make a pilgrimage to Mecca. While in Damascus in 1503 di Varthema made friends with the captain of a Mameluke escort assigned to accompany and protect a pilgrim caravan bound for Mecca from the depredations of Bedouins. The Bedouins, though Muslim themselves, did not hesitate to attack and rob other Muslim pilgrims, usually when they had stopped at an oasis to refresh themselves and were thus relaxed and unwary. Di Varthema, using his wits and very likely his money as well, managed to persuade the Mamelukes to let him join the caravan as one of them.

As a Mameluke di Varthema took the Arabic name of Yunos and, uniformed in the splendid Mameluke robes and supplied with a horse, set off on the 40-day march to the holy cities of Mecca and Medina. The latter was less important than Mecca and was not an officially required part of the pilgrimage, but Medina was still revered as the site of Muhammad's tomb. The Italian was one of a vast army of pilgrims: altogether he estimated that there were 40,000 accompanied by a Mameluke escort of about 60. When the caravan reached Medina, after crossing land so barren that di Varthema reported traveling 16 days without seeing a single animal or bird, they visited the prophet's tomb, which he described carefully in order to disprove the legend current in Europe at the time that Muhammad's coffin was suspended in air. (In fact to this day the coffin is difficult to observe closely, since it is enclosed within an interior tower of a mosque which has three small windows through which the faithful may offer their blessings.) Near Muhammad's tomb are two others—that of Abu-Bakr, his father-in-law and successor, and of Umar, the second caliph.

After leaving Medina the caravan stopped for a day to allow for the ritual washing and donning of the *ihram*, the two white cloths of the pilgrim. Then, as now, assuming the ihram involved special prohibitions. The pilgrim must not quarrel or take life—

Above: di Varthema's caravan on its way to Mecca. He described the group as follows: "The pilgrims travel with wives and children and houses like a Turkish tent made from wool. . . . The caravan was going in two groups . . . 60 of them Mamelukes for saving the people. One part of the Mamelukes were going first, another one in the middle, and the third part behind the group. We traveled night and day."

Right: the mosque of Muhammad in Medina, where the Prophet is buried. The visit to Medina is now part of the Muslim pilgrimage and, as in Mecca, the prayers to be performed are very precisely defined. The tomb itself is enclosed within an interior tower.

Di Varthema at the Holy City

Left: a Mameluke exercising his horse as seen in Egypt in 1801. By that time the Mamelukes no longer ruled Egypt. Many were recruited from Christian prisoners of war who were willing to embrace Islam, and they became an elite guard that ruled much of the Middle East in di Varthema's time.

he is even forbidden to frighten an animal or to cut a blade of grass. A pilgrim may not anoint himself with oils or perfumes, or dye, shave, or cut any of his hair. Any irregularity demands that a penance be done; according to tradition only the prophet achieved a perfect pilgrimage.

Upon entering Mecca, di Varthema found it not only a shrine but a bustling center of trade where Muslims from many Eastern countries gathered. In his opinion, many of the Indians, Syrians, Persians, and Ethiopians were as interested in the trading possibilities as in their devotions.

Having completed the pilgrimage without mishap, di Varthema challenged discovery by deserting the Mameluke guard and remaining hidden in Mecca until the pilgrim caravan had left on its return journey to Damascus. He faced either of two grave dangers: desertion from the guard was punishable by death, but if he admitted he was not a Mameluke, and thus not subject to their discipline, he faced almost certain execution as an infidel on holy ground. However, posing as a skillful gunmaker, he managed to find a refuge in Mecca in the house of a merchant whose commercial instincts were roused. The merchant's niece became greatly enamored of the mysterious stranger. Alas, wrote di Varthema, "at that tyme, in the myddest of those troubles and fears, the fyre of Venus was almost extinct in me." He eventually managed to creep out of the city secretly at night and headed for Jiddah, the Arabian port on the Red Sea about two days' journey away. He reached the port and, still in danger of recognition as a Mameluke deserter, took refuge in a mosque where he pretended to be ill. For three weeks he spent his days groaning in

First Europeans to Reach Mecca

Above right: woodcut from an early edition of di Varthema's book about his adventures, showing some Mameluke guards accosting a townsman.

Below: Ulrich Jaspar Seetzen, a German botanist who visited Mecca in 1809. He was murdered in the desert near Ta'izz in 1811.

the mosque and his nights creeping around the city to buy food surreptitiously and observe the city's inhabitants from the shadows. At last he managed to get aboard a ship bound for Persia, and by 1510, after an adventurous journey which included being jailed in Yemen and visiting Persia and India, he had reached Italy where his book was published.

For centuries di Varthema was not just the first but the only European to have seen Mecca. The next visitor was Joseph Pitts, an English seaman who did not make the trip until 1685. His was not a voluntary adventure: he was captured and enslaved by Barbary pirates off the north coast of Africa in 1678, sold to a Muslim cavalry officer, and—having been forced to accept Islam—he eventually made the pilgrimage with his master. He subsequently escaped and managed to return to England, where he wrote a book about his adventures.

By the beginning of the 19th century Europeans had acquired a definite taste for exploration and adventure. They crossed and recrossed the face of the earth, describing and naming places previously known only to those who lived there. But Mecca offered a far greater challenge. Not only was there the lure of the unknown, but there was also the excitement of doing something forbidden, at enormous risk. European adventurers took the prohibition against unbelievers entering Mecca as a gigantic dare. The promise of success—and of publicizing that success—was the bright, glittering reward for the completion of a dangerous deed.

The first man to succeed after Pitts' involuntary pilgrimage was a mysterious Spaniard who called himself Ali Bey. He reached the holy city in 1801 and managed to bring scientific instruments with him, which he used to fix the geographical location of Mecca by astronomical observation. He was said to have been a Muslim prince, but his actual identity remains a tantalizing enigma.

A German botanist named Ulrich Jaspar Seetzen journeyed to Mecca and Medina in 1809, but he did not live to tell the tale.

Above: Ali Bey, a mysterious Spaniard who managed to fix the geographical location of Mecca with scientific instruments in 1801.

Left: a band of pilgrims on their way to Mecca, in a miniature from a 16th-century Persian manuscript.

Below: John Lewis Burckhardt, the Swiss explorer, wearing the Muslim clothing in which he disguised himself for the journey to Mecca. He was a careful observer and kept a detailed journal.

His disguise eventually failed him, and he was murdered somewhere in the desert near Ta'izz in 1811. The next person to try his luck was a Swiss explorer, John Lewis Burckhardt, who was fluent in Arabic, well versed in the Koran, and even possibly a convert to Islam—although the sincerity of his conversion is debatable. Burckhardt had been employed to seek out the sources of the Niger river by a British scientific association, but while waiting for a caravan at Cairo in 1815 he decided to make the Meccan pilgrimage first. Unlike di Varthema, Burckhardt was an unobtrusive, systematic man with no taste for daring adventures. His journals are clear, factual, and unembroidered. He obviously took the pilgrimage seriously, and his notes covered not only its spiritual aspects but the secular life of Mecca as well. No longer a political center—indeed, the post-Muhammadan government had been shifted first to Medina and later to

Burton and "The Huge White Blot"

Damascus—it was still an important city for trade and held a unique position as the meeting place of Islam. Unfortunately, Burckhardt did not long survive his journey: he contracted dysentery at Medina, and, in 1817, he died in Cairo from a second bout of the disease.

Possibly the best-known infidel intruder into Mecca was the Englishman Richard Burton. As flamboyant in his own way as di Varthema was in his, Burton, after a career as an intelligence officer in the Indian Army, resolved to explore "the huge white blot which in our maps still notes the Eastern and Central regions of Arabia." However, he was prevented from beginning the journey, which he expected would take three years, on the grounds that it was too dangerous. Defiantly Burton resolved to visit Mecca, which would be a shorter but even more hazardous enterprise, in order "to prove, by trial, that what might be perilous to other travelers was safe to me."

During his years in India he had become a master of disguise, and, due to a remarkable gift for languages, he was by then fluent in both Arabic and Persian in addition to Hindustani and several European languages. He set off from England in 1852 disguised as a Persian Muslim. He quickly discovered that this was a mistake, as the Arabs tended to look down on the Persians. Therefore in Alexandria he pretended to be an Afghan doctor, and it was in this role that he made the pilgrimage. Although he met some suspicion at the beginning of his journey, he was able

Above: Burton's Arab shoes, loose and comfortable, the heels of which have been worn down.

Right: Burton's drawing of Medina, from his book *Pilgrimage to El-Medinah and Meccah*, published in 1855. This vivid account of his journey brought him considerable fame as an explorer.

Opposite: Richard Burton in Arab dress. Burton's gift for languages and his thorough knowledge of Islam made it possible for him to pass as a Muslim among Muslims. He identified himself so much with every aspect of their life and faith that he almost became a Muslim. After his journey to Mecca he was accepted as a *hajji*—someone who has completed the holy pilgrimage.

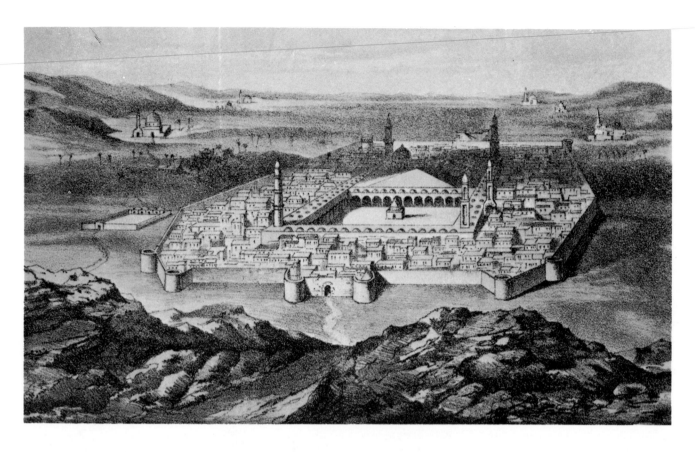

Above: sketch of Medina by a native artist, published along with his own drawings by Richard Burton in his 1855 book about the holy cities of Islam.

to join a group of Muslims whose homes were in Medina and Mecca, and it was with them that he made the pilgrimage. He traveled on a pilgrim ship from Suez to Yanbu, the port of Medina, and then continued inland to Medina and on to Mecca. When Burton was actually face to face with the Kaaba he found himself swept by emotion, echoing the tumult of those around him. He wrote later, "I may truly say that, of all the worshipers who clung weeping to the curtain, or who pressed their beating hearts to the stone, none felt for the moment a deeper emotion than did the Haji from the far-north . . . But, to confess the humbling truth, theirs was the high feeling of religious enthusiasm, mine was the ecstasy of gratified pride." Unlike Burckhardt, Burton returned safely to Europe where, in 1855, he published a vivid account of his pilgrimage. This brought him considerable fame and launched him on his later career as an explorer in Africa.

Over 50 years later another Englishman, A. J. B. Wavell, repeated Burton's feat of visiting Mecca in disguise—in this case as a Zanzibari pilgrim. By this time the pilgrimage had become somewhat modernized and the well-to-do were able to take the train from Damascus to Medina, a journey of only four days as opposed to the month or more required for the slow camel caravans. Wavell made his pilgrimage in 1908, but although he reported some innovations (like the phonograph brought along by two Turks who provided recorded readings from the Koran for the fascinated passengers), in the main the procedure was very little different from that originally reported by di Varthema in his book four centuries earlier.

Mecca-The Unique City

The temper of the 20th century has not encouraged further Christian attempts on the sacred ground of Islam. Even Burton encountered criticism at home for his duplicity, and today the idea of assuming a disguise to enter a holy place would be interpreted not as an adventure but as an intrusion on the privacy of others. No longer is it necessary for non-Muslims to enter Mecca in order to satisfy the curiosity of the outside world: capable Muslim writers and photographers have amply recorded the pilgrimage. Nor would the present rulers of Saudi Arabia, within whose domain Mecca lies, wish to have the blood of an unbeliever on their hands. The danger to modern infidels apprehended in Mecca is less from the government than from the rash fury of other pilgrims. Some inquisitive tourists have been literally torn to pieces, while others, who have strayed into the sacred precincts by a combination of ignorance and bad luck, have found themselves imprisoned for their own safety.

Mecca, guarded by its stone pillars, is both a city like other cities and at the same time unique. Hundreds of thousands of pilgrims now converge upon the sacred city each year; some arrive by the luxury of jet airliners and modern ships, while others walk as their predecessors have walked for centuries. But all assume the same plain ihram of seamless cloths, and all of them, ruler and ruled, rich and poor, make the same seven circuits around the Kaaba, pushing and shoving through the crowd to touch or, with luck, kiss the black stone at the corner. Meccan businessmen charge what the traffic will bear for lodging and food for the endless throngs. The keepers of the Kaaba sell pieces of the kiswah, the cloth covering the Kaaba which is replaced annually, for pilgrims to take with them as a sacred souvenir. Islam is a practical religion, and in Mecca sanctity and trade have long walked hand in hand. There are now over 500 million Muslims in the world who represent all the known races of mankind. One out of every seven human beings today subscribes to the faith of Islam, and each of them, if at all possible, is obliged at least once in his or her lifetime to make the holy pilgrimage. But for the other 85 percent of humanity Mecca remains as it has been for 13 centuries, a forbidden city.

Above: A. J. B. Wavell in Damascus in 1908. Like Burton half a century earlier, Wavell made the journey to Mecca disguised as a Muslim pilgrim.

Left: modern Muslim pilgrims from Africa arrive at Jiddah airport on their way to the holy city of Mecca. During the annual pilgrimage the population of Jiddah swells to many times its usual numbers as buses and planes full of pilgrims disgorge their passengers.

Chapter 11
The Quest for Timbuktu

Timbuktu is a nursery rhyme name that in many languages has become synonymous with the back of beyond, a faraway, half-mythical place impossibly remote and distant beyond all imagining. Since the 14th century Timbuktu has captured the imagination of many people, but for most of that time no one knew precisely where the city was located. More of an idea than a place, Timbuktu stood for almost any fabulous, gold-roofed, utterly mysterious city. It gleamed like a distant jewel—guarded from the outside world by endless miles of desert sands to the north and dense jungle to the south. Many of those who tried to find the city died in the attempt. But a handful succeeded—what did they discover about Timbuktu?

All that was known for centuries was that Timbuktu lay somewhere in the vast expanse of the Sahara desert, and that the only way to reach it was by camel caravan. Even that was far from certain. The Sahara was, and still is, one of the least hospitable areas of the globe, and by any standards it is immense. At its broadest it stretches about 3200 miles from east to west; from north to south it covers 1400 miles. Its area is similar to that of Europe, but instead of the busy tapestry of villages, cities, roads, and fields, the Sahara is empty. For hundreds of miles there is absolutely nothing to guide a traveler—no clearly distinguishable features, no human life—it is simply a wasteland. The popular image of the Sahara is of a sea of sand, and indeed miles upon miles of undulating sand dunes are rippled by the harsh desert winds. But a far greater proportion of the Sahara is made up of rocky plateaus and barren rolling plains. Over this apparently endless nothingness cross the ancient caravan trails, which follow traditional routes from one oasis or well to the next. These routes sometimes involve detours that may double the distance of a long journey. But these detours must be made, for without water the caravan will perish. Sometimes wells go dry; caravans thousands strong have vanished into the desert and never been heard of again. The Arabs, who know the desert better than any except the native tribesmen, believe that four or five successful crossings of that empty vastness are the most that a person can hope for in one lifetime.

Opposite: the Sahara desert on the edge of the Niger river in Mali. Barren of life for mile after empty mile, the Sahara forms a natural barrier which isolated Timbuktu from the outside world for centuries.

The "White Man's Grave"

To the north and northwest the Sahara stretches to the shores of the Mediterranean Sea and the Atlantic Ocean. In the east it meets the Nile. But in the south is a deadly obstacle—the hot, steamy tropical bush. It is swampy and disease-ridden, known grimly as the "White Man's Grave." Somewhere beyond that ominous jungle, beyond the desert barrier, lay the city of Timbuktu.

The fabulous wealth of Timbuktu had first come to the notice of the outside world in 1324, when the emperor of Mali, Mansa Musa, left Timbuktu to cross the desert on a pilgrimage to Mecca. The merchants of Cairo, though accustomed to Oriental opulence, were so astonished at the riches of the caravan—particularly the gold—and so impressed by the emperor's extravagant benevolence that gossip soon spread far beyond the Arab world. The magnificence of the caravan lost nothing in the telling, and the name of Timbuktu was thus first heard in Europe in connection with unlimited gold. Only a few years later, in 1353, the Moroccan sheik Ibn-Batuta arrived in Timbuktu. He had traveled halfway around the world observing and reporting on the Arab world of his time, and in his account Timbuktu was ranked among the most magnificent cities. To distant Europeans, Timbuktu acquired a glamorous aura of opulence and sophistication which was enhanced by its inaccessibility.

In the 15th century the Portuguese heard further stories of the richness of Timbuktu as a trading center, where gold, silver, brass, pepper, and slaves changed hands before being transported northward across the desert. Later, in 1565, an official attempt was made to reach the city: the envoy, Diego Carreiro, wrote a hopeful letter to the Portuguese king in which he explained his plans and announced that he was on his way. Nothing further was ever heard of him.

Opposite: detail of a Spanish map attributed to Abraham de Gresques, showing the European idea of northwest Africa at the lower right. Lavishly ornamented and on fine parchment, it was probably made for Charles V of France in the 14th century.

Right: Timbuktu in relation to the rest of northwest Africa and the Atlantic coast.

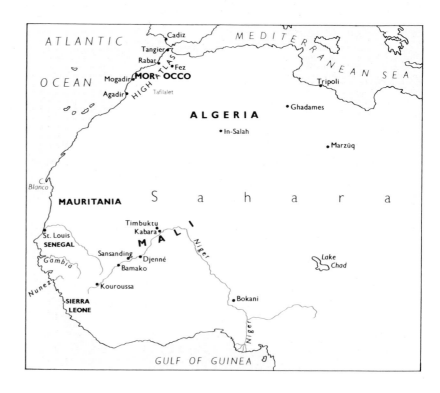

Two African Mysteries!

Above: miniature portrait of Mungo Park (1771-1806). He was the third man the African Association recruited to explore Africa, and his assignment was to find the source and the mouth of the Niger river.

About the time of that first abortive attempt, a tale of another traveler was published in Europe. The writer, called Leo Africanus, was a Moor born in Spain who had been sent on a diplomatic mission to Timbuktu (which he called Tombuto) by the Sheriff of Fez (in modern Morocco) in 1526. The Italian translation of his Arabic journal was published in 1559, and an English translation became available in 1600. Leo Africanus reported "a most stately temple to be seen . . . and a princely palace . . . The rich king of Tombuto hath many plates and scepters of gold and keepes a magnificent and well-furnished court . . . Here are great store of doctors, judges, priests, and other learned men . . . The coin of Tombuto is gold." Leo Africanus detailed the king's lavish hospitality and display—one of the scepters of gold, he said, weighed 1300 pounds. In short, his journal confirmed all the marvelous visions of fantastic wealth which had been circulating for the previous two centuries.

Not only Europeans were dazzled by the vision of the wealthy desert city. In 1591 the Sultan of Morocco sent out an army to capture the riches of Timbuktu. It was the largest military force ever to cross the desert, and included 5000 mounted men and 2000 infantry armed with specially imported English artillery and supplied with 9000 camels and horses. Those who survived the grueling four-month march fought a Negro army beneath the walls of Timbuktu on March 13, 1591, and the Negroes—who had never seen firearms before—were massacred. But the triumph was illusory, for the Moorish army was unable to recross the desert wastes. Caravans bearing spoils worked their way back to Morocco, but the army itself remained where it was. The men intermarried with the women of Timbuktu, and gradually their descendants became indistinguishable from their neighbors. The master of Timbuktu might have been replaced, but the caravans filled with slaves, gold, and spices continued to supply themselves in Timbuktu, and still no one except the caravan leaders themselves knew exactly where the city lay.

By the middle of the 18th century the mystery of Timbuktu had become linked with the mystery of the Niger river of West Africa, whose place of origin, direction of flow, and point of contact with the sea were all unknown. Timbuktu was believed to lie near the Niger, and the two mysteries, thus joined, were irresistible to the armchair geographers of a Europe which was gradually exploring and mapping the rest of the world. In London the Association for the Promotion of the Discovery of the Interior Parts of Africa was founded in 1788, and that very year it sent an American adventurer, John Ledyard, on a journey to Timbuktu. Ledyard went first to Cairo to find a caravan he could join, but in the event he contracted dysentery and died there. It was not a promising start.

The next person commissioned to find Timbuktu, a British army officer named Daniel Houghton, did no better. He landed at the entrance to the Gambia river in 1791 and set off eastward toward Timbuktu. He wrote one letter to his wife in England (and a short note to the African Association in London), expressing his expectation that he would be in Timbuktu in a month's time. He was never heard of again.

After Houghton's disappearance a young Scottish surgeon with a passion for natural history took up the task. Mungo Park made two expeditions, also starting from the Gambia river, in 1795 and 1805. On the first he succeeded in reaching the Niger river and determined that it flowed eastward; on the second, after a ghastly march inland during which 40 of the 45 Europeans died, victims of dysentery and malaria, Park managed to push as far as Sansanding on the Niger. Then the party, reduced to Park himself, a lieutenant, and three soldiers, one of whom was raving mad, embarked on a nightmare journey down the river to the sea, wherever that might be. After having been repeatedly robbed and once imprisoned by natives for the three months of his first solo expedition, Park was determined to keep to the river and avoid any contact with the local people. He ruthlessly gunned down any boats that approached, and in the final stages he was apparently, according to the natives, shooting anyone he saw. In the end his craft was caught in an ambush by vengeful tribesmen, and Park plunged overboard, clutching one of the soldiers who could not swim. Both men vanished in the swirling waters. By then they had traveled 1200 miles down the river and,

Above: one of Mungo Park's last letters, written from Sansanding, to Sir Joseph Banks, founder of the African Association. In this letter he explains his plan for the expedition's next stage: "It is my intention to keep [to] the middle of the River and make the best use I can of Winds and Currents till I reach the termination of this mysterious Stream."

Above: slave caravan in the Sahara around 1820. Robert Adams was forced to walk across the desert to Timbuktu with such a slave caravan after he was shipwrecked. This drawing is by George Lyon, who published it in his book, *A Narrative of Travels in Northern Africa*, in 1821.

if they had only known, were only 400 miles from their destination.

Neither Park's nor Houghton's experiences had indicated that the approach to Timbuktu from the south was particularly promising, and for the next attempt, this time by a German theological student named Frederick Hornemann, the desert route was tried again. Hornemann left Cairo in 1798 with a caravan going west, but he was last heard from in Marzūq, south of Tripoli, in 1800. Years later other explorers discovered that he had indeed crossed the Sahara far to the east of Timbuktu and had died, sometime early in 1801, at an obscure village called Bokani, only a day's journey short of the Niger river.

None of these disappearances did anything to subdue the public curiosity about Timbuktu—on the contrary, they probably added to it. The fire was further fed with the publication in 1809 of a book by James G. Jackson, an English merchant trader who lived in Morocco. Jackson called his book *An Accurate and Interesting Account of Timbuctoo, the Great Emporium of Central Africa*, and in it he wrote, apparently relying on the reports of slave traders, that Timbuktu was 12 miles in circumference and that the climate was "salutary and extremely invigorating, insomuch that it is impossible for the sexes to exist without intermarriage ... The natives, and those who have resided there any considerable time, have an elegance and suavity of manner.'' The stage was thereby set for a bizarre interlude which occurred in 1814.

A mulatto American sailor called Robert Adams was found starving in the streets of London by a man who had seen the same man before in Cadiz, Spain, where he had been told that Adams, who was then calling himself Benjamin Rose, had been to Timbuktu. Adams was promptly taken to the offices of the Africa Committee, a group of merchants interested in promoting trade with Africa, where he was interviewed and his story verified. While appreciative of the food and clothing provided by the Committee, Adams was not particularly interested in telling of his adventures. He was far more concerned with returning home to America as soon as possible. He was eventually induced to spend a few weeks in London while a report was made, with the promise that he would be paid for his time.

His story was extraordinary. After being shipwrecked on the African coast (probably near Cape Blanco), the entire crew of his vessel were seized as slaves by a party of Moors. Stripped naked and left to shamble alongside the camels, the captives were forced to walk across the desert. En route most of them— all but Adams and a Portuguese slave captured earlier—were sold to another band of Moors, who took them north. Adams and his captors continued on to Timbuktu. At times they had no water and had to drink the urine of their camels to survive. After 16 days of torment they reached a hilly area with some small trees, where the Moors themselves were surrounded by a large group of blacks who beheaded most of the Moors and took the rest, with their two slaves, on to Timbuktu. Once inside the city, his Negro captors treated Adams as an honored guest, and he was allowed to move around the town freely.

The sailor was neither an observant man nor particularly impressed at having reached the mysterious city. During the interviews in London he was apparently unable to volunteer any information: only when his attention was directed to a subject by questioning did he seem to remember anything in detail. In any case, the Timbuktu he described had nothing in common with European expectations. It was dirty and dull, he said. The houses were built of sticks and clay and had no furniture. Nobody wore silk, which refuted the word of Leo Africanus, who had claimed that silk was everyday garb. Adams did not see any mosques in Timbuktu, but he did report a broad river just south of the town.

Adams' journey back from Timbuktu was as grueling as the march there. Another party of Moors arrived who ransomed the two slaves along with their own countrymen and took them north across the desert. The crossing was so terrible that some of the Moors were simply abandoned to die in the sand. Adams survived and was passed from one master to another, by whom he was often beaten and once almost killed. At last near the African coast, south of Agadir, Adams was purchased by Joseph Dupuis, the British consul at Mogador in Morocco. Dupuis had been authorized by his government to purchase Christian slaves, and he duly restored Adams to freedom in

A Bizarre Interlude

Above: tortures undergone by an Arab slave, from a book published in 1675. The treatment of captured slaves by the Moors was terrible in the extreme.

Above: the rooftops of Timbuktu, a sight probably much the same now as in the early 19th century when Adams was there.

Opposite: Hugh Clapperton (top), one of the first Europeans to see Lake Chad. Richard Lander (bottom), in Arab dress, wrote a book about his and Clapperton's African expedition.

October 1813, by which time Adams had been in Arab captivity for nearly three years. After remaining in Mogador for seven months with Dupuis, he went on to Tangier and then Cadiz in the hope of joining an American-bound ship. Eventually he had to settle for a Welsh brig bound for Holyhead, and from there he begged his way to London. By leaving the brig he officially became a deserter from the British Navy, which is why he had adopted the false name of Robert Adams. His true name and the one by which he had been known throughout his harrowing adventures was Benjamin Rose.

Having told his story, Benjamin Rose/Robert Adams managed to return to America, where he returned to the obscurity from which he had so startlingly emerged. The Africa Committee published a book about his odyssey, which was savagely attacked on all sides. Adams was alleged to be an imposter and a liar, for his Timbuktu bore no relation to the city described by others. The nearby river was only one of the details to be seized upon and challenged: Leo Africanus had stated clearly that the Niger was some miles south of the city. Adams had said there were no mosques, whereas it was well known that Timbuktu had a large Muslim population. Most importantly, what Adams had described was merely an uninteresting and impoverished desert crossroads, which was not the image the world had come to expect. After a flurry of denunciations the matter was laid to one side and forgotten. From the beginning the consul Dupuis, who knew Africa well, believed Adams' eye-witness story. The geographers of Europe did not.

Benjamin Rose, restored to his family, his country, and his own name, never defended himself. It is unlikely that he even knew of the controversy in any case, for he was illiterate.

Meanwhile explorers continued recklessly to spend their lives in the attempt to clarify West African geography. The problem of the Niger was investigated by a Scottish naval lieutenant named Hugh Clapperton and his servant Richard Lander, who continued the exploration after Clapperton died of dysentery in 1827. The mouth was eventually tracked down, in 1830, as a great delta in the Gulf of Guinea which had been known to Europeans for more than three centuries. One of the mysteries was thus solved, but the golden riddle of Timbuktu still glittered. The curious episode of the American sailor had by this time faded from memory, and the imagined riches of Timbuktu shone as brilliantly as ever.

The next man to challenge the desert was another Scotsman, Alexander Laing. He became interested in African exploration when he was stationed as a junior officer with the British Army in Sierra Leone in West Africa. Laing was young, poor, and passionately eager to make his mark on history, and a dramatic discovery seemed the surest method. By this time the British government had itself undertaken to support exploration, and Laing peppered the authorities with letters proclaiming the advantages of the West African approach route to Timbuktu and his own fitness to make the journey. Lord Bathurst, through whom as secretary of war application for official support was made, eventually accepted Laing as a serious candidate but was not impressed by his chosen route. He pointed out that no traffic was known to exist between the west coast and Timbuktu, whereas Muslims had traveled south across the desert for centuries. What Arabs and Moors could do, said Lord Bathurst, Europeans could do as well. In the end Laing reluctantly agreed to follow the northern route, and in 1825 he sailed for Tripoli.

Laing arrived wan and sickly after suffering an illness at Malta en route, and the British consul Hanmer Warrington insisted he remain in Tripoli to recover before undertaking the difficult journey south. During his enforced rest Laing spent much of his time with Warrington's daughter Emma, and their friendship gradually ripened into love. Her father was astounded and appalled, and he promptly forbade their marriage. As Laing, passionately insistent, made his final preparations for departure, the girl wept wildly while her father stood by, baffled and explosive. In the end Warrington yielded, but only partially. He agreed to conduct a marriage service for them but, unsure of its legality, he would not allow the marriage to be consummated. With this uneasy compromise the matter was settled. On July 14 Alexander Laing and Emma Warrington were married, and two days later Laing left Tripoli to cross the Sahara on his way to Timbuktu. They exchanged miniatures as keepsakes.

Laing set off with a small caravan guided by a sheik named Babani, traveling quite openly as a Christian in European clothes. Babani eventually persuaded him to wear Turkish clothes as they traveled in order to avoid attracting attention, but Laing had no intention of seriously attempting to disguise himself. He sent letters back to Tripoli by courier—to Warrington and his be-

Laing Sets Out

The Territory of the Tuareg

Above: Alexander Laing. Not a strong man, Laing was plagued throughout his life by ill health. His expedition to Timbuktu proved that he had the will to endure crushing hardships, but the loneliness and danger of desert travel constantly preyed on his mind.

loved Emma—and they record his struggle with the desert, himself, and his ambitions. The first stopping place, Ghadames, was less than 300 miles southwest of Tripoli, but a large loop detour they had to make to avoid a local war in the hinterland meant that they had traveled twice that distance by the time they arrived. Laing reported that during the journey he was continually pestered for money, with the threat of robbery or death if it were not forthcoming. The heat was unremitting—temperatures of 120°F were common—and for nearly a week before reaching Ghadames the travelers had no food at all. From Ghadames Laing sent several letters back to Tripoli. His guides were unwilling to set out on the next leg of the journey, and, aside from being impatient at the delay, he was becoming increasingly aware of the dangers of his position as a self-confessed Christian carrying large amounts of money and valuable gifts. His response to any trouble was to pay out more money, and not surprisingly the demands increased. Meanwhile Warrington innocently exacerbated his worries by sending word that Clapperton had arrived in Africa to seek the outlet of the Niger. Laing became convinced that he was involved in a race with Clapperton to reach Timbuktu, and the delays were more frustrating than ever.

At last he left Ghadames and traveled as far as In-Salah in present-day Algeria. His letters tell of the increasing humiliations he suffered on the march. He was often left to unload his camels himself, although he had paid his guides well. They were now in the territory of the proud and suspicious Tuareg, a tribe of Berber warriors who wrapped themselves in indigo veils that stained their faces, for which they were given the nickname of the Blue People. To them foreigners were unwelcome; Christians were at best distrusted and more often hated. Babani guided the caravan away from particularly hostile areas, but Laing was aware that his presence threatened the safety of the others, and that in spite of his payments that presence was resented.

The residents of In-Salah had never seen a European before, and curious natives followed Laing so insistently that in the end he boarded up his door. More worrying was a rumor that he was Mungo Park. The stories of Park's murderous progress down the Niger 21 years before had reached as far as In-Salah, and although Laing would have been a child when Park made his mark on African bush history, he was nevertheless in fear of his life. His letters from In-Salah show his sense of isolation, his passionate concern for Emma back in Tripoli, and his increasing obsession about Clapperton. In spite of it all, however, he wrote that he still took pride in his mission for no other reward "than that which I shall derive from the consciousness of having achieved an enterprise which will rescue my name from oblivion."

On January 9, 1826 he at last left In-Salah. He believed he would reach Timbuktu in about four weeks, but in fact he was less than halfway there, though he had left Tripoli six months before.

The track from In-Salah to Timbuktu was then particularly dangerous, which was why the caravan had delayed much longer than usual in In-Salah in the hope that the unrest would die down. Laing's impatience forced the caravan on, but most of its

Above: traveling through the desert in a sand wind, in a drawing by George Lyon, who unsuccessfully tried to reach the Niger from Tripoli in 1818. All Europeans searching for Timbuktu had to first survive such natural hazards of desert travel.

members were still wary of traveling with him at all. They especially resented his insistence on venturing forward when by a longer delay they might have traveled in greater safety. But Laing persisted, and the caravan reluctantly moved on toward Timbuktu.

Three weeks out of In-Salah the Tuareg struck. They attacked only Laing's part of the caravan, but they were both fierce and merciless. Laing was asleep when he was shot through the side of the tent, and a ball passed through his hip. Before he could arm himself the Tuareg were in his tent slashing about with swords and daggers. His camel driver was cut, two of his servants were killed, and Laing himself received 24 wounds, 18 of which he described as severe. His face, head, and hands were deeply cut; later it was reported that his right hand had been cut off altogether. Laing himself wrote only that three of the fingers were broken and the wrist cut most of the way across, but from that time all his letters were written with his left hand.

Above: modern Tuareg tribesmen gathered around the light of their campfire. These fierce desert nomads were rightly feared by all who crossed the Sahara. Although they adopted the Muslim religion they retained their own language, and these legendary "veiled men" consider themselves the aristocrats of the desert.

Although the rest of the caravan was untouched, the others hastily struck camp and prepared to move away for fear of further attacks. Laing, still bleeding, was tied to a camel, but he was unable to keep up with the fleeing caravan and only rejoined it long after his erstwhile companions had stopped for the next night. The next day Laing was again forced to travel almost alone as he followed the swiftly moving group ahead of him. Babani was of no help to him; Laing was left to struggle on alone day after day, only reaching the caravan late at night, exhausted, sick, and utterly disillusioned. At last they reached the lands of a friendly sheik called Sidi el Muktar, who took pity on Laing and saw that he was cared for properly. After three weeks of rest and recuperation Laing felt ready to go on, but then another devastating blow struck him. Plague struck the oasis, and the sheik and Laing's two surviving servants all died. Laing himself was stricken, too, but his remarkable physiology stood him in good stead and he slowly recovered. At this point he was disfigured, worn, and had had all his money stolen in the Tuareg attack. All he had left was his iron determination to reach Timbuktu.

In late July or early August 1826 he set out on the final stage. Those around him solemnly advised him to return by the route he had come. Timbuktu was in a state of ferment, and it would not be safe for a Christian. Laing was deaf to the warnings. He had come too far, gone through too much, to turn back now.

Laing wrote one letter from Timbuktu. He said, "I have no time to give you my account of Timbuctoo, but shall briefly state that in every respect except in size (which does not exceed four miles in circumference) it has completely met my expectations . . . May God bless you all . . . I have begun a hundred letters to [Emma] but have been unable to get through one; she is ever uppermost in my thoughts . . ." The letter was dated September 21, 1826.

It was the last letter ever received from Alexander Laing. Later it was learned that he had left Timbuktu on September 22 under the protection of Sheik Labeida, a religious fanatic. To strengthen his geographical achievement Laing was determined, against all advice, to take a different route home, heading toward Arouan (north of Timbuktu), doubling back south to the Niger at Sansanding, and then continuing up the Niger toward Bamako to end up hopefully in the Sierra Leone territory he knew well.

On the third night out of Timbuktu Labeida and his men fell upon Laing while he slept; he was killed with a sword and then decapitated. His Arab boy servant was also killed, and his Negro attendant, the only survivor, escaped execution only by feigning death. After the rest of the caravan had moved on, leaving Laing's mutilated body unburied, a passing Arab took the servant back to Timbuktu, and it was this servant who reported what had happened to Laing.

Not until August 1828 did Warrington and his daughter receive the entire story, rumors of which had reached them the year before. In 1829 Emma married a vice-consul at Tripoli, but she died six months later of consumption.

The Death of Laing

Below: digging for Laing's remains by the French official inquiry of 1910. After the murders a passing Arab buried the bodies. The nephew of Sheik Labeida, 82 years old by this time, still possessed a golden brooch his uncle had taken from Laing's body. It had been a parting gift from the explorer's wife Emma.

Above: a Timbuktu water hole. Laing expected Timbuktu to be a great metropolis, but all he found was a small slave market in an undistinguished town.

While Laing sought fame in the desert another man was dreaming of Timbuktu. René Caillié, a slim, boyish-looking young Frenchman, had a burning ambition at least as strong as Laing's. His father was a baker who had died in prison for petty theft; his mother had died shortly afterward, and young René and his lame sister were cared for by an uncle. Caillié adored his sister, and it was for her sake as much as his own that he was determined to achieve some great feat of glory for France. An early interest in Africa brought Caillié to St. Louis, a French settlement in Senegal, in 1816. There his path to fame and glory suddenly became obvious to him: he must get to Timbuktu and back. It was as simple as that.

Caillié was very clear in his own mind about how the feat was to be accomplished. There was to be no nonsense about traveling as a Christian and a gentleman: in Senegal Caillié had learned enough of Africa to realize that it was suicidal for anyone but a Muslim to launch into the interior. He therefore went to live for nine months in a primitive village among the Braknas, a nomadic Moorish people who lived in what is now Mauritania. He told them that he wanted to become a Muslim, having been greatly impressed by the Koran in translation, and that he had come to them to learn Arabic and the wisdom of Islam. The Braknas accepted his story, though with some skepticism, and after nine months Caillié could pass as an Arab.

Financing his journey was another problem. Although he sought government aid from the French and British, the French were unresponsive and the British felt obliged to let Laing have his chance first. Caillié was not deterred. If he could find no official support, he would do it himself. A promise of eventual reward also encouraged him: in 1824 a French geographical society offered a prize of 10,000 francs for the first person to return with information about Timbuktu. One requirement was that the would-be explorer must penetrate the interior starting from the Senegal region on the west coast, and therefore Laing was ineligible for the prize. Using his own carefully hoarded savings, Caillié equipped himself with Arab clothes and a little bundle of silver, gold, and portable merchandise. He also provided himself with a cover story. He was an Arab born in Egypt; he had been carried away to France in his infancy by a French soldier under Napoleon and eventually had been brought to Senegal by his master, who set him free there. He was now traveling to Egypt to seek his family. This slightly improbable story was not universally believed, but René Caillié had enough charm to make even those who found his tale hard to accept inclined to help him when he needed it.

Caillié set out in March 1827, having chosen as his starting point the Rio Nunez estuary between Sierra Leone and Senegal. He joined a small caravan going to Timbuktu, and in spite of the veiled skepticism of his own hired guide and the more open curiosity of the local strict Muslim tribesmen, who were naturally suspicious of Caillié's comparatively fair complexion, he was generally accepted. Despite his frail appearance he had incredible stamina: he walked all the way, in spite of suffering from malarial fevers. Early in June the caravan reached the Niger at Kouroussa. Caillié pressed on, but his fever was worsening, and in August he limped into a small village where he collapsed. An old Negro woman took care of him. He was afflicted with malaria and ulcers on his feet and legs, and then, as his original ailments improved, he was tormented by a new scourge, scurvy. The bones on the roof of his mouth peeled away as his teeth loosened in their sockets, his body ached, and his head throbbed unbearably. He was sustained by rice water and a bark brew brought to him by Manman, the kind old woman. Slowly, though Caillié in his despair prayed for death, his health returned. In January 1828 he was able to go on to Djenné, on a tributary of the Niger.

At Djenné he boarded a boat for Timbuktu. It was not a pleasant experience. As an obvious outsider, Caillié was treated insolently, fed the miserable food given to the slaves on board, and forced to sleep among them in their cramped quarters while the crew and other passengers had cabins. Again Caillié became sick; at his most ill he was grudgingly allowed to share a cabin with one of the crew and his female slave, but he was given so little room that he could not lie straight.

After three weeks they entered desert country, where the river flowed improbably past the dry sands. Here the Tuareg ruled,

René Caillié and Timbuktu

Above: René Caillié (1799–1838), the first Frenchman to reach Timbuktu, in 1828. He had no particular scientific interest in exploration, but his passion for travel had been kindled when he was still very young.

Mystery into Anticlimax!

Above: Caillié in Arab dress, "meditating upon the Koran."

Below: Koran boards from the Mandingo area near Timbuktu.

and Caillié was astonished to see the boat's crew acquiesce meekly to the nomads' arrogant demands for plunder. Caillié himself was bundled below decks to stay hidden lest he be taken for a Moor (and thus presumably wealthy) and thereby tempt the Tuareg to increase their demands. Not until they reached Kabara, the port of Timbuktu, was Caillié allowed to reappear on deck. By then he had been traveling for a year, and in that year he had covered 1500 miles, two-thirds of which he had walked.

From Kabara it was only a short way to the mysterious city itself. Although a suspicious Tuareg warrior who joined the caravan eyed Caillié with wary attentiveness, he was not openly challenged, and within a few hours the city was there before him. "On entering this mysterious city, which is an object of curiosity and research to the civilized nations of Europe," he wrote later, "I experienced an indescribable satisfaction. I never before felt a similar emotion and my transport was extreme. I was obliged, however, to restrain my feelings, and to God alone did I confide my joy."

He had indeed reached the fabled town, the golden city of Timbuktu. Anticlimax, however, followed sharply. Timbuktu was nothing but a mass of badly built houses made of earth. The spires of three mosques were outlined against the desert sky, but the grandeur and opulence he had expected simply did not exist. As the illiterate sailor Benjamin Rose had reported to a disbelieving world, Timbuktu was merely dirty and dull. Caillié was provided with a small house (which, he discovered by carefully casual inquiries, was directly across from the house where Laing had stayed so briefly), and his visit lasted for two weeks. His first impression of the city was not altered by further acquaintance. The famous market of Timbuktu was "a desert" compared with the thriving market of Djenné. "Timbuktoo and its environs present the most monotonous and barren scene I ever beheld," he wrote drearily. In addition, the city was held in thrall by the Tuareg, who prowled the surrounding desert and swept into Timbuktu to demand whatever took their fancy: food, slaves, or the scanty gold available (one of the local specialties was braided straw jewelry made to look like gold). The city was entirely dependent upon food and water brought from outside, and thus placating the Tuareg, who might otherwise have cut the city off to suffer certain starvation, was a grim necessity.

Although the city was not what Caillié had anticipated, he liked the people. "The people of Timbuctoo have some idea of the dignity of human nature," he wrote, and commented, "I saw some women who might be considered pretty." He drank tea with the locals and made what discreet inquiries about Laing that he could without arousing suspicion. He used the mosque, which was usually deserted, in which to make his notes, and once he was surprised there when a middle-aged Moor came up to him and gravely slipped a handful of cowrie shells, the local currency, into his pocket. Caillié approved of "this delicate way of giving alms."

Having achieved his goal, Caillié had still to survive the return journey in order to win the prize and the fame he coveted. Sensibly, he decided to return via Morocco, so that no one could accuse him of having simply lived in the bush for a time as they

might have if he reappeared on the west coast. His hosts in Timbuktu were reluctant to let him go, but Caillié persisted, and on May 4 he left for Morocco with an immense slave caravan. Four days out of the city the scene of Laing's murder was pointed out to him. Caillié glanced briefly at the remains of a camp still lying in the sand and then looked away, masking his emotion.

During his desert crossing he experienced most of the horrors of Saharan travel. Between the scattered wells water was rationed by carefully measured sips. Thirst seized and obsessed him; he humiliated himself by begging for an extra mouthful from the rich merchants, though he had been warned that this was forbidden—everyone was rationed. His disguise provoked taunts and suspicion. He was insulted by men who threw stones at him and laughed contemptuously, saying "He is like a Christian." Caillié said nothing. He watched the mirages floating before him, tried to ignore the skeletons of dead men and camels which littered the route, and simply endured day after endless day. At last, after two long months, the caravan moved slowly out of the desert to the oasis area of Tafilalet south of the high Atlas Mountains. Six weeks later he finally reached Fez, in Morocco. It was a populous city, and Caillié was able to slip away from the caravan unnoticed. He then made his way to Rabat on the coast, where he had been told there was a French consul, hopeful that there his hardships would at last be at an end.

Unfortunately, it proved to be nearly as difficult to abandon his disguise as it had been to assume it in the first place. The consul at Rabat was unwilling to involve himself with Caillié's

Above: a camel caravan moving across the desert at night.

Below: the house in which René Caillié lived in Timbuktu, opposite that of Laing. Above the door the French, who held the city for over half a century, placed a plaque commemorating Caillié's achievement.

The Legend that Endures

predicament, so he went on, still dressed as an Arab. By now he had hardly anything of value. In Tangier it was only by the greatest persistence that he could persuade the French consul-general to house him while Caillié changed his identity. Dressed as a sailor he was smuggled on board a French sloop and, after 10 days, he arrived at Toulon. He was received as a hero, and though his story was questioned he quickly gained influential supporters, and within 11 weeks the award of 10,000 francs was presented to him. René Caillié, the baker's son, became one of the most celebrated men in France.

The British were less delighted. Warrington, Laing's father-in-law, had convinced himself that the French, by underhanded means, had succeeded in suppressing Laing's journal, which he had probably left behind in Timbuktu, and by vigorous correspondence he shared his suspicions with all and sundry. Some people were therefore quite prepared to believe that Caillié had simply drawn his information from Laing's notes. When his book actually appeared, however, that line of reasoning was quietly dropped by most of his opponents, for although his book was no literary masterpiece it was clearly the work of an honest man. The controversy bubbled on, but what ironically persisted, especially after Caillié himself died in 1838, was the fabled vision of Timbuktu as a city of splendor. It seemed impossible that Caillié's drab town was the glittering goal which had drawn so many to their deaths.

Below: a street in Timbuktu. Once the rich city of legend, its glory was fading even as Europeans first heard of its existence. Now Timbuktu is a provincial city in the modern state of Mali.

It was a humorless, methodical German who finally laid to rest the myth of a fabulous Timbuktu. Heinrich Barth was originally recruited as part of a British expedition in 1849, and he eventually became leader when John Richardson, who had organized the mission, died in the desert, probably of sunstroke. They set off from Tripoli in 1850 to settle the question of the exact position of Timbuktu, which was still disputed since Caillié was not a particularly reliable geographer. Traveling by way of Lake Chad, Barth reached the city in September 1853. Once there he verified Caillié's observations entirely. Timbuktu was simply a desert crossroads, distinguished only by its position between the Niger and the desert.

It may indeed have once been the rich city of its legend, but its glory was fading even as Europeans learned of it. After Leo Africanus visited it—just after it had reached its peak of affluence and splendor—the Moors sacked it. As Moorish influence waned, weakened by distance and the difficulties of crossing the wide Sahara, the Tuareg took over. They systematically milked the city, and it quietly and steadily declined. By 1600, when the writings of Leo Africanus were translated into English, the Timbuktu he had described no longer existed. Glittering, golden Timbuktu was gone.

Timbuktu today is a typical Saharan crossroads. The French, who colonized West Africa for many years, have gone after controlling the city for nearly 70 years. The population, which at its peak may have been more than 50,000, was 5000 in the French census of 1940. In 1960 the independent state of Mali was established and Timbuktu became a provincial center. It has an airstrip, and curious tourists, eager for a stamp in their passports that includes the mysterious word "Timbuktu," can make stopovers there. The names of Caillié and Laing are half-forgotten, while the name of Timbuktu lives on. Men, it has been said, die easily. Myths die hard.

Above: a drawing of Ghāt in the Sahara by Heinrich Barth (1821–1865). He spent five years traveling around the southern fringe of the Sahara between Lake Chad and Timbuktu. Barth was a methodical, humorless, and unemotional man, well prepared for his African task.

Index

Picture Credits